Draftee

Vietnam, A Draftee's Story, A War Fought by Draftees, and an Opportunity to Change America

Francis Epplin

Copyright © 2022 by Francis Epplin

Cover Designer: Maya Taylor

Cover Editor: Fiona Suherman

Supervising Editor: Shannon Marks

Editing Assistants: Avery Timmons

Publishing Assistant: Lisa Wood

Paperback ISBN: 978-1-958503-22-5

Hardback ISBN: 978-1-958503-23-2

All rights reserved.

No part of this book may be reproduced in any form or by any electronic or mechanical means, including information storage and retrieval systems, without written permission from the author, except for the use of brief quotations in a book review.

Contents

Preface — vii

Part One
A Draftee's Story: One Among 2.6 Million

1. Introduction — 3
2. A Child During the Cold War — 14
3. December 1969 Draft Lottery — 20
4. May 1970 Kent State University Tragedy — 24
5. Report for Induction — 29
6. KP (Kitchen Police) – Spilled Milk and Guilty Bystander — 37
7. Fitness, Blisters, and Poison Ivy — 42
8. Advanced Individual Training 13E20, Field Artillery Fire Direction Control — 53
9. Next Stop, Vietnam — 63
10. Replacement Battalion to Artillery Battery — 66
11. Fire Support Base Wilson — 70
12. Christmas 1970 — 78
13. Life at Wilson — 83
14. Encounter with Dental Version of M*A*S*H's Dr. Frank Burns — 89
15. Life at Wilson: Neighboring Rice Paddies — 91
16. Calm at Wilson, Disasters Near the DMZ — 97
17. Vacating Fire Support Base Wilson — 100
18. Ship to Shore to the Cam Lo Cemetery — 104
19. Camp Carroll – Keystone of the McNamara Line — 108
20. Rookie Aerial Observer — 117
21. Duck and Cover — 122
22. ARVN (Army of the Republic of Vietnam) – the South Vietnamese Army — 125

23. Leaving Carroll	131
24. Albright's Forecast	137
25. Leaving Vietnam	140
26. Headed for Home	143
27. Fort Hood	147

Part Two
A War Fought by Draftees: A Mess for the U.S.

28. Jesuits Following their Call	157
29. World War II Intervened	161
30. U.S. Leaders Discuss	170
31. 1954 Geneva Accords	182
32. Bao Dai and Ngo Dinh Diem	187
33. Pawn in a Cold War	194
34. President Johnson	204
35. Nixon Elected	215
36. President Nixon	219
37. Fair and Impartial Random (FAIR) Draft Lottery	222
38. No Secret Plan Only Secret Bombing	227
39. Official Paris Talks and Unofficial Kissinger-Le Duc Tho Meetings	232
40. Kissinger's October Surprise	239
41. Rationalizing a Loss	250

Part Three
Opportunity to Change America: Freedom to Choose

42. Family Tradition	265
43. Military Drafts in the United States	268
44. Paving the Way to an All-Volunteer Force	292
45. Economists and the Draft	296
46. Push Back	308
47. Flawed Plans to Revise the Selective Service System	313

48. Free to Choose on Citizenship Acknowledgement Day	324
49. A More Random Selection System	332
Epilogue	342
Maps	347
Notes	351

Preface

I was drafted into the U.S. Army on July 7, 1970. I served with an artillery battery in Vietnam in 1970-71. Approximately 2.6 million U.S. military personnel served in Vietnam. Each of them had a unique experience depending on when they were there, where they were, and what they were doing. For many years, I managed to suppress issues related to my military experience. I was preoccupied with other life issues and did not choose to allocate time to decipher my army service.

Soon after I retired in 2017, the U.S. Public Broadcasting Service aired the Ken Burns and Lynn Novick 10-part series titled "The Vietnam War". For the first time, after more than 40 years of marriage, my wife and I, after watching the films, discussed Vietnam. A few weeks later, my third-grade granddaughter invited me to a veterans' appreciation ceremony. Most of the veterans in attendance were too young to have served in Vietnam. The children sang. Flags were waved. Several children approached me and repeated, "Thank you for your service." They were well coached and very respectful. I tried to smile and thank them for the ceremony. None of them asked when I served, where I served, or what I did in the military. These events triggered some old concerns and rekindled my interest. Retirement enabled time to explore a number of issues that had concerned me, and that I had managed to suppress. These issues may be categorized into three sets.

The first set of issues concerned my specific situation as a draftee. For several months in 1971, our artillery battery occupied locations a few miles south of the Demilitarized Zone (DMZ) that formed the border between North Vietnam and South Vietnam. The locations that we occupied and the activities that we conducted enabled a unique insight into the strategy of our enemy, the performance of our allied South Vietnamese draftees, and U.S. administration policy.

The second set of issues concerned U.S. involvement and the motivation of South Vietnamese draftees. During our time along the DMZ, we had the opportunity to observe ARVN (Army of the Republic of Vietnam, the South Vietnamese Army) soldiers. The vast majority of the ARVN troops did not appear to be motivated to fight. If they were not interested in defending their country, why were we there? When we left the region in late September of 1971, it was clear to us that (A) the North Vietnamese Army (NVA) was planning a major offensive and (B) that the ARVN that we observed would surrender rather than fight. During the 1972 "Easter offensive", 194 days after we departed the region, as we had expected the ARVN surrendered rather than defend the location. Why did the ARVN soldiers lack motivation to defend their country? Why, after the war, did some U.S. military personnel, including some Vietnam veterans, and politicians proclaim with great certainty that South Vietnam would have survived as a thriving democracy if the U.S. military had not been required to fight with "one hand tied behind their back"? The "denied permission to win" narrative was not consistent with what I had observed.

Preface

The third set of issues concerned the military draft. Any objective observer could easily ascertain that the selection system that had evolved in the years after World War II was unfair and contributed to civil unrest during the Vietnam War. Draft boards across the country were not consistent in awarding deferments and exemptions. Young men of draft age were well aware that the draft was not fair. The lottery system introduced to aid with selections beginning in 1970 reduced, but did not eliminate, the inequity. The U.S. transitioned to an all-volunteer military in 1973. However, since 1980, all 18 to 25-year-old male U.S. citizens and male immigrants are legally required to register with the Selective Service System. It is estimated that approximately 10% who are required to do so do not bother to register, and most suffer no adverse consequences. Why does the U.S. retain the Selective Service apparatus? In the event of a national emergency of such enormity that Congress and the President deem it necessary to conduct a draft, would there not be a fairer, more equitable, and more transparent selection process?

This manuscript is presented in three parts. Part I includes my personal story. Part II includes my understanding of how the U.S. got into and eventually out of the Vietnam War and why an independent democratic South Vietnam did not result. Part III includes a proposal to replace the legacy Selective Service System and local draft boards with a fairer system than that used for prior U.S. military drafts.

Part One

A Draftee's Story: One Among 2.6 Million

Chapter 1

Introduction

"We are not here."

The alarm rang. It was August 1971. I was in a bunker at an artillery fire support base called Camp Carroll about nine miles south of the DMZ (Demilitarized Zone). Camp Carroll was also known as Artillery Plateau and firebase Tan Lam.[1] We were Northwest of Hue and Northeast of Khe Sanh. The DMZ extended for approximately three miles on both sides of the border between North and South Vietnam. The border and the DMZ had been established by the 1954 Geneva Accords. I shut off the alarm and crawled out from under the mosquito net. We used the nets to keep rats from nibbling on us while we slept. The rats had been in charge of the bunker since the U.S. Marines abandoned it in December of 1968. I put on my combat boots and other garb, including a flak jacket and helmet, grabbed my M16, and along with Bill Deal and Harv Harden, stepped out of the sleep bunker and walked the 100 feet to the Fire Direction Control (FDC) bunker. It was time for our three-man crew to begin our next eight-hour shift. Shift changes typically began with an informal briefing regarding activity for the last eight hours from the other three-man crew, as well as any ongoing fire missions.

We were greeted by Ron Albright, who got our attention when he began the briefing with: "We are not here."

I responded, "What do you mean? We are not here?"

Albright: "We are not here."

I was confused. "If we are not here, where are we?"

Albright: "I don't know."

I asked, "How do you know we are not here?"

Albright: "According to U.S. military brass in Saigon, there are no U.S. combat troops within 200 miles of the DMZ. So, we can't be here. We must be someplace else."

In addition to his FDC duties, Albright also served as the battery's RATT RIG (Radio Teletype set (rig)) operator. (That is, until the rig was destroyed by an NVA rocket. But that story will have to wait.) During a trek from the FDC bunker to the RATT RIG that was mounted on a three-quarter ton truck, Albright encountered a reporter who had hitched a ride on an ammunition resupply truck. The French reporter explained to Albright that he was surprised to find U.S. troops in the area since he had been told by U.S. military officials in Saigon that no U.S. combat troops were within 200 miles of the DMZ. The reporter traveled to our location to witness how the South Vietnamese troops were doing without U.S. help.

At the time, the bulk of news reports about activities of U.S. forces in the Vietnam War were paraphrased from press releases prepared, censored, cleared, and disseminated by the U.S. military. For example, an *Associated Press* article dated July 10, 1971, included "The sector is now defended on the ground almost exclusively by South Vietnamese forces following withdrawal last week of American troops from their last two fire bases...",[2] and on July 22, 1971, "The last American combat battalion was withdrawn from the area just below

Draftee

the demilitarized zone..."³ Given the newspaper reports, presumably based on U.S. military press releases, it would be reasonable to conclude that we were not there. We did not have access to newspapers other than the military's *Pacific Stars & Stripes* that was usually two weeks old upon arrival. The story that "The last American combat battalion was withdrawn from the area just below the demilitarized zone..." was news to us.

We were the FDC crew with a U.S. army artillery battery (Battery B of the 6th Battalion 32nd Artillery of the First Field Forces). Our battery of about 100 men (and boys) was assembled to operate two self-propelled 175-mm guns (M107 "long skinny") and two self-propelled eight-inch howitzers (M110 "short stubby").⁴ Since we used maps to calculate elevation and deflection settings for aiming the artillery, we knew our exact location. On July 10th, we had traveled through the city of Hue, crossed the Perfume River, and set up camp, a temporary firebase, next to a cemetery near Cam Lo, about six miles south of the DMZ. On July 20th, we broke camp at Cam Lo and traveled by road to Camp Carroll, about five miles southwest of Cam Lo and about nine miles south of the DMZ. The range of the 175-mm guns exceeded 20 miles. From our location, they could deliver 147-pound high explosive projectiles to targets as far east as the South China Sea, southwest to the Laotian salient, and north into and over the DMZ. We were a northernmost U.S. battery in South Vietnam. We were on the front line of a war that had no front line.

Albright continued the briefing, bringing us up to date with activity (radio traffic, fire missions) for the last eight hours and expected activity for the next eight hours. He then, along with the other two members of his three-man crew (German and Turnbull), put on his helmet, flak jacket, grabbed his M16, and headed out for the sleep bunker to rest for what remained of the eight hours.

Our battery included a minimal number of FDC troops to man two crews for accepting requests for and preparing artillery firing data, for conducting fire missions. At least one three-man crew was on duty at all times. Since we had arrived at Cam Lo, our routine was eight hours on and eight hours off. We averaged twelve hours per day. It was a pattern that we had determined was better for eating, sleeping, and remaining alert, than twelve on and twelve off. However, there were times of intense activity and housekeeping duties, such as burning feces, when shifts extended beyond eight hours. Since Albright also had to spend some time in the RATT RIG, he seldom had eight hours off.

For the most part, life in the FDC bunker was very businesslike. We were not officers. We had been drafted. We had no responsibility other than to do our jobs. A junior officer (second or first lieutenant) was present during fire missions. Usually, the officers stayed out of the way, observed, and helped when appropriate. The officer on duty was the final arbiter of the firing data provided to the cannon operators.

Deal took up his position at the radio table and shook his head. "Well, don't that beat all? No wonder we can't get replacement parts for the generators and Molly and other supplies. We ain't here." Molly was the name given to the three-quarter ton Dodge multi-fuel (Diesel or gasoline) truck assigned to our FDC unit. Molly was used to transport us and our FDC equipment (generators, radios, antennas, computing equipment, maps, charting table, batteries) as we moved from one location to the next. Deal usually drove; he assumed an unofficial responsibility for Molly's maintenance and sensed that Molly's water pump was close to failing.

Deal continued, "Do you suppose they have forgotten about us?"

Draftee

I responded, "No, I don't think so. They still send us ammo, Diesel fuel, and fire missions".

Harden: "And food, such as it is."

Deal: "The NVA sure as heck knows that we are here."

Indeed, they did. They all too frequently fired rockets that landed and detonated on our base. There was a 30-day period during our encampment at Carroll during which we endured incoming NVA rockets every day. Years later, I learned that the September 1, 1971, edition of the *Pacific Stars & Stripes* reported that "ARVN soldiers at Fire Base Carroll 10 miles south of the DMZ suffered light casualties Sunday when Communist gunners hit the base with 60 122-mm rockets..."[5] We were at Carroll from July 20 to September 22, 1971. There was no mention of our battery in the article. There was no mention of U.S. soldier casualties. Perhaps the U.S. military spokesman was not permitted to mention us as they had already proclaimed that we were not there.

Unfortunately, we did suffer casualties. Rueben Aragon's (Vietnam Wall Panel 2W Row 20) local Colorado newspaper reported that SP4 Rueben T. Aragon "died ... of wounds suffered in a rocket attack Aug. 15 on an artillery position near the Demilitarized Zone separating North and South Vietnam..."[6] Deal continued, "Sort of makes you wonder. The enemy knows that we are here. And our own Generals deny our existence."

It was August of 1971. it was 45 months, almost four years, since Defense Secretary McNamara explained in a November 1967 memo to President Johnson that the U.S. "could not win the war in Vietnam..."[7] Approximately 58,220 U.S., 5,100 South Korean, 500 Australian, 40 New Zealand, and 9 Philippine soldiers lost their lives as a direct result of the war (another 300,000 were wounded and 75,000 of those were severely disabled). Of the 58,220 U.S. soldiers, 69% died after McNamara's memo to his commander in chief. In addition, an estimated 250,000 ARVN soldiers, over a million NVA and Viet Cong combatants, and two million Vietnamese civilians were killed.[8]

It was August of 1971. It was 25 months since Neil Armstrong and Buzz Aldrin walked on the moon.

It was August of 1971. It was 31 months since President Nixon had been inaugurated. During his campaign he pledged to end the war.[9] Unlike McNamara, President Nixon was the commander in chief. In spite of his pledge, 35 percent (20,309) of the total number of U.S. soldiers who lost their lives in Vietnam, were killed after President Nixon was inaugurated in January of 1969.

Harden said, "One thing about our commander in chief. He can sure keep a secret. Of course, it would be easy to keep a secret if it never existed." In March of 1968, candidate Nixon pledged that he would "end the war," but when asked about his plan to end the war he responded, "Let me tell you why I won't tell you that. No one with this responsibility who is seeking office should give away any of his bargaining positions in advance..."[10] This statement was interpreted by some as an affirmation that candidate Nixon had a "secret plan" to end the war.

Our conversation was interrupted by radio traffic calling for a fire mission. Our focus quickly shifted to the job at hand. The remainder of the shift was normal, to the extent that calculating and transmitting artillery firing data with the expressed purpose of destroying "targets" that often included human beings can be normal.

On a personal level, our primary interest was survival of self and survival of colleagues. That is why we wore helmets and flak jackets when we were not in a bunker. For the most part, we were too busy to concern ourselves with "not being there." We knew where we were, and we knew that the likelihood of our survival depended at least in part on remaining alert and focused on our jobs. It reminded me of a line in Remarque's description of German soldier activity in the World War I epic *All Quiet on the Western Front*: "Every expression of life must serve only the preservation of existence, and is absolutely focused on that ... that is the only way to save ourselves..."[11]

After the shift, as I headed back to the sleep bunker, my thoughts returned to our whereabouts. Why are we here? What are we doing? How did we get into this mess? What are we hoping to achieve? Was candidate Nixon lying in 1968, or had he implemented his "intensive diplomatic, economic, and political programs," and did they fail to work? Were we part of his "plan"? Or was his ambiguous "plan" simply campaign rhetoric designed to attract votes?

The Gulf of Tonkin Resolution gave U.S. presidents authorization, without a formal declaration of war by Congress, for the use of conventional military force in Southeast Asia. It was enacted August 10, 1964. However, the start of direct U.S. military involvement in the war can be traced to the 1954 Geneva Accords. The U.S. Defense Department lists Richard B. Fitzgibbon Jr. as the first U.S. soldier killed in the Vietnam War on June 8, 1956. Dwight Eisenhower was President. U.S. soldiers continued to die in the country until the war formally ended, when NVA forces captured Saigon, and South Vietnamese President Duong Van Minh surrendered on April 30, 1975; Gerald Ford was the President. Charles McMahon and Darwin Lee Judge were killed in a rocket attack on April 29, 1975: one day before the official surrender, and almost four years after Albright had learned that "we were not there." They are considered to be the last two U.S. soldiers killed in Vietnam during the Vietnam War.

Approximately 2,594,000 U.S. servicemen served "in country." Each had a unique experience that varied considerably depending on when they served, where they served, and their specific military duties. My experience was limited to specific locations. For example, I did not travel south of Phan Rang, which is more than 200 miles northeast of Saigon, the capital city of what was South Vietnam. (After the war, Saigon was renamed Ho Chi Minh City, to honor the leader of the revolution that defeated the French. Ho Chi Minh was the first leader of North Vietnam.) Most of the time we spent on firebases (some of them quite temporary) about the size of a couple of football fields, surrounded by concertina wire. We did not routinely wear rank insignia; it was not necessary. We knew the rank of the small number of fellow soldiers with whom we interacted. We did not salute officers. The highest-ranking officer with our battery was a Captain. Captain Wayne Smoot was in charge until March 10, 1971, when he completed his time in the country and was replaced by Captain Larris Hunting. During my time in Vietnam, I seldom saw a higher-ranking officer.

For our predicament, less shine was preferred to more. We did not polish boots. We did keep our M16 assault rifles oiled, ready, and always in close proximity. Some of our locations were very temporary, others less so. The lack of polished boots and rank insignia was seldom a problem; one exception was on September 22, 1971, the day after we left Carroll and traveled from Camp Evans to Camp Eagle. When we arrived at Eagle, after months on remote firebases, we were stopped by Military Police (MPs) for not wearing proper insignia, for not having polished boots, and for our unprofessional appearance. Indeed, we were filthy, but we had grounds for being so. Fortunately, somebody in authority agreed, and we were spared time in the brig.

Draftee

It is estimated that of the 2.6 million U.S. military personnel that served in Vietnam, 80% did not fight in combat and were not regularly exposed to enemy attack. For example, Appy writes that: "At least four of five American troops in Vietnam carried out noncombat duties on large bases far away from those snake-infested jungles..."[12] Similarly, Ward et al. reported that "Eight out of ten Americans in Vietnam never heard a shot fired in anger, never saw a bomb dropped or a village burned. They were men in combat support..." and that "Private American contractors constructed 100 airfields ... created seven deep draft ocean ports ... Six giant dairy plants ... more than 40 ice cream plants..."[13]

The largest American base was Long Binh. It was "20 miles north of Saigon ... roughly the size of Manhattan ... As many as 60,000 Americans made it their home. Tens of thousands of South Vietnamese filed through its gates each day to see to the Americans' needs. Vietnamese cooks prepared their meals. Vietnamese maids and laundresses tidied up their barracks and made sure their uniforms were clean and crisply ironed..." Ward et al. reported that Long Binh had "about the same facilities you might find stateside" including swimming pools, golf driving ranges, football fields, air conditioned clubs, bakery, go-cart track, plus a 24-hour "massage parlor."[14] Kelly reports that Long Binh covered eighteen square miles and at one time housed over 100,000 U.S troops.[15] Our locations near the DMZ were 600 miles and a "world away" from Long Binh.[16]

During time in transit, I spent a few days at several bases that encompassed an area much larger than the typical area that our battery usually occupied. These bases located near Cam Ranh Bay, Nha Trang, Phan Rang, and Da Nang were much larger than what we were accustomed to but smaller than Long Binh. From my brief experience, life for some of the soldiers on these bases appeared to be similar to life on bases in the U.S. For example, it appeared that some soldiers on these bases did not routinely wear flak jackets and helmets or routinely carry weapons. However, most of these bases were under constant threat of potential rocket attacks and potential attacks from saboteurs. I suppose that it could be concluded that many of these soldiers did not fight in combat and were not regularly exposed to enemy attack. But they were a long distance from family, friends, and the peaceful existence of most U.S. communities.

Over the years, I have not engaged in many conversations about Vietnam. Family and friends that knew me prior to my service did not ask. I suppose that they assumed that it would only bring up sad memories. I did show them the few pictures that I had taken. Photos of bunkers and destroyed military equipment were sufficient evidence that our battery was engaged in a war. When someone did ask what I did in Vietnam, I would usually respond with "I ducked." That was often interpreted as a signal that I wanted to change the topic of the conversation.

On more than one occasion, when someone learned that I had spent time in Vietnam, rather than ask about my experience, for some reason, they felt a need to tell me the story of their cousin, or perhaps their cousin's brother-in-law. I tried to listen politely. I interpreted that as a signal that they had no interest in my story, because it could not possibly compete with what they already thought they knew. Some, who were near my age but did not serve, explained why they were fair and squarely (legally) not drafted. I recall one exchange during which I was told how veterans, such as me, were given a multitude of advantages relative to a nonveteran, such as the speaker. Perhaps that explains why, according to the 2000 U.S. Census, 13,853,027 U.S. residents falsely claimed to have served with the U.S. military in Vietnam. In actuality, peer-reviewed research published in the *American Economic Review* found that "Social Security administrative records indicate that, in the early 1980s, long after their service in Vietnam was ended, the earnings of white veterans were approximately 15% less than the earnings of comparable nonveterans. The experience-earnings profiles estimated imply that white veterans suffered an earnings reduction equivalent to the loss of two years of civilian labor market experience..."[17]

There were 2.6 million unique experiences and 2.6 million stories. No one story is any more or less important than any other. I caution the reader that while there are 2.6 million credible stories, since 13,853,027 falsely claimed in the 2000 U.S. census to have served in Vietnam, some stories may be less than authentic.

More than 50 years have passed since Albright proclaimed that "we are not here." I have come to believe that to understand why we were there on that August day in 1971, the story must begin many years before 1971. But, from the perspective of an individual draftee, there are two stories. There is the story of how the individual got into the mess, and a separate story as to how the U.S. got into the mess. I begin with my personal story as best as I can recall. My mother told us that there are three versions to most stories: there is "his" story, "her" story, and finally, there is "what really happened." In honor of her, I will try to tell "what really happened."

Chapter 2

A Child During the Cold War
"What is a calm-u-nist?"

It was late afternoon on a typically damp, cloudy, cold, fall day in Southern Illinois in 1954. I was in the first grade and had recently celebrated my sixth birthday. My two older brothers, older sister, and I were dropped off a school bus and walked a little more than a half mile to our home. The bus carried first through twelfth grade students. Our school did not have preschool or kindergarten.

My brother James opened the back door, and we walked into the warm but drafty farmhouse kitchen. Mom had prepared snacks that, as she said, "would tide us over until supper." Snack time enabled my mother to gently pry into the day's happenings at school. My oldest brother James was in the seventh grade. He was usually relatively quiet, but this day, he began the debriefing with:

"Mom, the boys on the bus say that President Eisenhower is a communist."

Mom: "Which boys said that?"

James:"The high school boys."

Draftee

Mom: "He'd better not be."

James: "Well, that's what they said McCarthy says."

I squeezed in a question. "Mom, what is a calm-u-nist?"

Mom: "I don't know, but he'd better not be one."

After arriving from the bus, it was routine for the young scholars to change from school clothes to work clothes, to eat a snack, and for the two older boys to head outside to complete their evening farm chores. There were chickens, hogs, and cattle to water and feed, eggs to gather, and cows to milk. My sister in third grade helped with laundry, cleaning, egg cleaning, and food preparation. My chore load was limited to activities where I could do the least damage, such as setting the table and drying dishes. I worked hard to shirk any additional work assignments.

Neither of my parents attended high school. Both of them grew up on farms. Mom had two older brothers and two younger brothers. She was eight when their mother died, and for a time was sent to live with an aunt's family. Her uncle was a World War I veteran. Several years later, her father married a widow who had three children. Soon after graduating from the eighth grade, which for her contemporaries was considered to be a terminal degree, she moved from the farm to work as a live-in maid for a family in town. Two of my mother's brothers, and one of her stepbrothers, served during World War II.

Our father didn't talk about his formal education in the one-room school located near the intersection of three rural trails, about a mile from his home. One day, my sister found his report cards and was surprised to learn that he was marked absent every other day in both the seventh and eighth grades. Upon learning our father's attendance record, she asked if she could skip school every other day, but Mom said "no." The discovery of routine absenteeism, however, required an explanation. Dad explained that when he entered the seventh grade, he knew that the teacher taught seventh grade material one day and eighth grade material the next. On the days she taught eighth grade, the seventh graders were responsible for maintaining the stove, the grounds, and keeping the building and outhouses clean. Dad initially proposed to attend and participate in academics both days and complete both grades in one academic year. The school board members, who were all neighboring farmers that he knew, denied the request, probably for two reasons. First, it would have set a bad precedent, and second, by law, he was required to attend at least fourteen weeks per year until his fourteenth birthday. The school year was 7.5 months, so even if he skipped every other day, he could technically fulfill the fourteen weeks requirement.

This enterprising seventh grader negotiated a deal to do his fair share of the work details before and after classes on the alternate days that he attended. He mastered sufficient material with the alternate day schedule for two academic years to earn an eighth-grade diploma. At the age of fourteen, he became fully immersed in a farming career. Given the lack of electricity, the livestock activities (cows to be milked, hogs to be fed and eventually butchered and processed, eggs to be gathered and cleaned) and the crop activities (crops to be planted, cultivated, and harvested; hay to be harvested and stored), "full time" meant seven days a week, year after year.

Dad was born in 1909. He was four when his mother died. He was almost six when his father married a childless widow. He was too young to serve in World War I; he was 32 on December 7, 1941. He had been a full-time farmer for eighteen years. I did not ask, but I assume that the local draft board classified him as either a II-C (deferred in agriculture) or III-C (deferred both by reason of dependency and agricultural occupation). His younger brother, who was also a married farmer

Draftee

when the U.S. formally entered World War II, was exempted as well.

My parents did not discuss world events. They did not discuss politics. I learned that some of my uncles had served in the military from discussions that they had when they visited, and from pictures of them in military uniforms proudly displayed in my grandparents' home. I also knew that my mother was concerned about the health of her brothers who had served — what years later would be classified as post-traumatic stress disorder.

My parents had limited access to news beyond the local area. Their lives were too busy with farm and family obligations to allow much time to ponder national events. They subscribed to a local newspaper that was delivered a day after publication six days a week by the rural free-delivery mail service. They were appreciative of rural free delivery. The Saturday paper arrived on Monday, and the newspaper did not publish a Sunday edition.

In 1954, our family did not have a television. We had one radio in the kitchen and listened, at a few specific times during the day, to a local station. Dad was interested in the weather forecast and, depending on what he had to sell, grain and livestock prices. Mom was interested in the hospital reports. A less than cheerful announcer read the names of those admitted, those discharged, and births (Mom was always offended when he mispronounced a name of someone that she knew). This was followed by a listing of death notices, complete with information regarding time and location of funeral ceremonies. The announcer also read a brief account of the national and international news from the United Press International wire. Evidently, the local announcer had some discretion as to what he read. I recall frequent accounts of President Eisenhower's golfing habits. Mom was okay with the

President golfing, as long as he kept the United States out of war.

Given the limited access to information, it is not surprising that the family did not discuss world events. Even if more information had been available, given their work activities, there was little to no time for talking about things over which they had no control. They would not have paid much attention to Wisconsin Senator Joseph McCarthy's long list of disagreements with fellow Republican, President Eisenhower.[1]

As a practicing Catholic, Mom knew that the Catholic Church had described communism as a religion without God. She was no doubt familiar with the ongoing battle between Catholicism and communism as practiced in Eastern Europe. In 1949, the leader of the Catholic Church in Hungary, Cardinal Mindszenty, was sentenced to life in prison by the communist authorities for treason and leading an organization concerned with the overthrow of the Hungarian government. New York Catholic Cardinal Spellman was quoted as referring to communists as "men depraved and deranged, men who as their gods know only Satan and Stalin..."[2] That was all my mother needed to know about communism.

Down on the farm, the east/west struggle, the Cold War, was relatively simple: it was us against them. They were bad and we were good. The spread of communism was seen as a sinister movement by the Soviet Union to take over the world and to deny the existence of God. Albania, Bulgaria, and East Germany "fell" in 1945; Romania, Poland, and Hungary in 1947; Czechoslovakia and North Korea in 1948, and Mainland (we called it Red) China in 1949.

My mother's response that President Eisenhower "better not be one" ended the discussion. It was a clear message that "calm-u-nists" were bad. At the time, I had no idea why they were bad. It did not matter. I had lived long enough to know that Mom did not want to extend the conversation. I also knew that a continuation of the discussion might lengthen the time until supper was ready, and I was hungry. For my six-year-old self, food was more important than information about "calm-u-nists."

Chapter 3

December 1969 Draft Lottery

"October 30 is zero three eight."

During the Fall 1969 university quarter, I was a senior at Southern Illinois University (SIU) majoring in Agricultural Education. At the time, education majors who desired to obtain a certificate to teach high school students were required to complete a class commonly referred to as student teaching. I was assigned to fulfill the student teaching requirement with a wonderful veteran teacher at a high school about 30 miles from my parents' home. Since it was within commuting distance, to avoid the expense and hassles of finding a place to live for only twelve weeks, I chose to live at my parents' home and commute. Thus, on the evening of December 1, 1969, I sat with my parents in their living room to watch the televised military draft lottery on our local CBS station.

The program began with: "Because of the Special CBS News Special Report which follows, Mayberry RFD will not be shown tonight ... The Draft Lottery, a live report on tonight's picking of the birth dates for the draft. Here at Selective Service headquarters in Washington is CBS news correspondent Roger Mudd..." We watched quietly as Roger Mudd

Draftee

read the dates in the order selected. He read the first 34 dates selected and then continued, "For number 35 it is May 7, August 24, May 11, October 30, December 11..."[1]

Mom said, "He said October 30th. What number was it?"

Me: "October 30 was number 38."

Mom: "What does that mean?"

Me: "That means that I don't have to worry about finding a job."

My parents were silent and continued to stare at the television as Roger Mudd continued to read what was, for me, meaningless dates and numbers.

Me: "Mom, are you sure that I was born on October 30th?"

Mom: "That is what I remember, but I'll check your birth certificate. I am sorry."

After October 30th was called, I was only interested in two other dates: October 29th and October 31st; October 31st was the 79th number called. Delaying my birth by a day would not have helped. Throughout the years, I thought it was best to not share a birthday with Halloween.

As Roger Mudd explained, the Defense Department expected that those with numbers 001 to 120 were almost certain to be drafted. (Eventually, most of those with the first 195 birth dates selected were drafted.) My number was 38; that removed the ambiguity. I was quite certain that my student deferment would continue until my expected graduation in June of 1970, after which I would be reclassified and drafted.

October 29th was the 229th date drawn. In a statement that I regretted for years, I said, "I should have come a day earlier," to which my mother responded, "Well, I feel awful." I am sure that she did. My idiotic comment was not helpful.

To confirm my assessment, several weeks later, I visited the local draft board number 186 office at the Post Office building in Du Quoin. The board's executive secretary was Linda Sherman. She was aware of my situation, as well as that of every male my age in Perry County. She confirmed that my 2-S student deferment would remain in effect until I graduated in June, at which time my status would be changed to 1-A (eligible for military service). She told me that, based on previous Board action, I could expect to be drafted in July.

I completed the student teaching assignment in December and returned to campus in January. A typical conversation among male students for the first few weeks of 1970 on campus began with "What's your number?" "38." "That's a shame." "Yours?" If the response was greater than 250, my response was "congratulations." After a few weeks, we returned to our normal routine of completing assignments and preparing for exams.

I was seventeen when I graduated from high school and entered college. I registered with the Selective Service System when I turned eighteen during my freshman year. For the most part, during my time in college, I was successful in ignoring the conflict in Vietnam. I shared a room with two other students in a large, converted house in which about 30 male students resided. There was one television in a communal "TV" room. It displayed a lousy picture from a signal obtained from an over-the-air antenna. During the four years that I lived in the house, the only show I recall trying to watch on the television was *Monday Night Football*. One of my roommates subscribed to *Newsweek* magazine. He offered to let us read its weekly offering. I chose not to read stories about Vietnam. During my sophomore and junior years, many of my former high school classmates who did not attend college were drafted, and many were serving in Vietnam. My mother's friends kept her informed and she relayed the information to me, usually ending the story with "You should pray for him."

The U.S. drafted young men for military service during the

Draftee

Civil War, World War I, and World War II. Three years after World War II, the 1948 Selective Service Act became law. Facing the draft became a rite of passage for young men. My brother James was drafted in 1964. He served from February 27, 1964, to February 27, 1966. After basic training at Fort Leonard Wood, Missouri, he served the remainder of his two years of active duty at Fort Richardson near Anchorage, Alaska.

In 1969, one way to avoid the draft and reduce the probability of serving in Vietnam was to join the National Guard. Members of Guard units typically served a two-week summer camp and a weekend per month. Those who joined the Guard were referred to by regular army soldiers as "weekend warriors" or as "adult boy scouts." A few Guard units did serve in Vietnam (a few thousand guardsmen out of a total of hundreds of thousands). However, President Johnson did not want to call up Guard units for active duty. It is generally assumed that he feared calling up Guard units for service in a foreign country would reduce support for the War.[2] For Presidents Johnson and Nixon, increasing the number of draftees was more palatable than calling up the Guard. By 1969, the Guard was an alternative for those about to be drafted, the alternative to avoid Vietnam. But there was a catch: by 1969, most Guard units were "full." Slots were limited, and it was generally understood that in some states, political influence was required to secure a spot.[3] For example, one Guard unit in Texas found slots for seven members of the Dallas Cowboys; George W. Bush, son of Congressman George H. W. Bush; Lloyd Bentsen Jr., son of Senator Lloyd Bentsen; John Connally III, son of Governor John Connally Jr., and others with "connections." I did not know anyone in the Guard. I certainly did not have any political influence, and thus for me, the National Guard was not a viable option.[4][5][6]

Chapter 4

May 1970 Kent State University Tragedy

"Southern Illinois University closed indefinitely."

The SIU spring quarter began on March 30, 1970. It was to be my last quarter as an undergraduate student, with ten weeks of classes, finals week, and then graduation, scheduled for June 12, 1970. I was enrolled in seventeen hours. I was busy. The good news was that I did not have to concern myself with finding a job. The bad news was that I was scheduled to be "selected" by my local draft board soon after graduation. I was not alone. Approximately half of the male seniors scheduled to graduate who were physically fit and not already affiliated with a military service branch had learned during the December 1, 1969, lottery that they were likely to be drafted before the end of 1970.

The first five weeks of the 1970 spring quarter on the SIU campus were relatively normal. Things changed during week six. On Thursday, April 30, President Nixon addressed the nation to announce that he had ordered an American invasion of Cambodian territory controlled by the North Vietnamese.[1] On Monday, May 4, 1970, Ohio National Guardsmen fired live rounds into a group of students, killing four Kent State

Draftee

University students and wounding nine others. A group of Kent State students had assembled to demonstrate their opposition to the invasion and bombing of Cambodia. The Ohio National Guard had been activated to maintain order. Two of the four students killed were not involved in the protest. They were walking from one class to the next.

Many college students across the country were very sensitive to happenings in Vietnam and Cambodia. Many had close high school friends who had been drafted and served, or were still serving in Vietnam. The killings at Kent State added fuel to the tensions on college campuses all across the country. Headlines taken from the SIU student newspaper, the *Daily Egyptian*, tell part of the story:[2]

Tuesday, May 5: "Kent State confrontation, 4 students die."

Wednesday, May 6: "Chancellor suspends Thursday classes."

Thursday, May 7: "Police, students clash; several hurt."

"Demonstrators ransacked offices in Woody and Wheeler Halls starting at least two fires and causing heavy damage with brick-borne assaults ... Late Wednesday night a group of about 500 demonstrators moved down South Illinois breaking windows in businesses ... plans call for (Illinois) National Guardsmen to supplement Security Police on three-man patrols scattered all across campus ... some 650 (guardsmen) were mobilized..."

Friday, May 8: "Police gas crowd; then, violence."

"A crowd of 2,500 students blocked the intersection of Main and Illinois for two hours ... A smaller group sat down on the Illinois Central tracks and halted two trains ... Tear gas was fired after orders to clear the tracks were ignored..."

Saturday, May 9: "Calm returns to Carbondale; curfew still on."

"Carbondale Mayor ... issued an order Friday extending a state of civil emergency to prohibit any gatherings of 10 or more persons within the city..."

Tuesday, May 12: "SIU officials plan meeting on state of campus." "$100,000 damages to city, SIU — 356 arrests."

Wednesday, May 13: "SIU closed indefinitely."

"Chancellor Robert W. MacVicar made the announcement at 11:30 p.m. Tuesday..." "The closing had been authorized by Gov. Richard B. Ogilvie in consultations with University officials..."

Thursday, May 14: "Closure continues; Board to decide future of campus."

Friday, May 15: "Closure voted by students; reopen say faculty-staff."

The SIU Board of Trustees met on Friday, May 15, and officially terminated the 1970 spring quarter classes. They ordered students to leave on-campus living facilities. I packed up my things, picked up a cousin who was told to vacate his on-campus residence hall, and drove home. SIU was one of hundreds of U.S. institutions of higher education that suspended some normal activities in the spring of 1970.[3]

Many students were sincerely concerned about the execution of the war. During his 1968 campaign, President Nixon implied that he had a secret plan to end the war. When students learned that the President expanded the war by bombing and invading Cambodia, they were not pleased. Many of the college students who participated in the May 1970 demonstrations cared about the draft and only indirectly about the war. Almost all of the 23,000 students on the SIU campus in the spring of 1970 knew someone who had been drafted and was serving in Vietnam. Many knew someone who had been killed or seriously injured. Approximately half of senior male students had learned on December 1, 1969, as had I, that given their lottery number, their deferment would end upon graduation, and they expected to be drafted before the end of 1970.

Many draft susceptible students found the Kent State shootings exceedingly offensive for another reason. The fatal shots were fired by members of the Ohio National Guard, the Weekend Warriors, the adult Boy Scouts. By 1970, many draft-vulnerable college students had come to believe that slots in the National Guard were reserved for those of privilege. Those who occupied the slots were not seen as patriots, but rather, rightly or wrongly, as recipients of undeserved advantage of family "connections."[4][5][6]

The vast majority of the 23,000 SIU students did not engage in unlawful behavior. The *Daily Egyptian* reported that 2,500 (about 11%) were involved in the May 7th protests. My roommates and I were in our room studying on the evening of May 7th, less than a half mile from the main gathering of protestors. We did witness National Guard vehicles on the streets adjacent to our house and detected tear gas that penetrated our open windows. It "burned" our eyes. We elected to close the windows.

The *Daily Egyptian* did not publish after May 15th until summer school started in late June. Few classes were held after May 6th, which was in the sixth week of the planned eleven-week quarter. The administrators were placed in a difficult situation. We later learned that the university elected to keep our tuition and fees, to continue to pay the faculty and to issue credit and assign a grade of "S" for classes. The transcript also includes the following statement: "CLASSES SUSPENDED MAY 12, 1970. ONLY GRADES OF S AND U USED EXCEPT WHEN DEAN APPROVED USE OF LETTER GRADE."

Francis Epplin

Name **FRANCIS MICHAEL EPPLIN**

COURSE TITLE	DEPT.	Course Number	Qtr. Hrs.	GRADE
C8 SPRING QUARTER 1970				
PRIN AG MECHANIZAT	AG	412	4	S
PLANT GENETICS	PL	315	4	S
SOIL FERTILITY	PL	407A	3	S
SOIL FERTILITY	PL	407B	2	S
FORAGE CROP MANAGE	PL	419	4	S

CLASSES SUSPENDED MAY 12, 1970. ONLY
GRADES OF S AND U USED EXCEPT WHEN
DEAN APPROVED USE OF LETTER GRADE.
SEE EXPLANATION SHEET FOR DETAILS.

Part of My Official Transcript

The Transcript Explanation Sheet included the following explanation for the "S" grade: "S — Satisfactory. Ordinarily used for non-credit courses only. Exceptions: 1) Used for credit courses as well during spring quarter, 1970..."

There was a period of time during which it was not clear if credit toward degree completion would be awarded for the spring quarter classes that had been prematurely terminated. However, the University did not want to refund tuition and fees and the faculty expected to be paid. The decision to award credit for the courses with an assigned grade of "S" enabled my graduation and completion of teacher certification requirements. I was relieved. I was not doing well in the classes.

For the remainder of May and June, I helped my family on the farm. On Friday, June 12, 1970, we drove back to campus for the graduation ceremonies. Campus had been closed for five weeks. Graduation was not a joyous occasion.

Chapter 5

Report for Induction

"So help me God."

On June 25th, my local draft board mailed the notice ordering me to report to the Illinois Central Railroad Depot in Pinckneyville at 6:15 a.m. on July 7, 1970. My parents and I left home at 5:50. The Illinois Central train — a few ancient passenger cars pulled by a freight engine belching Diesel exhaust — rolled in at 6:40 a.m. I said goodbye to my parents and boarded the train along with the other Perry County inductee, Jerry Duvardo. The train traveled northwest out of town, past the cemetery where one set of my grandparents, two sets of my great grandparents, and one set of my great-great-grandparents are buried. The train followed a rather long route, traveled north of St. Louis, crossed the Mississippi River, traveled south through the tunnel under the St. Louis Arch grounds, and eventually into Union Station at about 9:00 am.

Francis Epplin

```
                SELECTIVE SERVICE SYSTEM          Approval Not Required.
                ORDER TO REPORT FOR INDUCTION

                                         LOCAL BOARD NO. 186
                                         SELECTIVE SERVICE SYSTEM
                                         POST OFFICE BUILDING
The President of the United States,      MARION, ILLINOIS 62959
  To   Mr. Francis Michael Epplin
       R R 1, Box 57                           (Local Board Stamp)
       Pinckneyville, Illinois 62274         JUN 2 5 1970
                                              (Date of mailing)

                                         SELECTIVE SERVICE NO.
                                         11  186  48  144

GREETING:
        You are hereby ordered for induction into the Armed Forces of the United States, and to report
   at      Illinois Central Railroad Depot, Pinckneyville, Illinois
                                    (Place of reporting)
   on     7 July 1970        at    6:15 A7M7 MORNING
             (Date)                     (Hour)
   for forwarding to an Armed Forces Induction Station.
                                        Donald A. Barrett
                                    (Member, Executive Secretary, or clerk of Local Board
```

Order to Report for Induction

We used a meal voucher that had been provided by Local Board 186. We then departed Union Station and walked the half mile to the Induction Center at 12th and Spruce. After several hours of waiting at station two, we were told to strip for inspection by the physician on duty. The doctor asked if there had been any change in our physical condition since our last physical. We replied "no" and were told to dress and report to station four. The folks at station four told us to report to station seven. At station seven, we were asked to complete a form to designate a benefactor for our army-provided life insurance policy. We were then issued a meal ticket and told to be back at 12:30.

We returned to station seven at 12:30. While waiting at station seven, a man dressed in a Salvation Army uniform distributed Bibles and prayed for our safety. We were then ordered into a yellow carpeted "ceremony room." We were told to respond to a choice of either entering the army by taking one step forward at the call of our name, or face a $10,000 fine and five years in federal prison. When my name was called, I took one step forward. Then we were issued an oath: "I, (state your name), do solemnly swear (or affirm) that I will support and defend the Constitution of the United States against all enemies, foreign and domestic; that I will bear true faith and allegiance to the same; and that I will obey the orders of the President of the United States and the orders of the officers appointed over me, according to regulations and the Uniform Code of Military Justice (So help me God)." With that oath, I was officially awarded the title of Private E-1 (Pvt, E-1). Ranks for enlisted soldiers (non-officers) and noncommissioned officers ranged from E-1 (private) to E-9 (sergeant major). Ranks for officers ranged from O-1 (Second Lieutenant) to O-10 (General).

We received orders from station twelve at about 2:30 p.m., assigning us to the army reception station at Fort Leonard Wood, Missouri. Shortly after 3 p.m., we (thirteen draftees and eight "volunteers") were loaded onto a chartered bus and transported the 150 miles to the Fort; we arrived at 6 p.m. We were marched through a chow line and then to an orientation center. We filled out forms until about 8:45 p.m. and then marched to barracks 9121. Lights out were at 9:30 p.m. I was assigned to fire watch from 9:30 – 11:00 p.m.

We were awakened at 6 a.m. on Wednesday, July 8th, for a 6:10 formation and breakfast. After breakfast, we were marched to a "barber shop." A "barber" stepped out and said to "send in about 40." Lines formed in front of each of the three "barbers." We were told to have $0.85 in our hand. One at a time we were ordered to sit in one of the three barber chairs. Our head hair was mowed with three or four passes of electric clippers, reminiscent of 4-H sheep clippers. We stood, handed the $0.85 to the "barber," and filed out. The barbers did not need aprons, combs, or scissors. Their electric clippers were only silenced to enable verification of correct payment.

Next, we were trucked to the clothing center. No measurements were taken. A soldier looked at us and handed us a bundle. The pants in my bundle did not fit; they were too tight around the waist.

Next, mug shots were taken for base identification cards; then to the optometry station for visual screening, followed by a trip to a dispensary for a tuberculosis skin test and blood sample, and then to a mess hall for lunch. After lunch, we were told to put on our new boots (again, fit did not seem to matter) and then marched to a reception hall for orientation. We were told that if the boots were too big for our feet, we should roll up a sock or two and stuff them in the boot. We were not offered a "work around" for boots that were too small. My "work around" for the tight pants was to leave them unbuttoned and to use the belt to secure them in place.

We were shown two training films. The first was about the Uniform Code of Military Justice. The second was narrated by U.S. immigrant, professional comedian, and honorary veteran Bob Hope. He told us that if we did a good job (and, although he didn't say it, if we managed to survive), we would be rewarded with an honorable discharge, which, according to Mr. Hope, is a very valuable thing.

After viewing the films, we were marched back to the mess hall for dinner, and then back to the barracks, whereupon a drill sergeant explained how to make an army bunk. He told us that if properly made, a quarter could be dropped on the made bunk, and the quarter would bounce and flip. One of my fellow privates produced a quarter but was not permitted to conduct the flip test.

After bunk-making instructions, the drill sergeant told us that there are three "don'ts" to survive the army. Don't beg.

Draftee

Don't promise. And don't demand. He said that in civilian life, sometimes it would be okay to beg. He went on to explain the difference between officers and noncommissioned officers (NCO). He told us that the NCO "buck" sergeant (E-5; three chevrons) is the dumbest and worst rank in the army, except for the second lieutenant (O-1; single gold bar) officer.

On Thursday, July 9th, we received cloth strips on which our last name was stenciled. We were marched to a sewing room where three civilian ladies sewed the name strips onto our fatigue shirts and our field jacket.

The next stop was the post office. We were each provided a bag, in which we were told to insert our civilian clothes. A civilian lady used a machine to sew the bag shut. We taped an address label on the bag and tossed it into the back of a waiting truck.

Our next stop on the orientation tour was the dental center. A person, perhaps a dentist, looked into our mouth, yelled information to an assistant who presumably was recording something. (Note: I have not been able to retrieve any of my army medical records. My impression is that on some occasions, activities such as this were conducted for "show." In other words, I suspect that the only purpose of this exercise was to check for visual evidence of abscesses or other issues that needed immediate attention.) We were then marched back to the clinic where the tuberculosis skin test was read and the results recorded. After lunch, we were each paid $25 in cash and then marched to a location for mental testing.

On July 14th, we received orders effectively transferring us from the reception center to our Basic Combat Training (BCT) unit. I was assigned to Company A, 1st Battalion, 2nd Basic Combat Training Brigade (Company A-1-2). Our BCT training was to begin on July 20, 1970, one year after Neil Armstrong walked on the moon. The purpose of Company A-

1-2 was to provide eight weeks of basic combat training for 222 soldiers. The Company was divided into four platoons; those with last names beginning with A through F were assigned to the first platoon. The Company included two officers (company commander; training officer) and ten noncommissioned officers (NCOs) (first sergeant; senior drill instructor; four platoon sergeants; four assistant platoon sergeants). Days later, we were told that the WETSU (We Eat This Stuff Up) alligator was the company's mascot. During those rare times of indoor training, when chairs were available, if told to be seated, we were expected to yell "Alpha one two wetsu" and sit in unison.

Several days during time in the reception center, I, along with one other soldier, was assigned to work in the orderly's office. Evidently, I had checked a box on some form affirming that I could type. In addition to typing on forms, we completed charts and summarized data. In the process, I learned that 40 of the 222 (18%) had at least one four-year college degree; 50 of the 222 (23%) had not earned a high school diploma. The U.S. Census Bureau reported that in 1970, 22% of 20 to 24-year-old males had completed less than four years of high school; 14% of 20 to 29-year-old males had completed four or more years of college.[1] Company A-1-2 was composed of a very heterogeneous group of draftees and volunteers, and in terms of educational attainment, relatively representative of the U.S. male population.

I informally categorized the "volunteers" into three groups. One group (a very small percentage of the volunteers) included those who freely volunteered and thought, at least prior to arrival, that they wanted to be in the army. The second and largest percentage of "volunteers" included those who had a low draft lottery number and would have been drafted. However, they were convinced by an army recruiter that if they volunteered, they would be treated better by the army, would be taught a trade, and would reduce their chances of being sent to Vietnam. At the time, volunteers committed to three or four years of active duty, whereas draftees were expected to serve no more than two years of active duty. The third group of "volunteers" was composed of young men for whom a judge had offered the option of military service in lieu of prison time.

In the summer and fall of 1970, Company A-1-2 was one of many basic combat training companies in the U.S. army. One consequence of the draft lottery was that most were composed of a cross section of young men that included college graduates, high school dropouts, and convicted criminals.

During my time in the orderly's office, First Sergeant Thomas walked up and said, "You go over to the mess hall and tell the mess sergeant that the First Sergeant wants some cookies". I said "okay" and left. It took a while to find the mess sergeant.

"Yea," he said, "What do ya want?"

"The first sergeant asked me to come over and get some cookies."

"What first sergeant? There's a heck of a lot of um down there."

"The one from company A."

"Well, go to the supply room and get some."

I went to the supply room and a specialist gave me a box of army cookies. I walked back to the orderly's office and knocked on the First Sergeant's door. He took one look and said, "Git those gaud damn chocolate cookies outta here, tell that damn mess sergeant to git me some vanilla wafers or vanilla cream cookies or don't get me nuthin'."

I said, "Yes, first sergeant," and ran back to the mess hall supply room, put down the chocolate cookies, and grabbed a bag of vanilla wafers and ran back. The first sergeant said, "Put them by the coffee pot."

I do not know, but I expect that if during the first trip I had returned with vanilla wafers, I would have been told to return them and secure chocolate cookies. During our time in training, lack of precise directives was normal. Standard operating procedure was to provide ambiguous instructions that could then provide justification for verbal and physical abuse.

Chapter 6

KP (Kitchen Police) – Spilled Milk and Guilty Bystander

"Clean the place."

Friday, July 10th, while at the Reception Station, I served my first half day of Kitchen Police (KP) duty. During the morning we were administered a battery of written tests. At 11 a.m. we started KP. Eight of us were assigned to a mess hall; we washed, scrubbed, wiped, polished, ran, carried, cussed, laughed, peeled, and griped. Two of the eight, and perhaps the least experienced peelers, suffered cuts and bled — no extra charge for a little blood with your serving of mashed potatoes. We were released at 6:30 p.m. At the time, I did not realize that we had only experienced a mild form of KP. On Monday, July 13th, I was assigned to another mild form (4 a.m. to 10 a.m.) of KP duty.

Our eight weeks of BCT officially began on Monday, July 20th. On our second day, Tuesday, July 21st, 1970, I, along with Duvardo, Edgington, Ellis, and Emmerick, was assigned to KP duty. We were awake at 4 a.m. and were in the kitchen of the mess hall at 4:30. I was assigned to be storeroom man, but a cook grabbed me and told me to make toast. I worked at making toast until about 5:15 when we were ordered to eat. Head mess

Sergeant Shuster called off my name and asked me where the hell I was. I told him that I was making toast. He roared out that I was supposed to be the storeroom boy and that I had better be at the number one box. I said "okay" and moved through the line and ate breakfast. I then went back to the number one box, a walk-in refrigerator. Somebody yelled "clean that place." Which, it was explained, means to take everything out of the refrigerator and scrub the walls, shelves, ceiling, and floor.

I rolled out the four garbage cans of potatoes, pulled the two pots of potatoes, one huge pot of lard, and two large size (tea or Kool-Aid) drink dispensers. I was then told to move stacks of the milk out of the refrigerator and to scrub the floor on which the milk had been stacked. Each milk carton contained seven gallons (56 pounds) of milk. They were stacked four high with the fourth being higher than my shoulders. I began moving the milk out of the cooler.

After a period of time, a server came in, yelling that he needed a milk container. I turned to look and, in so doing, lost my grip on a carton. Two cartons (14 gallons) fell from the stack and milk splattered over a wide area. Milk flowed freely over the entire floor of the refrigerator and out into the kitchen. About the same time as it was rushing out the door, mess Sergeant Shuster came roaring. I looked him in the eyes, and he turned and walked away, evidently in search of some other problem. My urge was to laugh, but I decided it would not be prudent. Instead, I elected to remain calm and to continue with the original assigned task, now much more reasonable, of cleaning the refrigerator. I scrubbed the floor, restacked the remaining milk containers, and pushed, carried, or pulled the other items back to or near their original locations.

During the day, I repeated the cleaning process twice for this walk-in unit and three times for the other walk-in refrigerator. I spent a lot of time in the storeroom. I stacked 100-pound bags of potatoes. Shipments arrived throughout the day. One truck carried bread, another milk, a third pastries, a fourth meat, and a fifth ice cream. I carried the food items from the trucks to the appropriate places: either the storeroom, refrigerator, or freezer.

I took orders from a reservist specialist Gooch until about 3 p.m., and then he disappeared. Several cooks came into the storeroom about 3:30, complaining that mess Sergeant Schuster was out boozing. Evidently, they were supposed to stay until he officially told them that they could leave. At about 5:30, a drill sergeant, one individual in civilian clothing, and mess Sergeant Schuster drove up in a light tan Buick. Schuster was drunk. He managed to stumble up the steps to the loading dock, into the kitchen, and finally, into his office. I was cleaning the front refrigerator when I saw him trying to dial his office telephone. He had a half gallon bottle of Jim Beam bourbon with a handle that he held in his left hand. It was almost empty. By this time, the early morning shift cooks were very upset. They were finally permitted to leave after mess Sergeant Schuster almost picked a fight with one, when he went around yelling "I am the greatest," while waving the bottle of bourbon in his left hand. After about 30 minutes, a woman and man, both dressed in civilian clothes, walked in and succeeded, after another half hour of talking, in assisting the mess sergeant from the kitchen to their car.

I had my work completed by about 7:30 p.m., but one young cook decided that he ought to be able to see his reflection on the top of all the tin cans in the storeroom. I spent about an hour polishing the tops of the tin cans. Everything was in shining-top shape by 8:30 p.m., but we were made to stand around and polish equipment that had been polished at least three times since the last meal had been served. At 9:30 p.m. we were permitted to leave; we had worked a 17-hour shift. We then walked back to the barracks. I showered and shaved and got to bed a few minutes before 10.

During our time on KP, we did not participate in the scheduled training activities of the Company. We were told by our fellow trainees that one of the activities that we missed on July 21st was the Company photo shoot. They had been marched to a photo studio, dressed in white t-shirts covered by khaki outer shirts. A studio dress cap was placed on their heads and a headshot photo was taken. This activity was conducted in cooperation with a private company, Albert Love Enterprises, Inc. Publishers, 4070 Shirley Drive, S.W., Atlanta, Georgia 30336. Albert Love assembled the photos into a bound cycle book with other stock photos of army training activities and sold them to the troops and their families. (I wondered who in the chain of command was "on the take.")

I was curious as to whether photos of the five of us that had been on KP would be included in the book. Several of us inquired. Evidently, to stop more questions regarding the lack of our photos, more than a month later on Tuesday, August 25th, during BCT week six, the five of us were marched to the photo studio. Given that we were dressed in fatigues and helmet liners when our photos were taken, it was clear that this activity was orchestrated to stop us from asking questions. There was no plan to include our photos in the cycle book. The U.S. Army Training Center Company A, First Battalion, Second Brigade, 11 September 1970 cycle book does not include the names or photos of Privates Duvardo, Edgington, Ellis, Emmerick, and Epplin.[1]

In addition to KP duty, we were frequently required to function as "servers" at meals. These activities usually only required two to three hours at a time. The most annoying thing about "server" duty was that the servers were the last permitted to eat and only given a few minutes to eat the leftovers.

Later, during week six of BCT, on Saturday, August 29th, I was back on full-day KP. The routine was similar in that we were up at 4 a.m. and in the mess hall at 4:30. This time I was assigned to be the "outside man." I was assigned to keep the exterior area of the building and the garbage cans clean. Late in the evening, after the last meal of the day, a large, late model General Motors car with a huge trunk backed up to the loading dock. The occupants then walked into the mess hall and proceeded to transfer meat, mostly steaks, from the mess hall's freezer to the trunk of the car. I was not asked to help. It was the only time during the day that I was not a primary participant in moving materials to and from the loading dock. But none of the thieves seemed to mind that I was observing the activity. I also observed that other, more permanent mess hall workers, such as cooks, did not seem to be surprised or alarmed. It appeared to be a routine occurrence. After filling the trunk, the thieves closed the trunk, got into the car, and drove away. It appeared to be an extremely routine "inside job."

We were released from KP duty at 8 p.m. I do not know what happened to the frozen steaks that I last saw in the trunk of the car. I did not report the activity. At the time, it did not occur to me that I might have been a "guilty bystander."

Chapter 7

Fitness, Blisters, and Poison Ivy

"Before God, I swear this, the rifleman's creed."

Prior to being drafted, I had assumed that a major reason for BCT was to improve the physical fitness of the draftee. Fitness was measured by the Physical Combat Proficiency Test (PCPT). Our first PCPT was administered after the second week of BCT on Saturday, August 1st. It was scheduled to be given on Friday, July 31st. But, since the temperature on Friday afternoon was 102 degrees Fahrenheit and the relative humidity was 90%, the activity was delayed until Saturday morning. The PCPT was composed of five components — 40-yard low crawl; horizontal ladder; dodge, run, and jump; grenade throw; and one mile run. We were told that if we did not achieve the "standard" in each category on our last scheduled PCPT during week seven of BCT, we would be reassigned to a new training unit and would have another eight weeks of BCT.

Our second PCPT was administered on Monday, August 24th. Our third and last BCT PCPT was on Thursday, September 5th. (Later in the year, during Advanced Individual Training (AIT), while at Fort Sill, Oklahoma, I encountered

Draftee

the PCPT for the fourth time on October 31st.) A copy of my PCPT performance report, DA Form 705, includes my recorded scores.

PART II - PHYSICAL COMBAT PROFICIENCY TEST PERFORMANCE REPORT								
PRINT NAME (LAST, FIRST, MIDDLE INITIAL) EPPLIN, FRANCIS M			SERVICE NUMBER POT-E-1	RANK 21	AGE	HEIGHT (In Inches) 73	WEIGHT 160	
TEST NUMBER		FIRST TEST	SECOND TEST		THIRD TEST	FOURTH TEST	
DATE OF TEST		1 Aug 70	24 Aug 70			31 Oct 70	
WEATHER CONDITION (See Instructions)		TEMP COMP Clear	TEMP 60 COMP Good		TEMP 50 COMP Clear	TEMP 60 COMP Poor	
UNIT (Platoon - Company)		A-1-2-1	A-1-2-1			C-7-2	
EVENT	STANDARD	RAW	POINTS	RAW	POINTS	RAW	POINTS	RAW	POINTS
40-YARD LOW CRAWL	35 SECONDS	36	60	51	34	33	70	20	100
HORIZONTAL LADDER	36 RUNGS	69	93	46	70	59	83	60	84
DODGE, RUN AND JUMP	29.0 SECONDS	22	85	23	80	23.5	75	24	70
GRENADE THROW	15								
150 YD MAN CARRY		28	86	21	72	30	90	24	78
ONE MILE RUN	8 MINUTES AND 33 SECONDS	6:39	88	7:21	78	6:48	86	7:12	80
NOTE: TEST STANDARD - 300 POINTS. SEE REVERSE SIDE OF CARD FOR ADDITIONAL INFORMATION AND DIRECTIONS.		TOTAL SCORE	412	TOTAL SCORE	339	TOTAL SCORE	404	TOTAL SCORE	412
			SCORER		SCORER		SCORER		SCORER

Physical Combat Proficiency Test (PCPT) Performance Report

The recorded score in each category was lower in week five than in week two. This decline in recorded physical performance is due in part to the extremely poor physical training regime, and in part to differences in test administration. For example, the "mile" was one half lap longer in week five.

For perspective, these activities were conducted with combat boots and combat fatigues. The mile run was conducted on a nine-foot-wide, 440-yard (402-meter) track with 80 troops beginning at the same time. The "starting" point was not the same for all. Combat boots and foot blisters are not conducive to swift travel. Also, the horizontal ladder was restricted to 60 seconds.

On Sunday, August 30th, several troops who failed to score greater than 300 on the 5th week PCPT were removed from our Company and reassigned to a Company designed to assist people in poor physical shape achieve a sufficient score on the PCPT. We did not hear from any of the soldiers after they were removed from our unit. I do not know if the additional training was successful.

I did not have access to data, but my assessment is that many of the A-1-2 troops were in better physical shape when they arrived at Fort Leonard Wood then they were after the eight weeks of training. Much of this was a result of poor training methods. Low crawls on rocky ground tore up knees and elbows and resulted in scabs and infections. Boots that didn't fit resulted in blisters that hindered walking, jogging, and running. The fifth week bivouac, during downpours that saturated all clothing, was followed by a number of colds and sinus infections. Also, during a bivouac, we were ordered to set up camp — that is, pitch our pup tents — on a patch of poison ivy. Fortunately, I recognized the nasty vine and used my entrenching tool to cut and drag the poison ivy from the ground on which my shelter was pitched. Others were not so fortunate, and many contracted bad cases of poison ivy. I do not know if the experiences that we endured in Company A-1-2 were common or if they were an outlier. It could be that other training units on the base did a better job of physical training and had better outcomes.

In addition to assessments for physical condition, several other skills were evaluated. I managed to achieve the "sharpshooter" designation with the M16 rifle and an "expert" designation for grenade. The grenade score was based on a combination of distance and accuracy. Since I wanted to be as far from the explosion of the grenade as possible, I threw it as far as I could, and reasonably, straight toward the target.

Draftee

Basic rifle marksmanship training with the M16 was quite an adventure. We were first introduced to the "Rifleman's Creed": "This is my rifle. My rifle is my best friend. There are many like it, but this one is mine. I must fire my rifle true. I must shoot straighter than the enemy of my country who may be trying to shoot me. My rifle and I are a team. Together we are defenders of my country and are dedicated to its defense unto death. Before God, I swear this, the rifleman's creed..." At the time, I thought I should ask my mother how to reconcile the rifleman's creed with Jesus' response to heal the high priest's servant ear that had been severed by a follower.[1] But then I recalled that we needed to stop those godless "calm-u-mists."

During our training, we fired on several ranges. Range 41 had targets at 50, 100, 150, 200, 250, and 300 meters. I had difficulty seeing distant targets. Most of the ranges had pop-up targets — camouflaged human silhouettes. When hit, the target was supposed to flip to the ground so that we could see that it had been hit, and then pop back ready for the next shot. However, most of the pop-up targets were shot full of holes. Bullets would pass through the target, and the target would not move. On Friday, August 7th, we witnessed our SDI (A-1-2's highest ranking drill sergeant) Tilson, fire 27 rounds at representative porous pop-up targets. We observed that the 27 rounds managed to down one target. This activity was followed for a few seconds by stunned silence. Rifle marksmanship training would have been much more useful if the targets had functioned properly.

Later in the summer, during AIT at Fort Sill in Oklahoma, we were taken to a firing range and handed an M14. I managed to hit a sufficient number of targets to fulfill the minimum requirements for marksman qualification. That was the only time that I fired an M14 during my time in the army.

Late during BCT, on Saturday, September 5th, we were

marched to the G3 proficiency test site at 7 a.m. The G3 was designed to test our proficiency with marching drill, bayonet, first aid, individual protective measures (IPM, i.e., gas mask), individual tactical training (ITT, i.e., low crawl and camouflage), guard duty, hand-to-hand combat, map reading, military justice, and military courtesy.

We were divided into groups of about 20 and moved to our first station. Our first stop was labeled dismounted drill. Drill instructor Smith stood in front of the scorers' shack and gave us commands that were listed for our particular test. We were tested in groups of three. Our turn came. We fell in and were given commands, such as attention, right face, right flank, rear march, one step backwards, inspection arms, port arms, and lastly, "fall out, next group" (13 points).

At our second stop, we were given the first of two written tests. Fourteen questions were each worth 1/2 point (7 points). The written test at the third station consisted of 10 one-point questions and two three-point questions dealing with map reading. The tests were scored immediately after completion by the station NCO.

We moved on to the marches and bivouac station. We were asked to identify the best camouflage material. The choice was between a pile of fresh foliage and a pile of mostly brown dead foliage. We were asked how we would properly affix the straps of a bedroll and pack to a dummy's back. The last two questions dealt with water conservation and purification (5 points).

At the next station, we were confronted with abilities relative to the M16. We were told that this part of the evaluation was not a part of the G3 proficiency test, but rather is a part of the overall weapons qualification score (7 points). The NCO in charge told us that he would give us four points just to keep things going. We had to field strip an M16 in one minute and then reassemble it for one point, and answer two questions for the other two points.

First aid and IPM (Individual Protective Measures) were covered at our next stop. We were shown a dummy, told that "he" had a head wound, and were then told to perform life-saving measures. A — I cleaned his Airway. B — I applied pressure to stop the Bleeding. C — I elevated his head and covered his body to Control shock. D — I tied the first aid dressing around the head to Dress the wound. We then had to perform a neck drag on a fellow trainee; Emmerick was my partner.

For IPM, we were given nine seconds to properly secure our gas mask and then demonstrate what we would do if we had to maneuver through a gas-contaminated area (6 points).

To demonstrate our guard duty proficiency, for one point each, we ordered two guys to leave our post (2 points). As instructed, at the hand-to-hand station we executed a pivot kick, sidekick, counter to the rear arms free, and high parry. Each was worth two points.

At the ITT (Individual Tactical Training) station, we were given a brief orientation by a staff sergeant that went something to the effect of: "This is ITT. It's a damn farce. This whole G3 test is a farce. Unless you really goof up, you'll all get 13 points. You won't do this stuff right, but you'll get the damn 13 points. We know damn well you don't know how to do this stuff properly. It's just a farce (13 points)..." Farce or no farce, I was deemed to be G3 proficient.

Discipline

The unstated but seemingly overarching objective of BCT was to instill, or require, or indoctrinate, or use any means, to facilitate discipline. In this sense, BCT was similar to the first grade. The instructors were expected to teach soldiers when to keep their mouths shut, when to speak, and what to say when they did speak. They were expected to teach us how and when to walk, when to run, when to eat, when to sleep, when to urinate, when to smoke, and when to drink. As noted, about 18% of the Company's charges had at least one four-year college degree, whereas 23% had not completed high school.

Common punishments for alleged discipline infractions included push-ups, extra food service duty, extra guard duty, extra police calls[2], and lack of base privileges. I say alleged infractions because often a soldier was falsely accused. For example, during a first aid lecture one day, the soldier next to me was taking copious notes. For no good reason, one of the instructors grabbed him by the hair and told him to quit sleeping in class and to do push-ups. On more than one occasion, I was signaled out because my knees were not touching while standing at attention. It didn't seem to matter that my legs are crooked. (My mother told me that her physician told her that I had a mild case of polio as an infant. Perhaps that is why my legs were crooked. My father made it clear that he did not believe the physician. His sister, my aunt, had a serious case of polio and was paralyzed from the waist down. For my dad, there was no such thing as a mild case of polio.)

Prior to July 28th, because we had so little time, and since washroom space was limited in the morning, I shaved every evening just before going to bed. On Monday, July 27th, after the second hour of a first aid class, someone yelled for a formation. Drill Instructor Smith walked down the row and picked out those who he deemed had not been routinely shaving. I had shaved late the previous evening, but my name was entered in "the book" along with about a dozen other facial hair slackers. After inspecting everyone's facial hair, he informed us that he would call for the bearded ones later in the evening.

Later, after two more hours of first aid training in which we applied bandages to each other; four sets of 40-yard wind sprints; and a two-mile march back to the barracks, D.I. Smith

Draftee

yelled for all those who he had caught with beards to fall out. He held an old safety razor with a dull blade and handed it to the guy on the end, who tried to use it and then passed it on. I was third. The blade was no match for my beard, but I pulled it over my raw face. He yelled, "Still looks pretty rough."

"Yes, Drill Sergeant," I replied.

"Git outa here," he said. From that time forward, I shaved in the morning.

One weekend, four guys left the base and did not return at the scheduled time. They were Absent Without Leave (AWOL). My recollection is that they were not returned to our Company. We did not learn of their fate or punishment.

The next week, on August 11th, 1970, after a long day, at about 7:00 p.m., we were ordered to assemble. Platoon Sergeant Rolando read an Article 15 order. We were told that at some time during the previous week, one of the troops, Private Paul McChesney, walked from our barracks to an off-limits location for the purpose of using a telephone. Fortunately, he was not court-martialed. However, he was given an Article 15. Article 15, of the Uniform Code of Military Justice, provides the basic law concerning nonjudicial punishment procedures. He was given a punishment of 14 days of extra duty (probably KP), 14 days of restrictions, and a reduction of $29 in pay. We were not told if Private McChesney was successful in making the phone call.

Several weeks prior, on a Sunday afternoon, I had walked a short distance to a post library. At the time, I did not know that it was off limits. I suppose that I was fortunate to not incur an "Article 15." Perhaps my offense was not so egregious as making a phone call.

Vietnam on the Mind

Throughout our time at the reception center and during the eight weeks of BCT, references to Vietnam were common.

For example, on Tuesday, August 18th, during an ITT session, we were subjected to a one-hour lecture provided by a 2nd Lieutenant who claimed to have served a tour in Vietnam. (I was skeptical since he was a 2nd Lieutenant. Surely, after a year in Vietnam, he would have been promoted.) He told us that he sketched maps on his fatigue pants. He described various tactics used by the enemy, including booby traps. His "story" about "Saigon Sally" and how she used potatoes and razor blades did not enhance his credibility.

On Wednesday, August 26th, we were shown a film that described communists' tactics of guerilla warfare. The film contained a brief explanation of how well the U.S. was prepared to counter these activities. The following day, we were shown a film on Vietcong mines and booby traps. The following week, after a two-hour session of bayonet training, we were subjected to a lecture from Company Commander First Lieutenant Otto about the seizure of the U.S. Navy ship the USS Pueblo in January of 1968. Otto contended that the Navy "higher ups" were very upset with the response of Captain Bucher and his crew. I could not determine what information Otto was trying to convey. Perhaps he was saying that if we are sent to Vietnam and taken prisoner, we should be happy to know that someone will be upset?

Our third PCPT was administered during the morning of September 3rd. During the afternoon, we were subjected to a two-hour session conducted by Battalion Commander Lieutenant Colonel Stephen G. Beardsley. He was the highest-ranking officer in the Battalion. He showed several slides of Korea and Vietnam. He then proceeded to present a lecture roughly titled "why we fight." He presented his views regarding why the U.S. was fighting in Southeast Asia, plans for ending the war, and how the war was affecting the home front. For the first time during our time in the army, the officer in charge,

Draftee

LTC Beardsley, invited questions and comments. But he did not provide answers. Usually after a trainee made a statement or asked a question, Beardsley would respond by saying, "Yes, next man."

In hindsight, the grouping of slides from Korea with those of Vietnam was consistent with the views of many, if not most, high-ranking officers at the time. They did not understand that the situation in Vietnam was very different from the situation that had existed in Korea.[3] Their lack of understanding of the differences was very costly.

Someone asked if the U.S. would transition to an all-volunteer army. Beardsley responded that only society's flunkouts would volunteer, and as a result, the army would suffer severely. Beardsley's response was based on the assumption that factors, such as pay and training abuses, would remain the same.

Usually, there was no distinction between draftees and volunteers. However, during our time at the reception center, on Monday, July 13th, draftees were assembled. We were told that draftees were assigned the jobs that no one else wanted. The clear implication was that if we switched, that is, if we elected to "enlist" for three or four years of active duty (rather than our two-year active duty requirement as a draftee), we could select a military occupation that would reduce our chances of being subjected to infantry activity in Vietnam. None of the draftees took the bait.

The following day, on Tuesday, July 14th, the draftees were marched to a classification and assignment session. Individually we were called in to meet with a Spec-5 interviewer. He asked me to list my preferences for military occupation. Earlier, we had been given a sheet with a list of military specialties. Based on that list, I indicated a preference for either surveyor, automotive repair, finance, or clerk typist. He said, "I'll recommend you for surveying, but that is no guarantee of anything. Next."

Of the 222 soldiers in Company (A-1-2), two of us were selected for assignment to Advanced Individual Training (AIT) in the Military Occupational Specialty (MOS) of 13E20 (thirteen echo twenty), field artillery Fire Direction Control (FDC). I do not know the assignment criteria that were used to determine that I be sent to field artillery fire direction control training. Perhaps my poor eyesight influenced the decision. During our time in the reception center, prior to the start of BCT, we were given a battery of tests. It could be that assignment to artillery fire direction control training was based on findings from one or more segments of the exams. The classification and assignment specialist who told me that he would recommend that I be sent to surveying school did not mention artillery fire direction control and, at that time, I was not familiar with the occupation.

The artillery training center at Fort Sill, Oklahoma, included AIT for FDC. Later, we learned that of the 32 members of our AIT FDC training class, all but one had at least one college degree. All had excellent math skills. Several had completed PhDs. My recollection is that the one member who did not have a bachelor's degree was the sole National Guard member in the class. 17 of the 32 received orders to go to Vietnam.

Chapter 8

Advanced Individual Training 13E20, Field Artillery Fire Direction Control

"Thirty-one privates with college degrees."

On Saturday, September 12th, 1970, we completed our eight weeks of basic combat training. We were assembled on the parade grounds, performed a few fancy marches, endured a few speeches, and that was that.

On Sunday, September 13th, 1970, some of us who had been assigned to AIT training at Fort Sill were bused to Lambert International airport in St. Louis. Late in the day we were loaded onto a charter flight and flown to Lawton-Fort Sill Regional Airport at Lawton, Oklahoma. We were bused from the airport to the base and eventually to a World War II vintage barracks. I was assigned to Cycle 10-C-3, Battery C, 7th Training Battalion, 2nd Advanced Individual Training Brigade, U.S. Army Training Center Field Artillery, Fort Sill, Oklahoma. The barracks was our home for eight weeks of AIT and one week of Republic of Vietnam training.

We began our artillery Fire Direction Control (FDC) school on Monday, September 14th. Most of our eight weeks of AIT training was conducted in a classroom. In some respects, it was similar to a typical college class. The environment was much less abusive, more professional, and more respectful than what I had experienced in BCT. We had lectures, many of which involved a substantial amount of mathematics, followed by written exams. We did not have routine physical activity; we did not do KP duty. I gained weight and the pants that were too small when issued became tighter.

Historically, ground combat units included infantry (rifles, grenades, machine guns, mortars), cavalry (that over time evolved from armed soldiers mounted on horses [or camels] to armored tanks and also to soldiers transported by helicopters), and artillery (cannons). During the Vietnam War, the U.S. army employed four different sizes of artillery. The names assigned, such as 105-mm, referred to the diameter of the projectile (the inside diameter of the barrel). Three of them (105-mm, 155-mm, and 8-inch) were referred to as howitzers, and one (175-mm) as a gun. Howitzers were characterized by firing rounds with lower velocity and higher trajectories to a shorter distance. The muzzle velocity of the round depended on the charge (the quantity of propellant). Three levels of propellant, with charge one being the minimum available for use and charge three being the maximum, were available for the 175-mm gun. For a given elevation of the barrel, a round propelled by charge three would exit the barrel at a greater velocity and would travel a greater distance than a round propelled by charge one.

The 105-mm (4.1 inch) howitzer fired a 33-pound (15 kg) projectile. With a maximum charge (quantity of propellant), a velocity of 494 meters per second (1,621 feet per second) could be achieved, and given equal elevation above sea level of the howitzer and the target, the round could be fired a maximum distance of 11,270 meters (7 miles). The 155-mm (6.1 inch) howitzer fired 95-pound (43 kg) projectiles at a maximum velocity of 564 meters per second (1,850 feet per second) to achieve a maximum distance of 14,955 m (9.3 miles). The 175-mm (6.9 inch) gun could deliver a 147-pound (67 kg) projectile to a distance of 33,000 meters (20.5 miles). With the maximum propellant, a projectile velocity of 914 meters per second (2,999 feet per second) could be achieved. The 8-inch (203 mm) howitzer fired a 200-pound (91 kg) projectile at a maximum velocity of 701 meters per second (2,300 feet per second) a maximum distance of 17,000 meters (10.5 miles).

Artillery Fire Direction Control

During the Vietnam War era, the Global Positioning System (GPS) and laser-guided artillery rounds were not available. The U.S. Defense Department did not launch the initial GPS satellite until 1973. Historically, artillery rounds were fired in support of infantry activity. A forward observer could use a two-way radio to call for an artillery fire mission. Precise maps were critical. Accuracy required that the observer provide correct map grid coordinates to target.

The purpose of Fire Direction Control was to receive target grid coordinates, calculate the appropriate charge (propellant quantity), direction (deflection) to point the cannon, and the elevation (range) angle of the barrel (tube) that would result in the projectile hitting the target. Baseline estimates of appropriate charge (propellant quantity) and tube angle elevation for targets within relevant distances for each cannon size were produced by the army's ballistic research laboratories. These research laboratories were similar to those described in the book and movie *Hidden Figures*.[1]

A typical FDC center would include a charting table that included a map of the region that encompassed the range of fire of the cannons in the battery. A battery center pin would be placed in the map to designate the location of the most central cannon in the battery. When target coordinates were received, a temporary pin was placed in the map to designate the target location. A range deflection protractor was then used to produce an initial estimate of the distance and direction from the battery to the target.[2]

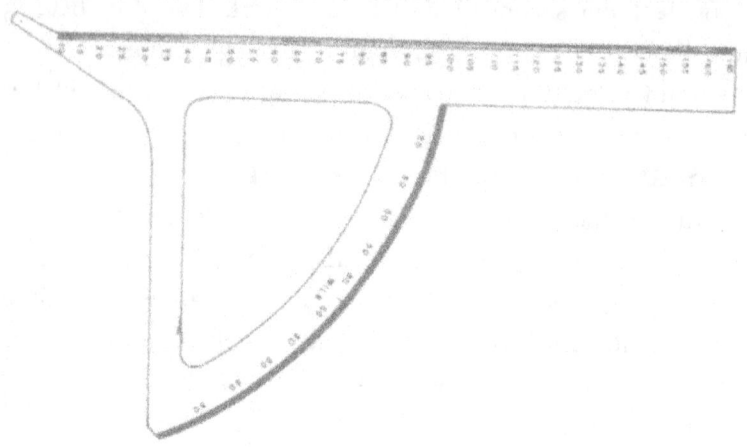

Range Deflection Protractor[3]

Information from the range deflection protractor was converted into charge, elevation (range), and deflection data via a slide rule device called a graphical firing table.

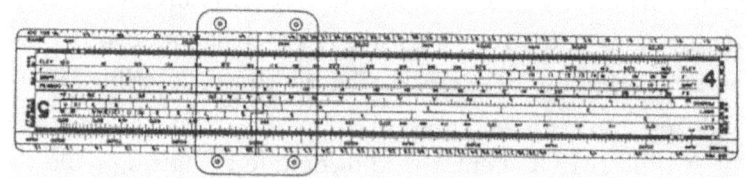

Graphical Firing Table[4]

The graphical firing table was designed to enable a quick

estimate of the information required to place the projectile on the target coordinates. Fire commands from the FDC center to the cannon operators consisted of the type of shell, fuse, charge, range (barrel elevation), and deflection (barrel direction).

If the firing data provided to the cannon operators was incorrect, the artillery round would miss the target and could explode at a location occupied by friendly forces — fellow U.S. soldiers — or by civilians, including children. None of the 32 FDC students wanted to be responsible for producing erroneous calculations that could result in artillery rounds exploding near U.S. soldiers or children. The potential consequences of an error provided sufficient incentive and motivation for attentive study.

The speed at which accurate firing data was calculated and provided to the cannon operators was also a point of emphasis. The cannons were not designed to hit moving targets. However, most targets of interest could not be expected to be stationary for an extended period. The objective was clear: be correct and be quick.

If the grid coordinates provided by the observer were correct, and if the earth was flat and did not rotate, and if there was no wind, and if the air temperature and density were constant at the baseline level, and if the propellant was identical to the baseline batch, and if the round weighed precisely the same as the baseline rounds, and if the rifling (rotating band) inside the barrel was not too worn, the process would not have been very complicated. Much of FDC AIT training was about accounting for factors inconsistent with the baseline.

In addition to distance and direction to the target, a major critical factor is differences in altitude between the location of the cannons and the location of the target. As anyone who has witnessed the operation of a T-shirt cannon at a sporting event knows: distance, direction, and altitude matter. For artillery projectiles expected to travel 7–20 miles, a number of other factors also may matter. Training was conducted to teach how to adjust for wind speed, wind direction, air temperature, air density, and curvature and rotation of the earth. For example, when firing from west to east, the earth will rotate under the projectile (reducing the distance to the target), whereas when firing from east to west, the target will be rotating away from the cannon. Similarly, flight times from New York to Los Angeles are greater than flight times from Los Angeles to New York. Flight times are also impacted by wind speed and direction. These distances and the appropriate adjustments for earth rotation differ depending on latitude.

Successful artillery targeting has had a long-standing association with mathematics. Students of calculus may recognize the name of Joseph-Louis Lagrange. Lagrange was one of the founders of the calculus of variations. Lagrange was also credited with developing techniques for constrained optimization: Lagrangian functions and Lagrangian multipliers. In 1755, at the age of 19, Lagrange was appointed mathematics assistant professor at the Paris Royal Military Academy of the Theory and Practice of Artillery.[5] My FDC classmates may not have been math prodigies, but their math skills were better than average.

The vast majority of our training time during AIT was conducted in a classroom with 32 students and one or two instructors. Experiences outside the classroom were limited. On October 23rd, we were introduced to the M14 rifle and taken to a firing range to fulfill minimum requirements for M14 firing qualification. We took our final PCPT on October 31st. Evidently, my body had recovered from the abuse of BCT, as I achieved the same total score as I had obtained during the second week of BCT, which was my previous high score. One day, we were trucked to an artillery firing range and observed as artillerymen set up and fired a 105-mm howitzer.[6] One morning, we were trucked to a missile range and shown a Pershing field artillery missile system. The Pershing was a nuclear-capable theater-level weapon with a range of 460 miles (740 km). The Pershing system was also capable of carrying and delivering non-nuclear high explosive rounds to targets. We were not trained to assist with the operation of Pershing missiles; they were not used in Vietnam. However, the field artillery professionals were quite proud that they had these weapons and used the opportunity to share their enthusiasm.

During a period prior to our arrival, it was determined that Fort Sill soldiers were involved in an abnormal number of automobile accidents. In response, base officers decided that each soldier on the base should complete a defensive driving course. For parts of two days our instruction was moved from the regular FDC classroom to a large auditorium that accommodated our FDC class, as well as a number of other soldiers. We completed the 6th edition of the National Safety Council Driver Improvement Program's defensive driving course. Several of my FDC classmates explained that the army wanted to keep us alive at least until we got to Vietnam.

FADAC

One day, we were shown and witnessed a brief demonstration of a Field Artillery Digital Automatic Computer (FADAC).[7] The FADAC was designed to compute firing data for artillery weapons. We were told that it was not intended to replace the traditional method of determining firing data, but rather to provide supplementary information. The old hands at the artillery school had learned to trust the traditional methods. It remained unsaid, but it was somewhat obvious that they did not understand this machine and were not inclined to trust it.

An operational FADAC system was composed of three units: computer, table, and generator. The computer was 24 inches wide, 14 inches high, and 34 inches deep. It weighed approximately 210 pounds. The FADAC field table weighed approximately 40 pounds and was designed to enable a level support base for the computer. The computer did not have a battery; it required a unique electrical power source: 3-phase, 4-wire, 400 hertz, 120/208 volts, approximately 750 watts. This power was provided by a gasoline engine driven, skid mounted, tubular frame, 3- kilowatt generator that weighed approximately 275 pounds. It was approximately 35 inches long, 24 inches wide, and 25 inches high. It had a 3.75-gallon gasoline fuel tank. A unique power cable was required to connect the generator to the computer. The total system weighed more than 525 pounds.[8] This 525-pound system probably had less computing power than a 1980s-era handheld programmable calculator.

We were not taught how to set up or how to use a FADAC. We were also not told that the FADACs were radioactive. At some point in time, after I had completed active duty, most of the FADACs were collected by the U.S. Department of Energy and disposed of as hazardous waste because they contained radioactive material.[9]

Draftee

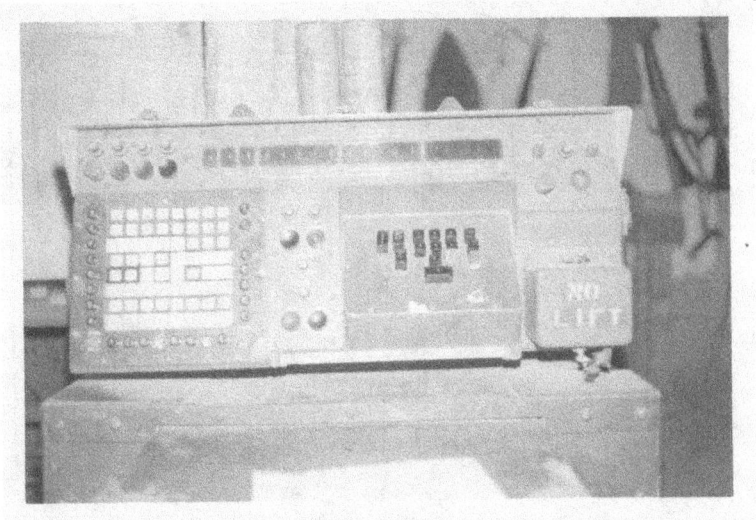

Field Artillery Digital Automatic Computer (FADAC) mounted on FADAC field table[10] [11]

We were also not taught how to operate and maintain the generator that was an essential component of a FADAC system. If the generator was not running, the computer would not work.

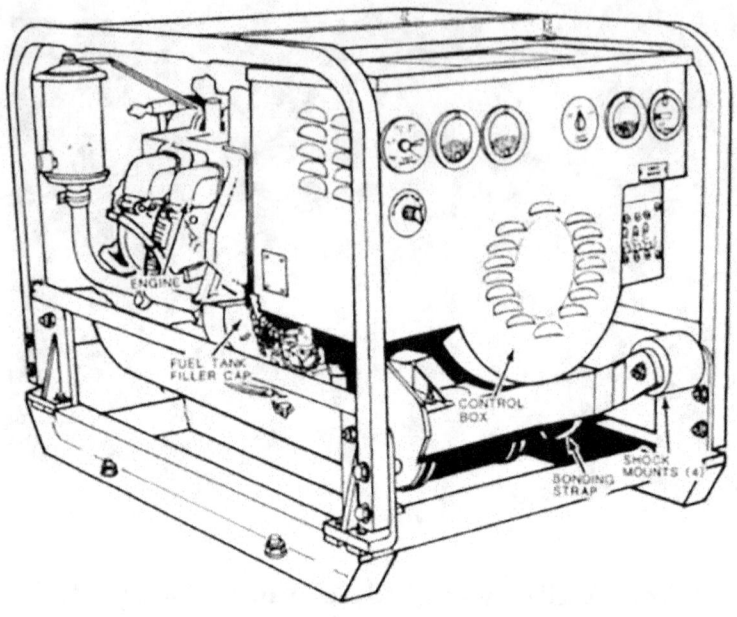

3-phase, 4-wire, 400 hertz, 120/208 volts, electric generator for powering a FADAC[12]

FDC AIT also included training in wireless radio and wired telephone operations. We memorized the phonetic alphabet and were taught procedures designed to enhance precision in communications.

During the course of study, we were administered a number of written exams including map and aerial photo, basic artillery math, firing data, area fire, precision fire, mean point of impact and high burst fire, high angle fire, meteorological data and velocity error, and a proficiency exam. These exams were administered and taken with more seriousness than any of the evaluations administered during basic combat training. All 32 students fulfilled the minimum requirements.

Chapter 9

Next Stop, Vietnam

"'Git' your affairs in order."

On November 4th, 1970, I was notified that I had been assigned to report to the U.S. Army Overseas Replacement Station at Fort Lewis in Washington state on December 1st, 1970. Fort Lewis was one of the Army locations at which soldiers from bases around the U.S. were assembled into plane loads for transport to Vietnam. On November 7th, 1970, we completed our 13E20 FDC AIT training. We graduated from cycle 10-C-3, were given a Certificate of Training from Battery C, 7th Training Battalion, 2nd Advanced Individual Training Brigade, U.S. Army Training Center Field Artillery, Fort Sill, Oklahoma, and that was that.

The following Monday, November 9th, we began one week of "Republic of Vietnam" training. Those of us who had completed FDC training (13E20) and who had received orders for service in Vietnam (17 of the 32 FDC graduates) were combined with dozens of others, most of which had completed 13B training, to serve as cannon crewmembers. Most of this week consisted of restating what we had previously been told regarding why the U.S. was fighting in Vietnam, to beware of booby traps, and to know that any Vietnamese that we encountered may be the enemy. One unique aspect of the training was a tour of a mock Vietnamese "village," during which many examples of potential hiding places for enemy soldiers were described.

We were told to get our affairs in order, and that if we owned assets that we wanted someone to manage while we were away, a JAG (Judge Advocate General) corps lawyer could help us prepare a power of attorney. I made an appointment, met a lawyer, and signed a power of attorney, authorizing my parents to act on my behalf. In other words, I gave them control over my car. I had no other assets other than the army-provided life insurance policy, on which they were listed as the benefactors.

My orders provided for a 15-day leave prior to reporting at Fort Lewis, Washington. I traveled home and had the opportunity to enjoy a Thanksgiving holiday with my family. On Tuesday, December 1st, 1970, my parents drove me to Lambert International St. Louis airport. I flew from St. Louis to the Seattle-Tacoma airport, traveled by shuttle to Fort Lewis, Washington, and reported to the U.S. Army Overseas Replacement Station. The Station processed hundreds of soldiers a month bound to and from South Vietnam and South Korea.

The Fort Lewis barracks were old and damp. Processing included additional vaccinations via a jet injector system. We had been introduced to the jet injector system during basic combat training. The jet injectors used high pressure — 1,200 psi — to deliver vaccines through a soldier's skin. The system provided a very efficient method for vaccinating a large group. We lined up with our shirts off. A medic or gun operator would caution us to relax our arms, then touch the skin with the end of the gun, pull the trigger, bam, and yell "next." I opined that the method of delivering vaccines was the most efficient thing that the U.S. Army did; in a few minutes, an entire company could be vaccinated. I estimate that the jet injector system was used to give us approximately 20 different vaccines. Years later, the Army discontinued the use of the system after learning that the injectors could bring body fluids to the surface, contaminate the system, and transmit viruses.[1,2]

We were issued a set of olive drab jungle fatigues, olive drab underwear, olive drab handkerchiefs, two pairs of olive drab jungle boots, and an olive drab hat. The days were dreary and depressing with overcast skies. The major activity for most days consisted of checking the flight manifest to see if we had been scheduled for departure. My name was included on a list for departure on December 8th, 1970. Our flight departed around 4 a.m. from McChord Air Force Base, and it included scheduled refueling stops in Anchorage and Tokyo. We arrived at the Cam Ranh Bay air base in South Vietnam on December 9th.

Chapter 10

Replacement Battalion to Artillery Battery

"No, not phone rang, Phan Rang."

We deplaned, found our duffle bags, and were loaded onto busses for transport to the 22nd Replacement Battalion. On the morning of Sunday the 13th, several of us received orders to board a C-130 transport. On the plane, Albright, who had completed FDC training with me at Fort Sill, and I received orders denoting that we were being assigned to the 6th Battalion 32nd Artillery of the First Field Forces. The C-130 flew north (approximately 100 miles) from Cam Ranh Bay and landed at an air base near Tuy Hoa.

We deplaned, grabbed our duffle bags, and walked to the terminal. We asked the Air Force clerk for directions to, as we read from our orders, the 6th Battalion 32nd Artillery of the First Field Forces. He looked up at us and burst into laughter. He stopped laughing and said, "The 6th Battalion 32nd Artillery headquarters moved from Tuy Hoa months ago."

I responded, "So, where should we go?"

He ruffled through some papers and said, "They moved to Phan Rang."

Albright said, "Phone rang?"

The clerk grinned and said, "No, not phone rang. Phan Rang, with a Ph. It is an air force base."

I inquired, "Where is it?"

The clerk responded, "I don't know. There is a C-123 headed back to Cam Ranh Bay. I'll get you seats on the plane. You can go back to the 22nd Replacement Battalion. They may eventually determine how to get you to Phan Rang. Don't be late. They will count you as AWOL." Then he laughed.

We grabbed our duffle bags, walked back to the tarmac, and boarded the C-123. When we arrived at the 22nd Replacement Battalion, we explained to a clerk that we were told by officials at Tuy Hoa that the 6th Battalion 32nd Artillery headquarters had relocated from Tuy Hoa to the Phan Rang air force base. He was not convinced. After an extended period of time and several phone calls, he said, "Hell, we send people assigned to the 6th 32nd to Tuy Hoa every week." It was implied that we were the first two to return.

The Phan Rang air force base was located about 30 miles south, southwest of Cam Ranh Bay. It was more than 200 miles northeast of Saigon, the capital city of South Vietnam. Saigon was renamed Ho Chi Minh City after the war. We arrived on Monday, December 14th. On Tuesday the 15th, we learned that Albright and I had been assigned to Battery B — that is, Bravo Battery 6th Battalion 32nd Artillery of the First Field Forces. We spent most of the week cutting weeds and painting the exterior walls of wooden buildings. Our most serious encounter during the week was with a many-banded krait snake. We had been told during our Republic of Vietnam training at Fort Sill that the venom deposited from the bite of one of these snakes could kill a human very quickly, before they could complete two steps. Hence, U.S. soldiers called them "two steppers." Fortunately, we had been provided with sickles, with which we had been expected to cut weeds. One of our fellow painters, Private

Hunt, who was awaiting transfer to Charlie battery, used his sickle to sever the head of the snake. The feared "two stepper" was dead.

The bases at Cam Ranh Bay and Phan Rang appeared to be very secure. We were not issued weapons at either location. Soldiers who were assigned to the bases did not seem to be too concerned about security. Most did not carry weapons and did not wear helmets or flak jackets. One major difference between these bases and bases in the U.S. was the smell. The stench at Cam Ranh Bay was intense. This was, in part, a consequence of the lack of waste treatment facilities. Rather than stateside sewage management systems, empty artillery powder (propellant) canisters were placed in the ground for use as urinals.

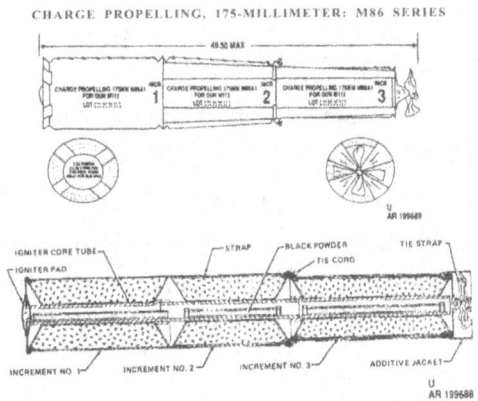

The M86 propellant for the 175 mm guns consisted of an adjustable three-increment white bag approximately 49.5 inches long and weighing 55 pounds.[1]

Draftee

M86 propellant charges used for the 175-mm guns were packed in metal containers.[2] The metal waterproof containers were approximately 56 inches long and 7 inches in diameter. They were used to store a 55-pound bag of propellant. To facilitate stacking and shipping, the round metal containers were surrounded by a "square" protective wooden case. After the propellant was removed for its intended use of propelling artillery projectiles, the metal containers could be repurposed. Some were filled with rocks and soil and used to fortify defensive barriers. Others were used as "piss" tubes. Both ends were removed; one end buried into the ground, with the other end exposed at an appropriate height for serving as a field urinal. During our time on the Cam Ranh Bay base, the stench from these "devices" was worse than that emanating from a 50,000 head West Texas cattle feedlot.

Chapter 11

Fire Support Base Wilson

"Front toward enemy."

On Monday, December 21st, Albright and I were provided a jeep ride from the Phan Rang air base to Fire Support Base Wilson, which at the time was the base location for B battery 6th 32nd artillery. Wilson was located on the east side of QL1, a little more than 20 miles north of Nha Trang, south of the village of Ninh Hoa.[1] QL1 was the main north-south road in the country. It was mostly a two-lane asphalt highway. Wilson was located near the coast of the South China Sea, and on the eastern side of the central highlands in what the U.S. army defined as "two corps," or military region II.

Bravo battery had two track-mounted, self-propelled 175-mm guns and two track-mounted, self-propelled 8-inch howitzers. The official name was Fire Support Base Wilson, but U.S. army occupants referred to it as "the hill." In addition to the battery of about 100 men, the hill served as a temporary home for a meteorological unit of about a half dozen U.S. soldiers. On most days, the MET section released and gathered data from a weather balloon every six hours to update weather data that was used to improve the accuracy of the cannons. The battery provided artillery support for a U.S. allied contingent of Republic of Korea (ROK) ninth infantry White Horse Division.[2] About 20 ROK soldiers lived on the hill and helped guard the perimeter. Over the course of the war, 5,100 South Korean soldiers lost their lives in Vietnam.

When we arrived at Wilson, only one gun and one howitzer were on the base. The other two cannons, along with a number of personnel, were at a remote location conducting what was described as a raid. Raids, during which the Battery was effectively split, were common and usually lasted a week or so.

The base was surrounded by several rows of concertina wire. Claymore directional anti-personnel mines, with the words "FRONT TOWARD ENEMY" embossed on one side, were strategically placed between rows of the wire. A number of guard bunkers, also called observation posts, were placed to ensure full coverage of the perimeter. The mines were remotely controlled by guards who occupied the nearest guard observation post bunker.

Albright and I were assigned to the Fire Direction Control (FDC) section. FDC occupied a bunker that housed two charting tables, one wall map, a FADAC, the base switchboard, and the wireless radios. The FDC bunker was easy to locate: it was the one with the RC-292 antennas. It was located a few feet south of the FDC hutch that would serve as our sleeping space while at Wilson. A generator shack that housed the FADAC generator was just south of the FDC bunker. Previous Wilson FDC hutch occupants had added a screened-in porch (some called it the patio), in which they constructed a rather serviceable bar that included a refrigerator and sound system with a reel-to-reel tape player, stereo speakers, and makeshift tables that could be used for card games. To the rear of the FDC hutch, they had erected a basketball goal and a rather primitive system that enabled mostly low-volume, cold-water showers.

The FDC section included a small group of talented young men. Among the group were Steve Fatz from Utah, Gary Powers from Alaska, Jim Glynn from Kansas City, Dana Frogen from North Dakota, Bob Kurpius and Bob Peterson from Illinois, Sp5 Roy from Georgia, and Bill Deal from Indiana. When we arrived at Wilson, half of the section's crew were away with the two cannons that were at the "raid" location.

The Hill was resupplied from a larger base at Nha Trang. On a typical day, a 2.5-ton cargo truck (known as a deuce and a half) with a metal-covered van bed made a round trip to Nha Trang to collect supplies and food. Hill residents referred to it as the bread truck. With proper permission from the officer of the day, soldiers could hitch a ride inside the covered bed of the bread truck for a trip to Nha Trang to visit banking, medical, and Post Exchange (PX) facilities. On December 23rd, two days after arriving at Wilson and 14 days after arriving in the country, Albright and I were issued M16 rifles. Mine was rusty, and his was inoperable. Nonetheless, we were instructed to hitch a ride on the bread truck to the finance facility in Nha Trang, and to open a bank account. I would have preferred to observe the countryside as we traveled along QL1, which ran mostly adjacent to Nha Phu Bay, but, from inside the covered truck bed, we could not see the countryside.

While at Nha Trang, we set up bank accounts with the Bank of America Nha Trang Military Banking Facility. By decree, U.S. military personnel were restricted to the use of Military Payment Certificates (MPC's). The Bank of America checks included the statement that "In the Republic of Vietnam and other areas where Military Payment Certificates are used, this check can only be cashed in MPC's and only by

Draftee

persons or organizations authorized the use of MPC's..." In addition to a bank, the base at Nha Trang was home to a retail store that was officially labeled as a PX. It was generally understood that those who had the privilege of riding the bread truck to Nha Trang were expected to return to the Hill with ample quantities of beer purchased from the PX. Our trip was completed without incident.

Francis Epplin

Military Payment Certificates 5, 10, 25 Cents

Draftee

Bank of America Check

In addition to rust and other problems, the rifles that Albright and I had been issued did not include slings. The following day, which was Christmas Eve, we trekked to the supply shack with our assault rifles. Supply sergeant Staff Sergeant Robinson was typing when we entered. He stopped and asked us what we wanted.

"Sergeant," I began, "We received rifles yesterday, but we didn't receive slings." He ordered his PFC assistant to locate slings for us.

Albright then said, "Sergeant, my selector switch is missing a spring."

Robinson interrupted, "Hold on now, one thing at a time." He told the PFC to "Take a look at his weapon."

The PFC inspected the selector switch and replied, "Yow, there is a spring missing."

Having won the initial point, Albright continued, "There's also something wrong with the bolt."

The PFC agreed, "Yow, there is something wrong with this bolt."

Robinson responded, "What's your name again?" as he

flipped through his index card box. "Take that weapon there on the floor."

I glanced on the floor and saw an M16 completely disassembled. "Yeah, go ahead and put it together and give me the serial number." Albright read the serial number. I kneeled and helped him assemble the M16. We now had slings, and Ron had a seemingly workable weapon. We stood and walked back up the hill to the Fire Direction Control bunker.

We placed the M16s in the rack. I walked outside and back down the hill. I stopped at a trash can, selected a relatively clean empty beverage can, and used my civilian pocketknife to remove the top. I then walked to the motor pool. Several guys were standing near the bunker door; when they saw me, they began to grin. Grins were the common expression when newbies with new fatigues appeared on the base. I explained that the M16 that I was issued was rusty and asked if they could spare some oil. One of them nodded. I followed as he walked toward an olive drab oil barrel with a spigot. I placed the beverage can under the spigot and caught a few ounces of the liquid. I thanked him and walked back to the FDC bunker.

I cleaned and oiled the rifle and placed it in the gun rack. Jim Glynn then gave Albright and me a brief but thorough introduction to FDC operations, Wilson style. He used the plotting board and wall map to describe typical targets and recent fire missions. He provided our call signs and demonstrated switchboard operations. This was our first encounter with a switchboard. (Later in the day, my thoughts drifted to recall discussions that my parents had regarding my mother's aunt, who operated the switchboard for a small rural Illinois phone service. It seems that she always knew a wealth of information.) The FDC bunker was the information center for the battery. On-base information traveled through the switchboard, while off-base information traveled through the wireless radio. Target information was plotted on the maps.

On occasion, the FDC section would receive a Sundry Pack (SP) box. The SP box contained items such as soap, toothbrushes, razors, shaving cream, writing paper, envelopes, cigarettes, Swisher Sweet cigars, Hershey tropical chocolate bars, candy, and gum. The SP contained items that we might have purchased at a PX if we had had access to a PX. The cigarettes were prized items, and since I didn't smoke cigarettes, that was fine with me. Most of the section members correctly assessed that Swisher Sweets were disgusting. Thus, there were usually several of these sweet cigars available for smoking. While on duty during the late night/early morning shift, I developed a bad habit of smoking Swisher Sweets. Hershey tropical chocolate bars were formulated to not melt in the warm climate. They had a unique taste that required acquisition.

The switchboard and radio were monitored 24 hours a day, 7 days a week. Albright was assigned the 19:00 – 23:00 — that is, 7 – 11 p.m. — shift. I was assigned the 23:00 – 03:00 shift. My first switchboard/radio shift began on Christmas Eve and ended on Christmas. At about midnight, Roy and Glynn radioed the raid site and wished them a Merry Christmas. After midnight, the switchboard and radio were relatively quiet. At 03:00 (3 a.m.), I woke Jim Glynn, who was next on duty. I then went to the sleep hutch.

On December 24th, I was officially promoted from PV2 (Private, E-2) to PFC (Private First Class, E-3): a routine order for newly arrived Privates. Other than that, Santa Claus had missed us.

Chapter 12

Christmas 1970

"FDC, PFC Epplin speaking."

At about 9 a.m. on Christmas Day, Kowalski hollered that a Catholic chaplain's chopper had landed. Albright and I walked down to the recreation bunker. The bunker, which was also called the club, was little more than a makeshift bar with a pool table. Since our FDC section had its own patio/porch/bar, we did not routinely visit the "club." For members of the gun sections, motor pool, food service, supply, and other units of the battery, it was the recreation center.

The priest grinned when he saw us and said, "Hey, two new guys." Once again, our unfaded fatigues signaled our newness. He handed each of us a medal with a chain.

"This is our Christmas present to you." We thanked him. He told us that he and his fellow military chaplains provided financial support to an orphanage in Nha Trang. They discovered that parents were bringing and declaring their own children as orphans. The parents expected that the orphanage would provide a better life for their children than they could. The chaplain expressed some concern over what would happen to the children after the U.S. military left the region.

Draftee

After the service, we walked back to the FDC bunker and waited for lunch. Soon after the chaplain's chopper departed, another landed. We were told that it carried General Brown of the First Field Forces, who decided to bless us with his presence at our lunch. The chopper left shortly after arrival; we did not see the General. For lunch, the written menu was impressive. In addition to a listing of the meal's contents, it contained a message from Commanding General Creighton Abrams and a prayer from Chaplain Colonel Stegman. We never met either of the gentlemen.

The bread and rolls that we received from Nha Trang were saturated with baked-in weevils and other baked-in bugs. It was rather obvious that the Nha Trang flour storage facilities had a serious pest problem. We could either eat the insects, try to separate them and eat the remainder of the bread, or not eat the baked concoction. I suspected that, in addition to the bugs, the bread probably contained insecticides, even though we could not see any baked-in pesticides. The weevils were not listed on the menu — no doubt, a bonus at no extra charge. As for the other components of the meal, well, they tried.

I slept most of the afternoon and was well rested for the 19:00 to 23:00 communications shift. The radio was relatively quiet. The ARVN (Army of the Republic of Vietnam, South Vietnamese Army) patrol locations came in code as usual. I decoded and posted them. It was routine to maintain locations of friendly troops on our maps, so that we did not intentionally fire at them. Every six hours, a member of the meteorological section on the base would bring a listing that included updated weather information. We were responsible for sending the MET data to other batteries in our vicinity. This was a tedious process that required the precise reading of rows of numbers from several lines of weather data. After sending the MET, the radio was relatively quiet.

Francis Epplin

CHRISTMAS PRAYER

Send, O God, into the darkness of this troubled world, the light of Thy Son; Let the star of Thy hope touch the minds of all men with the bright beams of Thy mercy and truth; and so direct our steps that we may ever walk in the way revealed to us, as the shepherds of Bethlehem walked with joy to the manger where He dwelt Who now and ever reigns in our hearts, Jesus Christ our Lord.

Leonard F. Stegman
LEONARD F. STEGMAN
Chaplain (COL) USA
Staff Chaplain

1970

COMMANDER'S CHRISTMAS MESSAGE

As we observe the birth of Christ, I wish to extend warmest season's greetings to each of you and to your families. Even though we are separated from our families and loved ones, we can take pride that they are celebrating Christmas 1970 in peace and security at home. As we face a coming new year, may we each pray for success in our mission of contributing to peace on earth and good will for all mankind.

Creighton W. Abrams
CREIGHTON W. ABRAMS
General, United States Army
Commanding

Christmas Day Dinner 1970

Shrimp Cocktail

Crackers

Roast Turkey   Turkey Gravy

Corn Bread Dressing   Cranberry Sauce

Mashed Potatoes

Glazed Sweet Potatoes

Buttered Mixed Vegetables or Buttered Peas

Assorted Crisp Relishes   Hot Rolls W/ Butter

Fruit Cake

Mincemeat Pie

Pumpkin Pie W/ Whipped Topping

Assorted Nuts   Assorted Candy

Assorted Fresh Fruit

Ice Tea W/ Lemon   Milk

Coffee

1970 Christmas Menu

The telephone switchboard was not quiet. The Observation Posts (OPs) (perimeter guard bunkers) used flood lights to illuminate their field of vision. Electricity for the lights was provided by a Diesel-powered generator. In addition to the generator, the lights depended on the integrity of the cables that carried electricity from the generator to the lights. I received calls from several OPs explaining that they were having trouble with lights. I notified the electrician, who quickly resolved most of the issues, except for a burnt-out bulb at one location. After a few more calls, I managed to get in touch with someone who promised to get the bulb replaced.

For me, the next issue began when the switchboard buzzed and lit a light, indicating a call on the Captain's line. Captain Smoot was the Battery Commander and the highest-ranking officer on the firebase. I plugged in the switchboard wire and began, "FDC, PFC Epplin speaking sir."

He responded: "This is Captain Smoot. Try to get in touch with the Officer of the Day, the Sergeant of the Guard, and the First Sergeant, and tell them that Dunn is out on the observation post and drunk. Tell them to get him back to the mess hutch."

I responded, "Yes sir. Did you say Dunn?"

He responded, "Yes."

I continued, "Sir, do you know where I could contact the First Sergeant?"

Smoot: "Try the mess hutch."

I responded, "Okay, will try."

I called the MET number because I thought the Officer of the Day might be there. I then left the switchboard and ran to the FDC hutch patio/bar for help. It was my second day on the switchboard, and I had not met most of the firebase occupants. A group was playing Monopoly, but Jim Glynn left the game and followed me back to the switchboard. I observed and learned as he quickly and efficiently facilitated a solution to the issue. I wrote a letter home and prepared postcards for my brothers. I woke Albright at 23:00 and watched the remainder of the Monopoly game; Lieutenant Elton folded when he landed on one of Roy's hotel streets.

"Shucks," he said, "I wonder if I could have done better if I had majored in economics instead of bugology?" Bill Deal folded next, and finally, Roy won. I found a cot and eventually slept. It was no longer Christmas Day.

Chapter 13

Life at Wilson

"Pound cake, that is good shit."

The raid party returned, and we met the rest of the Battery's FDC crew. Three things were quickly apparent. First, each member of the section was smart. Second, each conducted their assigned FDC duties efficiently and without whining. Third, they worked to make life in the FDC bunker and FDC hutch as livable as possible. Albright and I were quickly integrated into the routine.

The battery conducted several types of fire missions. Some were in response to a sensor hit. Sensors were placed along trails in the Central Highlands. When a sensor indicated abnormal activity, and if no friendly troops were known to be in the area, the battery would be called on to deliver high-explosive artillery rounds to the area in the vicinity of the sensor. Some sensors were frequently activated, and thus, some grids were frequent targets. A standard FDC crew assertion was that either the sensor was not working correctly, or perhaps a water buffalo, tiger, or monkey had crapped on it.

A second type of fire mission was referred to as harassment and interdiction (H&I). If the ROK infantry had plans to patrol an area, they would often request that we deliver high explosive artillery rounds to specific targets prior to their visit to the area. In the FDC, these missions were known as rocks and trees in the open.

The FDC bunker at Wilson included two charting tables with maps drawn in a 1:50,000 scale. This scale was necessary to accommodate the firing range of the 175-mm guns and to enable the use of the standard range deflection protractor. A wall map with the same scale was used to estimate the target's elevation above sea level. When a fire mission was called, chart operators plotted the target and used the maps, range deflection protractor, graphical firing table, and MET adjustments to compute firing data. The FADAC operator would jog to the generator shack and start the generator. He would then return to the bunker, switch the computer to "on" and wait for it to achieve operating conditions, prior to entering target grid information. Often the chart operators had agreed on firing information prior to a FADAC solution. The officer in charge preferred that all three systems converged on the same firing information. If the charts agreed and the FADAC was not too far off, information from the charts would be used. The team had grown to trust the charting system. The FADAC was a black box.

Someone in the FDC chain of command decided that I should learn more about the FADAC. I was ordered to attend a one week First Field Force Vietnam artillery FADAC operator course. On January 17th, I hitched a ride to Nha Trang on the bread truck and reported for training. I was assigned a cot in a hutch for transients. It soon became clear that I needed to learn how to effectively use a mosquito net. Every Monday while at Wilson, we were given a "malaria" pill (chloroquine-primaquine).[1] I always swallowed the pill; I didn't want to get malaria. While there were mosquitoes at Wilson, populations were small, relative to what existed at some locations, such as

Nha Trang. Some soldiers on the Hill did not like the malaria pill because it had a laxative effect. I reasoned that malaria would be worse, and I trusted that the pill was safe and effective.

The FADAC class began on January 18th for me and two others. On the first day of class, it was obvious that one of my fellow students did not have an effective mosquito net the previous night. His face, neck, and arms were saturated with evidence of mosquito feeding.

We were taught how to operate a FADAC with the third revision software, enabling the inclusion of 52 permanent storage channels, 12 working channels, space to store 88 targets, 21 no fire zones, and 9 forward observer locations. The training was effective in several regards. First, I learned how to efficiently use it to obtain firing data. Second, we were given substantial opportunity to practice, develop proficiency, and gain confidence. Third, we were provided sufficient information regarding the algorithms and software that the black box nature of the machine was reduced. I grew to understand what it could and could not do.

Francis Epplin

First Field Force Vietnam Artillery FADAC Operator Course

When I returned from FADAC training, I was expected to operate the machine during my shifts that were alternated with Jim Glynn. He had previously completed the course. Relative to me, Glynn was a short timer, which meant that he was much closer to completing 12 months in the country and much closer to a Vietnam departure date. Every six hours, we expected to obtain updated weather data from the MET station on the Hill. In addition to sending the information via the radio to other batteries, we entered the data into the FADAC. When the updated weather information became available, the FADAC operator on duty — either Glynn or myself — would start the

Draftee

FADAC generator, start the computer, and enter the MET data.

By default, as a FADAC operator, I assumed some responsibility for maintaining the 3 kW generators. It became clear that one of the machines needed a new carburetor gasket. Glynn and I reported the problem up the chain of command and requested a gasket. After a few weeks, the problem became worse, and no replacement gasket was forthcoming. I removed the carburetor, removed the gasket, and carried it into the FDC bunker. I found a heavy piece of cardboard, used the original gasket as a pattern, and, with my civilian pocketknife, carved a replacement. It was something that I had seen my father do on the farm when he needed a gasket for an unpressurized seal and did not have time to travel to a parts store. I returned to the generator shack and replaced the carburetor with the "new" gasket. The leak was fixed, and the gasket held — at least for the rest of my time as the unofficial generator maintenance provider.

Most soldiers were aware of the precise number of days until their 12 months in the country were to be completed. The appearance of someone in new fatigues was a reminder that it was another day closer to departure from Vietnam. Departures were cause for celebration. Arrivals were a cause for reflection: "That poor dude has more time left than me."

The arrival of Lieutenant Ed Hudson from Billings, Montana, was a memorable affair. Hudson was new to the country when he arrived at Wilson. He was a good-hearted guy, but sometimes, he tried too hard to fit in with the troops. Soon after he arrived, he was sitting with a group of FDC enlisted men while they were opening their C-ration boxes — technically Meal, Combat, Individual (MCI) boxes. Each box contained four cans, a meat-based can, a bread item can, a flat spread can, and a dessert can. Some dessert cans contained fruit, such as apricots, peaches, pears, or fruit cocktail. Other dessert cans contained cake, such as pound cake, fruitcake, or cinnamon nut roll. In what was probably his first C-ration encounter in Vietnam, Lt. Hudson observed that he had a can of pound cake. He held it up for all to see and said, "Pound cake, that is good shit." The veteran enlisted men broke out into laughter.

For the remainder of his time with B battery, Lieutenant Hudson was known as Lieutenant Pound Cake. Others in the Battery acquired nicknames. "Oatmeal" received his name after the group learned that his family produced thousands of bushels of oats on their North Dakota farm. "Thirteen-O-Five" acquired his nickname when he made the mistake of announcing that a baseball game was scheduled to be broadcast over the armed services radio network at 13:05. "Mormon" was from Utah. "Dogman" derived his name from a caricature of his facial expressions. But, none of the other nicknames were as persistent as Pound Cake.

Chapter 14

Encounter with Dental Version of M*A*S*H's Dr. Frank Burns

"Look at this overbite."

After a few weeks in the country, I realized that I had an infected tooth. I visited with the Battery's medic. He advised me to obtain permission to hitch a ride on the bread truck so that I could visit a dentist at the Nha Trang base. On March 16th, I traveled to Nha Trang and made my way to the makeshift dental facility. It consisted of an open room in a barracks type building. It housed several dental chairs. I was ordered to take a seat in one of the chairs. For a brief period after I was seated, the building lost power. When lights came on, a young man walked up and told me to open my mouth, and then to bite down. He did not introduce himself, but I assumed he was a dentist.

"Hey, guys," he said, "Look at this overbite." Two or three other young men who had been working at other dental chairs, and who I assumed were dentists, walked over and stared in my mouth. They then chuckled and returned to what they had been doing.

Next, the dentist proceeded to remove three of the teeth from my lower jaw. He placed a single stitch. He did not tell me that he was going to pull the teeth, did not discuss any alternative treatments, and did not tell me to return to have the stitch removed. Unfortunately, my one encounter with a medical professional in Vietnam was with a "Dr. Frank Burns," the fictitious, mediocre, combat surgeon of the M*A*S*H television series, rather than with a competent dentist. Several weeks later, I returned to Nha Trang and had the stitch removed. It was then that the dentist informed me I would learn to live without the bottom front teeth, the loss would not interfere with my army duties, and that I should thank him for curing the infection and enabling me to return to killing those godless communists.

For my remaining time in the army, and for several months after returning to civilian life, I did live with the gap. Eventually, after returning to civilian life, I found a caring, sensitive dentist who fitted me with a removable bridge. Every day as I remove the bridge and brush my teeth, it is a reminder that I was fortunate. I did not lose a limb. I did not lose my life. I did not lose sight. I only left three teeth in Vietnam.

Chapter 15

Life at Wilson: Neighboring Rice Paddies

"Thank you for a job very well done."

Life at Fire Support Base Wilson continued. During our time at Wilson, we did not encounter much hostile fire. Occasionally, a small rocket would land and explode on the base. However, except for when our cannons were firing, it was relatively peaceful.

From the Hill, we could observe local farmers as they tended rice paddies. Almost all of the farm workers that we observed were women, with only a few old men. I marveled at the sight of the women as they transplanted rice seedlings in the muddy paddy. They did not look in our direction. They seemed to tolerate our existence and activities by ignoring us. I wondered what they thought about our presence in their neighborhood, on their hill. What did they think when our cannon fire woke their children in the dead of night? They managed some of the paddies to produce three crops per year.[1]

My thoughts returned to home and Perry County. How would Illinois farmers respond if the tables were turned. I considered a thought experiment: suppose a group of militarily powerful, young, Vietnamese soldiers, confiscated an Illinois hill, set up an artillery battery, and routinely disturbed the evening quiet with sound of firing cannons with the intended purpose of killing or maiming other Illinois, or perhaps Wisconsin, citizens. How would my fellow, relatively militarily powerless, Illinois citizens respond? More importantly, would they be genuinely friendly with the Vietnamese soldiers, or would they be closeted hostiles? My conclusion was that most of the people that I knew in Illinois would be able to recognize when they were outgunned. They might smile at the Vietnamese occupiers, but deep down, they would be plotting for their removal. In other words, I would expect that many of the farm workers that I observed would prefer that either I did not exist or existed elsewhere. One benefit of being a draftee-enlisted man, rather than an officer, was that I was not paid to think.

I grew to gain much respect for the Vietnamese farmers and farm workers that I observed from our perch on Fire Support Base Wilson. These people worked hard; they were good rice producers. The methods that they used to manage paddy water demonstrated that they had a very practical understanding of hydrology.

Captain Smoot completed his year in the country in March. His clerk prepared and delivered a "Letter of Appreciation" to each of us. Smoot didn't sign the letters, but then, I am sure that he was a busy man.

Draftee

```
                    DEPARTMENT OF THE ARMY
                BATTERY B 6TH BATTALION 32D ARTILLERY
                       APO San Francisco 96350

AVFA-ATT-BB                                          10 March 1971

SUBJECT: Letter of Appreciation


Private First Class Francis M. Epplin
B Battery 6th Battalion 32d Artillery
APO San Francisco 96350



1. I would like to take this opportunity, at my departure, to express
my sincere appreciation for your outstanding performance of duty.

2. Commanding a unit is always a difficult task, however, when a
commander if fortunate enough to have soldiers of your quality and
ability as a member of the unit the job is considerably easier and
far more rewarding. Your high standards, loyalty and dependability
have been significant in making this one of the finest artillery units
in the Republic of Vietnam.

3. Again I wish to thank you for a job very well done and wish you
the best in your future endeavors. Your accomplishments have been in
keeping with the high standards and traditions established by the
"Proud Americans" of the 6th Battalion 32d Artillery.



                                        WAYNE SMOOT
                                        Captain, FA
                                        Commanding
```

Appreciation Letter from Captain Smoot

Captain Smoot was replaced by Captain Larris Hunting. There was no noticeable change in the management of the battery. We continued to conduct H&I missions in support of the South Koreans and continued to respond with fire missions in response to activated sensors. After Captain Hunting arrived, Albright and several others were promoted from Private First Class (PFC, E-3) to Specialist Fourth Class (SPC-4, E-4). Promotion was accompanied with a $69 per month pay increase to $305 per month. $55 of the $305 per month was for combat (hazardous) duty pay. I asked Captain Hunting why I was not promoted, but he said that he did not know. Evidently,

Francis Epplin

the battery had been allocated a fixed number of promotion slots, and Captain Smoot had decided who should fill the spots.

In April, I received a notice that I would be promoted. But in the notification of my promotion, there was a notice that the promotion that had been awarded to another PFC in March was revoked. Evidently, for me to be promoted, someone had to be demoted. I felt terrible. I did not know the PFC; he was a member of one of the four gun sections.

```
                    DEPARTMENT OF THE ARMY
                BATTERY B 6TH BATTALION 32D ARTILLERY
                      APO San Francisco 96350

UNIT ORDERS                                            7 April 1971
NUMBER    31

1.  TC 469.  Following orders are changed as indicated.

    Action:  Revocation
    So much of:
    Pertaining to

    As reads:    N/A
    How changed: Revoked
    Authority:   VOCO

2.  TC 422.  Following enlisted personnel APPOINTED/PROMOTED as indicated.

    EPPLIN, FRANCIS M.             PFC  13E20  Btry B, 6th Bn, 32d Arty
    (WA1T BO A)   APO San Francisco 96350

    Authority:  Para 7-15, AR 600-200
    To be:  Specialist Four
    Appointed by:  N/A
    Type:  Permanent
    MOS Awarded:  N/A
    MOS in which promoted:  13E20
    PMOS (how acquired):  A
    Effective date:  15 March 1971
    Date of Rank:    15 March 1971


                                        LARRIS A. HUNTING
                                        CPT, FA
DISTRIBUTION:                           Commanding

5 ea - Finance
3 ea - Indiv
2 ea - Btry File
1 ea - 201 File
1 ea - Records
1 ea - S-1
```

Promotion to Specialist Fourth Class (SPC-4)

Draftee

When I arrived at Wilson, the battery was engaged in a raid mission. Several additional raid missions were conducted during our time at Wilson. The battery would be split, with one of the 175-mm guns and one of the 8-inch howitzers remaining on the Hill, and the other two moved to a separate location. A raid required a convoy that included the two tracked cannons and a number of trucks. The trucks were used to haul personnel and supplies, including artillery rounds and propellant canisters. The tracked vehicles that carried the gun and howitzer were not reliable. On more than one occasion, a track from one of the cannons failed, resulting in an abrupt stop, often with bad consequences. During a convoy for one raid, a cannon stopped, and the 2½ ton truck that was following rammed into the rear of the cannon, inflicting damage to both the cannon and the truck. Fortunately, we did not incur hostile fire during these road trips to and from raids.

FDC equipment that included two charting tables, radios, antennas, a generator to charge the radio batteries, and FDC personnel were crammed into a three-quarter ton truck. We did not bring our FADAC and FADAC generator on the raids.

The typical raid location was further inland than Wilson, and thus would extend the battery's effective range to the west. These locations were usually in isolated regions that had been cleared, initially with the defoliant herbicide known as Agent Orange, followed by a few passes of a Corps of Engineers bulldozer equipped with a dozer blade. Agent Orange was the name given to a defoliant intended to be composed of equal parts of two herbicides, 2,4-D and 2,4,5-T. The name was derived from the orange stripe painted on the barrels in which the mixture was shipped. 2,4-D and 2,4,5-T decompose relatively quickly. Unfortunately, much of the 2,4,5-T was contaminated with excessive levels of TCDD, a dioxin that is carcinogenic and persistent.[2][3]

Each location required that the charting tables be fitted with maps of the locale. Battery location pins were inserted in what we hoped were the correct coordinates. After arrival, we would find and receive clearance for a remote, isolated, target location for firing to register the cannons. Standard operating procedure was to register the cannons to verify our coordinates prior to conducting fire missions and endangering "friendlies."

When all four cannons were at Wilson, it was rare that all four would be operable. A common problem was a failure of the hydraulic system, often resulting from hydraulic fluid leaking from hydraulic cylinders, hoses, or couplings. The cannon operators referred to it as situation normal, leaking cherry juice — the term applied to the red-colored hydraulic fluid. I was familiar with the use of hydraulic systems on farm tractors. My prior experience was that they were very reliable. After a few hours in an Illinois farm field, it was not uncommon for hydraulic hoses and couplings to be covered in dust and soil. However, farm machinery hydraulic system failure was not common. Based on the complaints that we received regarding leaking cherry juice, and the amount of time that one or more of the cannons was inoperable due to hydraulic system failures, I concluded that the cannon hydraulic systems were much less reliable than those that I had experienced on the farm.

Chapter 16

Calm at Wilson, Disasters Near the DMZ

"30 killed, 50 wounded at Charlie 2; Fuller overrun."

For several months in early 1971, life for soldiers of Battery B at Fire Support Base Wilson was rather peaceful. The bread truck made daily trips to Nha Trang. When the bar on the covered porch of the FDC hutch was low on supplies, at least one member of our FDC section could hitch a ride on the bread truck to the Nha Trang PX and secure provisions to keep the FDC bar well stocked.

Our numbers in FDC shrunk as soldiers completed their 12-month tours. A departure was cause for a party. For a number of months, Albright and I were the newest members of FDC. Albright was sent to a communications school to learn how to run a RATT RIG (Radio Teletype set [rig]). Albright contended that the training included six months of material in a one-week course. Albright also spent a month or so away from B Battery to serve as the only trained FDC member with our battalion's C Battery.

For the most part, I was oblivious to world news and news of activities elsewhere in Vietnam. We did receive copies of the *Pacific Stars and Stripes* newspaper. We called it the "Wars and Strifes." It was self-described as "An authorized unofficial publication for the U.S. armed forces of the Pacific Command."

On February 8th, the South Vietnamese army (ARVN) began Operation Lam Son 719. The operation had been planned to enable ARVN forces to demonstrate their ability to confront and defeat the NVA. The plan was for the ARVN to cross into Laos and attack NVA positions along the Ho Chi Minh trail.[1] This was the first big test of the ability of ARVN to function without U.S. infantry. Even though the U.S. provided logistical, aerial, and artillery support, the campaign was a disaster for the ARVN. It provided evidence to any objective military assessment that the ARVN, as managed by the Thieu government, would have a very difficult time operating, even with U.S. artillery and air support. They were not capable, or perhaps not properly motivated, to conduct successful combat operations against the NVA, independent of U.S. support.

Our battery was not directly involved in Operation Lam Son 719. It was conducted near the DMZ. We were many miles distant in military region II. For the ARVN, Operation Lam Son 719 ended in March of 1971. On March 13th, 1971, General Creighton W. Abrams, who was the senior U.S. military officer in Vietnam, noted in a briefing at his Pentagon East offices adjacent to Tan Son Nhut Airport near Saigon that "I think one of the side benefits of this — it may not be much — is that the South Vietnamese military is becoming an effective thing and it's going to be a thing you have to reckon with..."[2] The consequences of Operation Lam Son 719 did not end in March. Prior to, during, and after the Lam Son 719 operation, the NVA dug into positions at several points near and in the DMZ. These positions included several battalions armed with long range artillery and rockets.[3][4] For some reason, the U.S. did not bomb these positions during this time. Evidently, the U.S. continued to operate under a November 1st, 1968, pledge that they would not attack positions in the northern half of the DMZ if the North Vietnamese agreed to participate in peace talks.[5] The 1968 one-sided pledge enabled the NVA to use the DMZ as a safe haven for launching rockets and for artillery batteries. The North Vietnamese consistently denied that they had ever agreed to not use the land described as the DMZ for military purposes.

On May 21st, 1971, a 122-mm NVA rocket hit a bunker at Fire Support Base Charlie 2, just south of the DMZ. The blast killed 30 U.S. soldiers and wounded 50.[6] [7] [8] An *Associated Press* story of May 26th, 1971, reported that a stash of six-foot-long, 122-mm rockets were found three miles south of the DMZ.[9] On June 27th, 1971, the *New York Times* reported that two NVA regiments (approximately 2,000 soldiers) crossed the DMZ.[10] Fire Support Base Fuller, very close to the DMZ and not far from Charlie 2, was overrun by the NVA in late June.[11] These attacks effectively eliminated two U.S./ARVN firebases and substantially reduced the U.S./ARVN artillery fire power in the region. Meanwhile at Pentagon East, near Saigon, a U.S. military intelligence officer reported to General Abrams that "Enemy has 11 battalions north of the DMZ, one in the northern half of the DMZ, two in the southern half, and eight below the DMZ. There have been indications since 25 April of an enemy buildup for offensive operations..."[12] A typical NVA battalion at full strength included approximately 500 personnel. The NVA, after thwarting the ARVN in Operation Lam Son 719, were on the offensive.

Chapter 17

Vacating Fire Support Base Wilson

"Enjoy the cruise on USNS LST-546."

At Wilson, we were oblivious to the happenings near the DMZ; it was more than 400 miles north. During the late spring of 1971, some in FDC speculated that since our encounters with enemy activity had declined, our battery might soon be deactivated. Our knowledge of NVA and ARVN was about to change. Perhaps in response to NVA activity near the DMZ and the losses at firebases Charlie 2 and Fuller, and the relative lack of enemy activity near our location at Wilson, in late June, we received news that Battery B would be moving. Unlike the common raids during which the battery was split, we were informed that the entire battery was moving and would not return to Wilson. We were told to destroy letters from home and any other documents that provided information other than name, rank, and serial number.

Soldiers close to completing 12 months in Vietnam were told that they would remain at Wilson until transferred to a replacement battalion for their assignment on a return flight to the U.S. FDC personnel would shrink to Deal, German, and myself, as the rest of the section members had sufficient time in the country. Albright was a highly-skilled fire direction controller, but he had been reassigned to communications activities. The few acres that had been home to Fire Support Base Wilson would be abandoned, or perhaps more correctly stated, returned to the Vietnamese.

We were not told where we were going, only that we were moving north to military region I. We were not provided information that would have been necessary to prepare a charting table with a map of our new location. On the evening of July 6th, we said our goodbyes to FDC companions who would not be traveling north. As instructed, I reread the letters from home and then destroyed them. I loaded my clothes and other personal possessions into my duffle bag.

On July 7th, we loaded the FADAC, the generators, the radios, the antennas, the batteries, and all other FDC equipment on the three-quarter ton truck (Molly) that had been assigned to the section. We tossed our duffle bags onto the truck. And then, equipped with a helmet, flak jacket, and M16, climbed into the back of the truck for our final departure from Fire Support Base Wilson.

All four tracked cannons and all other battery vehicles were assembled. Deal maneuvered Molly into the convoy line. Slowly, we departed from Wilson. No one liked the place. No one was sad to leave. At the time, we had no idea that in a few days, we would have preferred to be back at Wilson. The convoy meandered its way south along QL1 for the approximately 50-mile trip to Cam Ranh Bay. Eventually, the procession terminated at a large lot near the harbor.

Adjacent to the dock was U.S. Navy ship USNS LST-546, a tank landing ship that had been built during World War II.[1] USNS LST-546 had been decommissioned as a regular navy ship (USS) in 1952, transferred to a non-commissioned status, and assigned to the Military Sea Transportation Service. The acronym USNS was used to designate United States Naval Ship (civilian-manned; in service). In other words, the boat was not operated by the U.S. Navy. Our assessment was that the Captain of the ship and all ship operating personnel were Japanese civilians.

USNS LST-546 was a flat bottom boat, about 328 feet long and 50 feet wide. The bow (front) of the ship had a large door that could be opened with a ramp for loading and unloading vehicles. LSTs had been designed to enable support of amphibious operations by carrying and landing vehicles and troops directly onto shore with no docks or piers.

One by one, the vehicles of Battery B were backed into the cargo deck of the ship and parked four abreast. After the four cannons and all other vehicles were loaded and secured, the ramp was raised, and the doors closed and sealed. All personnel were assembled on the top deck — it was the first time during my time with Battery B that all sections were together in one assembly. After it was determined that we were all present and accounted for, we were told times at which C-rations would be available, to make ourselves comfortable on the boat, and to enjoy the cruise. Someone asked where we were going and how long we would be on the ship. Neither question was answered; we were dismissed.

The ship included a small area with what were known as four deep sleeping quarters. Folding bunks were chained to the wall on both sides. When the bunks were lowered to "sleep" position, a narrow corridor separated the two sides of the quarters. The bottom bunk was about a foot above the floor, the second about three feet above the floor and two feet above the bottom bunk, the third two feet above the second, and the fourth two feet above the third and about seven feet above the floor. There were fewer bunks than soldiers; LST-546 was not

Draftee

built for troop comfort. Some elected to find sleeping places in the vehicles on the cargo deck.

The ship slowly eased its way from the shore and eventually out of the bay and into the South China Sea. We slowly traveled north. LST-546 was not built for speed, but we were not in a hurry. Time on the boat — even with the primitive sleeping facilities and the lack of beer — was more pleasant than time on a firebase. We were not subject to hostile fire.

Chapter 18

Ship to Shore to the Cam Lo Cemetery

"I thought we were stopping for lunch."

After three days of sailing, on July 10th, we arrived at the Tan My landing craft utility ramp and dock facility, near the mouth of the Perfume River north, northeast of the old imperial capital city of Hue. The ship's doors were opened, the ramp lowered, and the cannons and other vehicles were driven off the ship. The four cannons were loaded onto lowboy trailers powered by semi-tractors. The four tractor trailers and other trucks were formed into a convoy. We donned our helmets, flak jackets, and M16s and found a place on a vehicle. We traveled through the city of Hue, crossed the narrow Perfume River bridge, went slowly northwest for about 50 more miles along QL1 through the city of Quang Tri, and eventually along QL9, to a cemetery south of the village of Cam Lo.

It was late in the afternoon when we arrived at the Cam Lo cemetery location. Deal said, "I thought we were stopping for lunch." Instead of lunch, we were told that we were setting up camp. Cam Lo was about six miles south of the DMZ and about three miles south of firebase Charlie 2. Seven weeks earlier, on May 21st, 1971, 30 US soldiers were killed and 50 wounded from a single NVA 122-mm rocket that had penetrated and exploded in a bunker at Charlie 2.[1] Ten miles to the west of Cam Lo was Fire Support Base Fuller that had been overrun by the NVA in late June.[2,3] Thus, it came to be that on July 10th, 1971, B Battery, 6th Battalion, 32nd Artillery became officially attached to the 8th Battalion, 4th Artillery.

We were provided with empty sandbags that we were told to fill and place on top of half-round, corrugated steel culverts about six feet in diameter to provide cover for sleeping. However, prior to sleeping, those of us in FDC were expected to set up an operational FDC — that is, operational generators, radios, antennas, charting table, and FADAC. Adjacent to the cemetery was a half-round, concrete structure about 14 feet in diameter and about 12 feet in length that appeared to be an unfinished mausoleum. It contained trash and what Deal discerned was human feces. We were told to clean it and set up an FDC, in what we called the tomb.

We began the tedious process of setting up an operational FDC. The first order of business was to remove the junk from the tomb. We unpacked the equipment from the truck; set up the wireless radio, antenna, battery, and generator used to charge the radio battery; set up the wired phones for the cannons; then built a charting table and located and affixed an acceptable 1:50,000 scale map of the region to the table. This was a serious challenge for several reasons. When we arrived, we did not have a precise grid location, and we did not have weather data for the region. The French maps that we were given were not as high quality as those that we had used in military region II, especially with regards to altitudes. And we were not fully staffed.

German and Deal worked on setting up the radio and charting table and I set up the FADAC, FADAC generator, and the wiring to connect the two. We worked continuously for an extended period; evening turned into night, and night turned into morning. We settled on a grid location and altitude that we believed was relatively accurate. Seeing the close proximity of our location to Charlie 2 and Fuller was disconcerting. One consequence of being a fire direction controller is that we knew, perhaps more so than members of other sections of the battery, that we were in an extremely vulnerable situation. We were within close range of NVA rockets and NVA artillery. While others in the battery had laid out a strand of concertina wire around our perimeter, we knew that a single strand of concertina wire could be breached in a few seconds by a motivated enemy. It was not stated, but it was hoped that locating adjacent to a cemetery would discourage the enemy from attacking.

I entered a generic set of weather data into the FADAC. Eventually, we acquired a target location and registered the guns. The concussion of the outgoing round was followed by the sound of glass shattering in what we assumed was a Buddhist place of worship located across the highway from the cemetery. I was too exhausted to be concerned.

Captain Hunting observed that we needed help. He ordered Albright to add FDC to his communications workload. Deal and I alternated FDC time with Albright and German. Eventually, day turned into night, and I found a spot under a half-round, corrugated steel culvert that Albright had used for sleeping. Since we were alternating FDC time, it was convenient to use the same culvert. I was thankful that someone had covered the steel with a single layer of filled sandbags. Deal stayed in the tomb and curled up under the charting table, sufficiently exhausted to sleep through the activity that surrounded him.

My thoughts turned back to Illinois, and I considered another thought experiment: suppose a group of militarily-

Draftee

powerful, young, Vietnamese soldiers set up an artillery battery in a vacant lot next to an Illinois church cemetery? How would the Americans feel if the Vietnamese fired cannons whose concussion destroyed stained glass windows in a nearby church? This thought experiment was not helpful; I was not paid to think. But it was clear that the planners of this mission were not in the business of producing friendships with local residents. Our activities were not conducive to winning "hearts and minds."

When I woke, I returned to the tomb, and Albright returned to the culvert. During the night, it started to rain. It poured. Back in Illinois, it would have been called a gully washer. The tomb was not watertight. We managed to provide sufficient cover for the radios, charting table, and the FADAC so that they remained operational. Fortunately, the tomb was situated on relatively high ground, and ground water did not flow through it.

Meanwhile, Albright was not so lucky. Water rushed through the culvert, which had been strategically placed in a low spot, and washed the air mattress on which he was sleeping out from under the culvert. The pouring rain eventually woke him. He then "rowed" back under the culvert and managed to anchor his air mattress. The downpour was followed by mud.

We occupied the cemetery location from July 10th to July 20th. For some reason, the NVA chose not to attack. Perhaps the strategy to locate next to a cemetery served as a deterrent. Perhaps they read the *Associated Press* story in the July 11 issue of the *New York Times* or elsewhere that "The sector is now defended on the ground almost exclusively by South Vietnamese forces following withdrawal last week of American troops from their last two fire bases..."[4][5]

Chapter 19

Camp Carroll – Keystone of the McNamara Line

"We were sitting ducks."

On the 20th of July 1971, two years after Neil Armstrong and Buzz Aldrin walked on the moon, we were told to load the trucks and prepare for departure. We loaded the equipment, formed a convoy, departed from Cam Lo, and traveled to Camp Carroll — about five miles southwest of Cam Lo, about nine miles south of the DMZ, and eight miles southeast of firebase Fuller.

The U.S. had built Carroll earlier in the war. However, it was abandoned by the U.S. Marines in December of 1968.[1] On January 22nd, 1969, General Creighton W. Abrams, who was the senior U.S. military officer in Vietnam, noted in a briefing at his Pentagon East offices (adjacent to Tan Son Nhut Airport near Saigon) that "Camp Carroll is no more..."[2]

The following is from a marine who had served at Carroll in 1968 before it was abandoned: "I didn't like Camp Carroll. We were often sitting ducks ... The NVA already had their 'bead' on us and lobbed their rockets ... They wreaked so much havoc ... it was in the open. We were pigeons ... in many conflicts — we who are but serial numbers were left out in the open to draw attacks so that superior fire power from artillery and planes could reap the 'harvest' ... I hated Camp Carroll..."[3]

Carroll was one of several defoliated bases south of the DMZ, surrounded by several rows of concertina wire and claymore land mines. In 1967, Secretary of Defense Robert McNamara had proposed a barrier against NVA infiltration along the DMZ extending from the coast to the Laotian border and continuing on down along the border with Laos.[4] In addition to these bases, the plan was to insert a number of sensors along the DMZ and Laotian border that would be intended to detect infiltration. It was a high-tech plan that was never completed. In some circles, the plan was known as the "McNamara Line," a pejorative perhaps to remind folks of the ill-fated Maginot Line that the French built in the 1930s to insure against a German invasion. Of course, in World War II, the Germans bypassed the line. During our time at Fire Support Base Wilson in military region II, we did conduct a number of fire missions based on information from sensors.

From our location at Carroll, our field of fire included Khe Sanh to our southwest and the Rock Pile firebase to our west. Baho (Nui Ba Ho) mountain was about three miles almost straight west of Carroll.

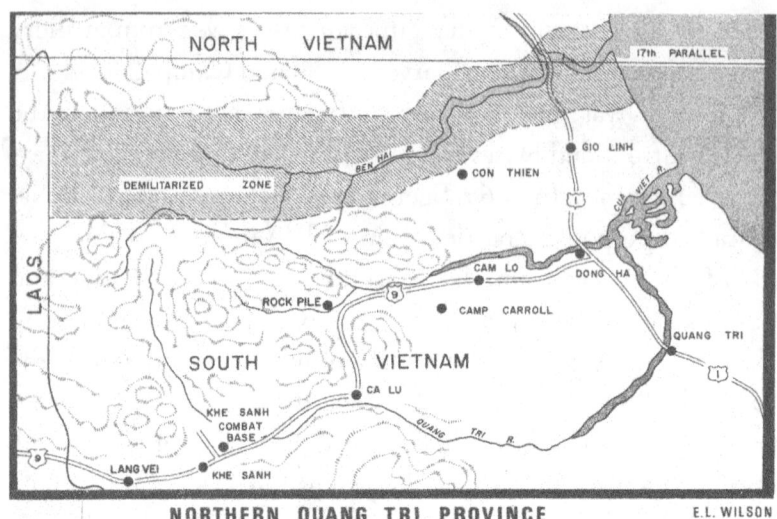

Area near the DMZ. Battery B occupied spaces near Cam Lo and later at Camp Carroll. Carroll was about nine miles south of the DMZ. Quang Tri is about 50 miles northwest of Hue along QL 1.[5]

I do not know why the U.S. army decided to reoccupy Carroll. The camp encompassed substantially more area than any prior location that we had used. It contained sufficient space to accommodate three artillery batteries. When we arrived, we occupied the area between a U.S. battery to our east and an ARVN battery to our northwest. The U.S. battery was similar to ours in that it operated two 175-mm self-propelled guns and two 8-inch self-propelled howitzers. We did not interact with them. They left Carroll several weeks after we arrived. The ARVN battery included six 105-mm towed howitzers.

We were assigned to two, rather ancient-looking bunkers:

Draftee

one for the FDC and the other for sleeping. While in the bunkers I did not feel as vulnerable to NVA rockets and NVA ground assault as at the Cam Lo cemetery. We set up cots in the very filthy sleep bunker. During our first attempt to sleep, we learned that mosquito nets could be used in an attempt to keep the rats from nibbling. I now had something in common with hall of fame St. Louis Cardinals pitcher Bob Gibson, who as a youngster lived, for a time, in a rat-infested environment. After the first attempt to sleep in the bunker, I made sure that an untorn mosquito net formed a tent that completely encircled my body. The rats used the top of the net as a trampoline.

After our arrival at Carroll, we welcomed two new members to our FDC crew: Harden and Turnbull. Both had been trained as surveyors and not as fire direction controllers. Our FDC section was now at six since we still counted Albright, even though he continued to serve as a communications RATT RIG operator in addition to his full FDC shifts. We formed two three-man crews: Albright and German were joined by Turnbull, and Deal and I were joined by Harden. The three-man crews enabled one person to handle the radios and switchboard, one person to use traditional charting techniques to calculate firing data, and the third person to operate the FADAC.

One three-man crew was on duty at all times. Our routine was eight hours on, eight hours off, for a net of 12 duty hours per 24-hour period. It was a pattern that we had determined was better for eating, sleeping, and remaining alert than 12 on and 12 off. However, there were times of intense activity and housekeeping duties, such as burning feces, when shifts extended beyond eight hours. Since Albright also had to spend time for his communications responsibilities in the RATT RIG, he seldom had eight hours off.

In addition to the rats, at Carroll, we were greeted with frequent NVA 122-mm rockets.[6] Unlike our stay near the Cam Lo cemetery, the NVA was not at all reticent to launch rockets targeted at Carroll. We soon learned to identify the sounds of incoming rockets. During our time in the sleep bunker, we learned to differentiate between the explosions of incoming 122s and the sounds of our outgoing 8-inch and 175-mm artillery rounds. There was a 30-day period during our encampment at Carroll that we endured incoming NVA rockets every day. Most of the time when we were not in a bunker, we wore our helmet and flak jacket, and we carried our M16. We did not assemble for any reason, including meals. The incident at Charlie 2, at which a single rocket killed 30 U.S. soldiers and wounded 50, served as a recent reminder to our superiors that we should remain dispersed.

Several weeks after our arrival at Carroll, Deal, Harden, and I arose from our now-routine, eight-hours-off rest in the sleep bunker, put on our boots, flak jackets, and helmets, grabbed our M16s, and walked the 100 feet to the FDC bunker. It was time for our three-man crew to begin our next 8-hour shift. Shift changes began with an informal briefing regarding activity for the last eight hours from the other three-man crew, as well as any ongoing fire missions.

We were greeted by Albright, who got our attention when he began the briefing with:

"We are not here."

I responded, "What do you mean? We are not here?"

Albright: "We are not here."

I was confused. "If we are not here, where are we?"

Albright: "I don't know."

I asked, "How do you know we are not here?"

Albright: "According to U.S. military brass in Saigon, there

Draftee

are no U.S. combat troops within 200 miles of the DMZ. So, we can't be here. We must be someplace else."

During his walk from the FDC bunker to the RATT RIG, Albright encountered a reporter who had hitched a ride on an ammunition resupply truck. The French reporter told Albright that he was surprised to find U.S. troops in the area, since he had been told by U.S. military officials in Saigon that no U.S. combat troops were within 200 miles of the DMZ. The reporter traveled to our location to witness how the South Vietnamese ARVN troops were doing without U.S. help.

At the time, the bulk of news reports about activities of U.S. forces in the Vietnam War were paraphrased from press releases prepared, censored, cleared, and disseminated by the U.S. military and the U.S. administration. For example, an *Associated Press* article dated July 11th, 1971 (one day after we arrived at Cam Lo), reported that "The sector is now defended on the ground almost exclusively by South Vietnamese forces following withdrawal last week of American troops from their last two fire bases,"[7] and on July 22nd, 1971 (two days after we arrived at Carroll), "The last American combat battalion was withdrawn from the area just below the demilitarized zone..."[8] Given the newspaper reports, presumably based on U.S. military press releases, it would be reasonable to conclude that we were not there.

We did not have access to newspapers other than the military's *Pacific Stars & Stripes* that was usually two weeks old upon arrival. The story that "The last American combat battalion was withdrawn from the area just below the demilitarized zone" was news to us.

The August 17th, 1971, *New York Times* reported under a headline — evidently based on press releases from the U.S. military and U.S. administration — that read "A Bitter Little War Raging Just Below the DMZ."

"North Vietnamese troops overran a South Vietnamese marine company's mountaintop post (Baho) south of the DMZ yesterday and inflicted heavy losses on the Government troops..." The article also said that "the last American troops sharing responsibility for the DMZ area have been withdrawn..."[9] Baho (also known as Nui Ba Ho) was about three miles almost straight west of Carroll. For perspective, the Lincoln Memorial in Washington, D.C. is 2.3 miles from the U.S. Capitol Rotunda.

During the NVA attack on Baho, our guns and howitzers were firing almost continuously for an extended period of time. After Baho was overrun, U.S. intelligence expected that Carroll was next in line. An estimated 20,000 NVA soldiers were involved in the "bitter little war" surrounding Carroll. Because of casualties (some by an accidental fire from burning excess propellant), our battery was at less than full strength and our gunners were exhausted. In addition to patching up casualties, our medic was humping ammunition. When the battery's ammunition was down to seven artillery rounds, Captain Hunting, the highest-ranking officer with our battery, ordered a cease fire. Hunting ordered the gun sections to prepare for close order combat.

8-inch howitzers and 175-mm guns were not designed for close order combat. The 105-mm howitzer ARVN battery that occupied the space northwest of us may have had access to beehive rounds that were designed for direct fire. A single 105-mm beehive round ejected 8,000 flechettes. Beehive rounds were not produced for 8-inch howitzers and 175-mm guns. The two 8-inch howitzers could have used their remaining few rounds for what was known as the "killer senior" direct fire technique. It was designed to explode a 200 pound, 8-inch-high explosive round approximately 10 meters above ground at ranges less than 1,000 meters.[10]

Draftee

Official Army manuals for 175-mm guns did not include a section for close order combat. However, during his artillery training at Fort Sill Oklahoma, Captain Hunting witnessed the demonstration of a close order combat technique for the 175-mm guns that could be used under dire circumstances. Hunting told the two 175-mm gun sections to open some of the remaining 5-foot-long propellant charge canisters, stand them on end, and pour as much Diesel fuel into the canister as the propellant would absorb. If the NVA entered the concertina wire that surrounded the perimeter, he would order the 175-mm guns to load and fire the Diesel-soaked propellant charges, without a projectile. This procedure was not in the manuals. Based on his training at Fort Sill, Hunting expected that one of these Diesel-soaked propellant charges would produce a fireball extending 300 meters. He was preparing for an anticipated NVA ground assault.

Given our ammunition situation, the call went out for air support. However, air support was limited by weather and constrained by NVA (and Russian) anti-aircraft activities. Fortunately, the expected ground attack was thwarted by back-to-back B-52 strikes. Most of the B-52s originated from distant air force bases, such as Anderson Air Force Base on the island of Guam and U-Tapao Airfield in Thailand. Usually, B-52 attacks were not effective against NVA infantry because of the time required between the decision to attack and the bomb drop — a minimum of 48 hours. This provided sufficient time for the NVA intelligence to obtain the information and warn NVA troops in the field to take cover prior to the drop. Russian radar provided early warning to the NVA of B-52s in flight and expected targets based on flight paths and U.S. air tactics. The NVA would evacuate the expected bomb drop area and then reoccupy the area after the bombs exploded. However, in the post-Baho bombing mission, the U.S. changed tactics by having a second B-52 strike shortly after the first. The second B-52 drop may have surprised the NVA, probably caused many casualties, and forced them to delay their plans to execute a ground attack on Carroll. It was effective to the extent that the anticipated ground attack on Carroll did not occur while we were there.

Chapter 20

Rookie Aerial Observer

"My gawd! They're building roads!"

The Army used single-propeller piston engine planes, including Cessna O-1 Bird Dogs, for reconnaissance and target identification. These small planes were capable of flying at 20,000 feet. However, aerial observation was often limited by weather and ground cover. A single engine plane flying at 20,000 feet is a relatively small target. Some requests for fire missions came directly from a Bird Dog pilot. Others were passed through various levels prior to arriving at our FDC bunker.

The default setting for our FDC over the air radios was "unsecure," meaning that the voice transmissions were not scrambled and could easily be monitored by the NVA. However, the AN/VRC46 radios were equipped with the AN/KY-38 secure voice system. All legitimate users of the secure voice system were provided with a monthly code book. Each day at 6 a.m. (that is, zero six hundred), users were expected to enter the codes for the day. When we received a radio call that we deemed should be scrambled, we would respond, "meet me green." If the caller agreed, then we would flip the switch to "secure" and continue the conversation. Then the NVA could listen only if their radio receiver was equipped with a stolen or captured secure voice system and if they had entered the stolen or captured daily code.

The secure system was cumbersome. If either party made an error in entering a character of the daily code, the system would not work. There was no easy way to determine if the codes had been entered correctly. I do not recall a situation in which a caller made a "meet me green" request. If we were using the secure communication system, it was in response to a request from us. Perhaps, given our location and vulnerability, we were more concerned about the negative consequences of compromised communication than those to whom we were communicating.

I recall one conversation with a rookie Bird Dog pilot. Our call sign was "Three Charlie." His was "Bravo Delta." It began:

Bird Dog pilot: "Three Charlie, Three Charlie, this is Bravo Delta over."

Me: "Bravo Delta, Three Charlie over."

Bird Dog pilot: "Are you the guys with the 75s down there, uh, over."

Me: "Bravo Delta, meet me green, over."

Bird Dog pilot: "Oh, oh, um, okay, over."

I flipped the radio switch to secure and waited for a response. I had assumed that the Bird Dog pilots were not responsible for entering the daily code updates. That tedious job had probably been assigned to some lower-ranking soldier. After encounters such as this, I was relatively sure that that was the case. After a few seconds he responded:

Bird Dog pilot: "Three Charlie, Bravo Delta, are you there, over."

Draftee

Me: "Bravo Delta, Three Charlie, roger, read you loud and clear." After which, for the remainder of the conversation, all radio formalities ceased.

Bird Dog pilot: "Hey, do you guys know what is going on up here?"

"My gawd! They're building roads! They've got bulldozers, road graders, and Tournapulls (wheel tractor-scrapers). They're building a road right through the DMZ. They have got heavy artillery. Let's see, I'll get the coordinates for you."

He sent the coordinates. I read them back.

Bird Dog pilot: "Roger that, let me know as soon as you fire."

By that time, Deal had plotted the target and realized that it was north of the border in the DMZ. Deal glanced at me and shrugged his shoulders.

Me: "Roger, the target is in the DMZ. We can request clearance, but I doubt if we can get clearance to fire."

Bird Dog pilot: "What the ... Why the hell not?"

Me: "Roger, Bravo Delta. We will put in a request. I'll get back to you as soon as we receive a ruling. Leaving green, over."

"Leaving green" was the term we used prior to switching the radio back to the unsecure setting. I was not sure how much more time the Bird Dog could stay aloft above the target. An experienced Bird Dog pilot would not reveal that over the air, secure or not, and I was not going to ask. We requested clearance, but as we had anticipated, clearance was not granted. That meant that someone or some group with more authority than us, for some reason, ordered us not to intentionally fire rounds to land north of the border in the DMZ.

Me: "Bravo Delta, Three Charlie, over."

Bird Dog pilot: "Yea, what did they say."

This guy was a rookie.

Me: "Bravo Delta, Three Charlie, meet me green, over."

I flipped the switch, waited a few seconds and continued.

Me: "Bravo Delta, Three Charlie."

Bird Dog pilot: "How soon can you start blasting these guys?"

Me: "Bravo Delta, Three Charlie, our request for clearance to fire was denied. Sorry about that."

Bird Dog pilot: "What the ... Did they provide a reason?"

Me: "No, but they are consistent. They haven't given us permission to fire at targets north of the border since we have been at this location."

Bird Dog pilot: "Do they not understand that these guys are building roads? It is easy to see that they plan to hook up with QL1. For gosh sakes, they have heavy artillery."

Me: "Roger, we conveyed the information, over."

Bird Dog pilot: "Damn, getting low on fuel, better head back to base. Geez."

Me: "Bravo Delta, Three Charlie, leaving green, over."

During our time at Carroll, we were routinely denied clearance to fire into the DMZ, north of the border established by the 1954 Geneva Accords. We followed orders and did not intentionally fire into the region. Evidently, the U.S. continued to operate under a November 1st, 1968, pledge not to attack positions in the DMZ if the North Vietnamese agreed to participate in peace talks.[1] The 1968 one-sided pledge enabled the NVA to use the DMZ as a safe haven for launching rockets that landed and exploded at Carroll. The North Vietnamese consistently denied that they had ever agreed to not use the DMZ.

The U.S. continued to bomb targets in North Vietnam. On September 21st, 1971, a day before we left Carroll, the U.S. dropped 200 plane loads of bombs on targets in North Vietnam in an eight-hour period.[2] Evidently, during these bombing runs, U.S. officials purposely chose to not attack the NVA artillery and NVA road building equipment in and close to the DMZ. However, Hastings has written that "Just as the Luftwaffe's 1940 blitz on Britain enabled Winston Churchill to energize the British people to meet it, so U.S. bombing proved a godsend to North Vietnam's leaders, empowering them to rally their citizens against a visible menace from the skies..."[3]

Chapter 21

Duck and Cover

"Epplin, what did you do to our bucket?"

Even though their rockets were relatively less accurate than our howitzers, given that our location was fixed, and given their sanctuaries in the DMZ, the NVA was very successful in landing and exploding rockets in our battery. It was generally understood that the radio antenna, perched adjacent to the FDC bunker, was the bullseye for the rocket launchers. During our time in the FDC bunker, we were usually too busy or too fatigued to be overly concerned.

We came to expect that a rocket could explode at any time at any location in the battery. When I was not in a bunker, I wore a helmet and flak jacket. During our time at Wilson, someone had secured a red three-gallon bucket. We found it to be useful, and someone placed it in the truck prior to our departure from Wilson. The red bucket traveled with us to Carroll, where it continued to provide utility.

The NVA pattern was to fire rockets in volleys, with each rocket separated by a few seconds. The key was to hear the first and take cover prior to the second, and the remainder of the volley. I was fortunate in that on more than one occasion, I heard the first and took cover, prior to the arrival of a later explosion that obliterated the space that I had previously occupied. One day, Deal, Harden, and I were walking from the sleep bunker to the FDC bunker. We heard the first rocket of a volley. Deal, who was following me, shoved me into the FDC bunker, just before the second round landed on our path and obliterated the blast wall outside the entrance to the FDC bunker. The blast wall was composed of a stack of several 175-mm propellant canisters filled with earth and rocks and secured in place with metal T-posts.

On another occasion, I was outside the FDC bunker with the bucket, conducting generator maintenance. I heard the first rocket, dropped the bucket, and dove into the FDC bunker. The second round hit very near the bucket. After what we hoped was the last rocket of the volley, I ventured out and retrieved what was left of the bucket — a part of the metal handle attached to a small piece of the original metal bucket — and returned to the FDC bunker. Lt. Riley glanced at me, stared at what I was holding, and sadly lamented, "Epplin, what did you do to our bucket?" Deal and Harden glanced up from their tasks, shrugged their shoulders, and continued on with the work of the FDC.

For several months, Albright had the combined duties of RATT RIG operator and full FDC shifts. The RATT RIG was mounted on a three-quarter ton truck, similar to a camper mounted on the bed of a large pickup truck. Operators entered the RIG via a door at the rear, where a tailgate would be on a pickup truck. Albright's standard operating procedure was to enter the RIG, close the door, and conduct the communications business in air-conditioned comfort — the only air-conditioned spot in the battery. The noise from the operating RIG and the air conditioner blocked out other noise from elsewhere on the battery, including the noise of exploding rockets.

After several weeks at Carroll, a replacement RATT RIG operator arrived. Albright was finally given a break from his RATT RIG assignments. During his first day of duty at Carroll, the replacement entered the RIG, but unlike Albright, left the door open. When he saw through the open door that some troops were rushing for cover, he left the RIG, and followed them into a bunker. The next rocket landed near the truck and destroyed the RATT RIG. The replacement was safe in a bunker and Albright, who would have been in the now destroyed RIG, was not harmed. However, the RIG was no longer operable.

The September 1st, 1971, edition of the *Pacific Stars & Stripes* reported that "ARVN soldiers at Fire Base Carroll 10 miles south of the DMZ suffered light casualties Sunday (August 29th, 1971) when Communist gunners hit the base with 60 122-mm rockets, spokesman said..."[1] Our battery was located at Carroll from July 20th to September 22nd, 1971. There was no mention of our battery in the article. There was no mention of U.S. soldier casualties. Perhaps the U.S. military spokesman could not mention us because they had already proclaimed that we were not there.

Chapter 22

ARVN (Army of the Republic of Vietnam) – the South Vietnamese Army

"Every single high-ranking member of the Saigon regime had been on the take."

During our time in military region II, while at Fire Support Base Wilson, we had little interaction with South Vietnamese military personnel. At Wilson, our battery provided artillery support for a U.S. allied contingent of Republic of Korea (ROK) infantry. About 20 ROK soldiers were stationed on the Hill. Their primary responsibility was to provide perimeter guard duty at several of the battery's observation posts. We had little interaction with the ROK troops. However, we observed that the South Koreans were professional soldiers.

While at Wilson, we routinely receive coded ARVN patrol locations. Standard operation procedure was to track locations of all (U.S., ROK, ARVN) friendly troops on our maps to prevent friendly fire incidents. Our first close interactions with South Vietnamese military troops were at Cam Lo. My impression was that they were less professional than the ROK soldiers that we had observed at Wilson. On paper, and based on the information provided by the U.S. military in press releases, there were several layers of South Vietnamese soldiers. There were (on paper) about 450,000 regular army troops (ARVN and South Vietnamese rangers and marines). These regular ARVN personnel were the ones expected to transition into activities that the U.S. soldiers had been doing prior to Vietnamization. The next layer contained about 430,000 regional and popular force soldiers; this group did not stray far from their home villages. Finally, approximately three million, mostly elderly men, were said to be in the people's self-defense forces. Most in this last group had zero military training.[1]

During our time at Carroll, we had opportunities to observe the behavior of ARVN troops. In addition to the 105-mm howitzers, the ARVN battery adjacent to our battery included several wire cages that were used to confine ARVN soldiers for what we assumed were disciplinary reasons. The cages were so small that even the typically diminutive ARVN soldier did not have sufficient space to stand or to lie. These cages were totally exposed to the elements and had no protection against incoming rockets. It appeared to us that a soldier was kept in the cage through at least one round of incoming rockets. The officers with our battery had no direct contact with the ARVN and had no input into their discipline methods. We did not discern which offenses resulted in this seemingly physically painful and potentially psychologically damaging incarceration.

A few ARVN infantry units were camped at Carroll. They conducted perimeter guard duty and exterior patrols. That is, they would move outside the encircling sets of concertina wire. We observed that usually a half dozen or so troops would be followed by the highest-ranking member of the group, who held his M16 pointing forward and ready to fire. It appeared that the regular ARVN troops had no interest in encountering the NVA. Their alternative was to move forward or to be shot by their own leaders, who were leading from the rear.

I suspect that there were many ARVN troops that were

courageous model soldiers. However, at the time, I was surprised that most of those that we observed seemed to have no interest in fighting. In 1970, fifteen percent of the ARVN troops were absent without leave.² As early as 1965, Langguth reported that thirty percent of ARVN draftees deserted during their first six weeks of service.³ Did they not know that if they did not defend their country against the NVA, their families would lose what little freedom they had and be subjected to godless communism?

It wasn't until later that I came to understand their situation. Most of the ARVN troops that we observed were draftees. "Drafted soldiers represented about 65 percent of the army's total troop levels, making it one of the most heavily conscripted armies in history..."⁴ As Brigham noted, "Corruption and abuse in the deferment system alienated many poor Vietnamese who had been forced into the army," while knowing that others escaped the draft because they knew someone in Saigon.⁵ There was a perception among the non-Catholics that "Catholics were receiving special treatment..."⁶ Brigham quoted a Buddhist monk as saying, "The cornerstones of freedom should be religious tolerance and the right to protest ... We were no better off than those living under communism..."⁷ ⁸

The Country's wealth and power were concentrated in a small group of mostly urban families. Draft-age sons of these privileged families often found their way to safe positions, some as university students in Europe and elsewhere. Sons of power who did serve were more likely to be officers and to be some distance from fighting. On the other hand, the draftees that we observed were more likely to be from poor rural families. These poor rural troops had little incentive to fight. For them, there was no reason to believe that their lives would be any worse if the NVA prevailed. "Ordinary soldiers had no reason to hate the enemy, because they had not seen what communism could do..."⁹

Income and class differences were not limited to South Vietnam. As Hastings noted: "There was also plenty of social injustice in the North. The poor people went to fight while others with political privileges were able to send their sons abroad to study, and some of them to enjoy luxurious lives..."¹⁰

"The communists enjoyed the critical propaganda advantage that they were almost invisible to most of the people most of the time..."¹¹ There was no free press to educate that Ho Chi Minh and Le Duan dictated over a brutal inhumane totalitarian regime. There was no free press in the North to report the massive loss of human lives that the North's leaders were willing to sacrifice. The ARVN draftees most likely did not know that the communists "executed village chiefs who declined to bow to their will, often by live burial before peasant audiences, after subjecting them to tortures of medieval ingenuity..."¹² During the war, and for many years after the war, the communists had total control over information reported regarding the North. It wasn't until many years after the War that witnesses of the North's brutal campaign of terror on its own citizens could relate what they had observed. One survivor, who lived through North Vietnam's terror campaign on its own citizens as a child, wrote, "I had seen many corpses beheaded, dismembered, eviscerated, even scalped..."¹³

As Hastings notes, "In most societies, including the modern U.S., rural dwellers feel an instinctive mistrust of metropolitan elites. This was especially acute in South Vietnam, where Saigon was seen as the embodiment of a French colonial rather than an indigenous culture. While few people had much interest in Marxist-Leninist theory, many were impressed by the promise of land reform that would cast off the yoke of land-

Draftee

lords and money lenders, promote government by and for Vietnamese, and expel foreigners..."[14]

The wire cages told the story. There was clearly a class system that enabled the superior urban officer to cage the inferior, and most likely rural, peasant. From the perspective of the peasant draftee, if the ARVN prevailed, the class system would continue. The draftees were not well educated, but they were not dumb. It is likely that some members of their families were well aware of corrupt members of the Thieu regime and had shared this information with the draftee. For example, "according to a post-war Rand study of 27 former senior officers and civil servants, every single high-ranking member of the Saigon regime had been on the take. A syndicate with connections that reach into the prime minister's office somehow smuggled out of the country 16,000 tons of brass shell casings worth $17.3 million. Province chiefs sold rice to the enemy, levied personal taxes on vehicles passing through their territories, and siphoned off funds meant for refugee resettlement..."[15] Evidently, the ARVN draftees that we observed were aware of the corruption, the concentration of power, the second-class nature of the peasantry, and not surprisingly, had little interest in seeing it preserved. They had little incentive to fight, other than for personal preservation.

One common post-war narrative was that the U.S. equipment was too complicated for the ARVN to operate. That is not credible. The NVA troops had no problem learning how to operate equally sophisticated Russian equipment. An anecdotal argument against the too-complicated narrative is that in April of 1975, pilots from the North flew, captured U.S. A-37 jets, and used them to bomb ARVN locations near Saigon. The equipment was not too complicated for pilots from the North to operate. If the ARVN had been properly incentivized, they would have learned how to use the equipment.

In retrospect, as U.S. soldiers, we had been trained to kill and to destroy. We were very good at killing and destroying. In May of 1965, President Johnson said that "the ultimate victory will depend upon the hearts and the minds of the people who actually live out there..."[16] We had not been trained how to win the hearts and minds of the vast majority of people who resided in Vietnam. More importantly, the South Vietnamese government either was not interested or did not know how to win widespread support. Ultimately, the hearts and mind battle determined the outcome. No amount of killing and no amount of destruction aided in the battle to win hearts and minds.

Chapter 23

Leaving Carroll

"Haul ass and let these other two guys fire back."

We occupied Carroll from July 20th until September 22nd. On Wednesday morning, September 22nd, 1971, we were told to assemble our personal belongings into our duffle bags and to disassemble the FDC equipment for departure from Camp Carroll. It was to be our first move since we arrived at Carroll on July 20th. It was the first day that we had not served alternating eight-hour FDC shifts since we had arrived at Cam Lo on July 10th. During our time at Carroll, our battery fired an average of 35 rounds per cannon per day.[1]

Departure was complicated. Some of the battery's vehicles had been destroyed, and others were damaged. Damaged vehicles that had functional wheels, tires, steering, and operable breaks were set up to be towed by the few that were operational.

Captain Hunting told one of the noncommissioned officers, Sergeant Rodriguez, that he was financially responsible for all FDC equipment. Rodriguez seemed nervous; we laughed. We loaded some of the FDC equipment into a CONEX (CONtainer EXpress shipping container) that was later loaded onto a

5-ton truck that would not start but could be steered. Patreno was in the driver's seat and was trying to start it. Two ammo trailers were attached to Patreno's truck that was towed by an operable 5-ton truck, driven by Wilson. The two trucks and two trailers formed a rather lengthy train. As we later learned, as the long train moved down the hill, that while the engine on Patreno's truck did not work, the brakes did.

We loaded the FDC section chests and the antennas, along with the FADAC and other FDC equipment, onto a trailer that was attached to Molly, FDC's three-quarter ton truck driven, as usual, by Deal. Our current second in command, executive officer Lieutenant Podkova, rode shotgun. Albright, German, and Harden sat on top of equipment piled in the back. I found a spot on top of duffle bags in the bed of Wilson's truck. We were securing our helmets and flak jackets and checking our M16s when Lieutenant Podkova walked up to Wilson's door.

"Okay, Wilson, don't stop for anything. If we get fire, just haul ass and let these other guys fire back." As long as the truck was headed downhill, perhaps he could haul ass with a 5-ton and two ammo trailers in tow.

Eventually the convoy started down the hill. I glanced back at Carroll, southwest to Firebase Sarge, west to Baho Mountain, and northwest to the scarred and desolate mountaintop that at one time was occupied and called Firebase Fuller. I then looked north toward the DMZ and North Vietnam. I, along with everyone in our battery, was glad to be leaving Carroll. Those of us in FDC knew how fortunate we had been to not have been overrun after the fall of Baho Mountain. We also knew that it was just a matter of time until the NVA made the next attempt to overrun what was left of Carroll.

We continued down the hill and drove past several Montagnard tribesmen who were on foot. They ignored us and moved to the side of the road. We arrived at QL9 and turned right. We made it to Cam Lo without any sniper fire. I assumed that any NVA snipers would be glad to see us leave and would have no desire to slow our departure.

We drove past Cam Lo where, on the 10th of July, our battery set up camp adjacent to a cemetery. The half-round concrete structure that we had used to house our FDC operations was no longer there. Perhaps the villagers destroyed it to prevent another occupation.

We continued on to Dong Ha, where QL9 intersected with QL1. We pulled into a small base at Dong Ha that was mostly deserted. We rendezvoused with four tractor trucks that were pulling empty lowboy trailers. All four of the tracked cannons had traveled on their own power to Dong Ha; three of them were loaded onto lowboys. Gun 3 was deemed to be in sufficiently good shape to continue the journey under its own power. That enabled the fourth lowboy to be used to haul one of the dead lined three-quarter ton trucks that had been towed to Dong Ha.

Operable trucks and Gun 3 were topped off with Diesel fuel. It was about 12:30 p.m. when Harden came and told me that they had room in Molly. So, I moved back to the FDC three-quarter ton truck and joined the FDC section for a C-ration meal. The convoy continued southeast on QL1, passed Camp Evans, and eventually made it to the Perfume River bridge at Hue.

Patreno's 5-ton truck, which had been started and running since Dong Ha, died on the bridge. Blocked convoys and bridges are not a good combination. Eventually, a tow was arranged, and the complete convoy crossed the bridge and traveled through Hue. The convoy then separated into two groups.

The lowboys carrying the three cannons, Gun 3 (still providing its own power), a 2½ ton (deuce and a half) truck, and FDC's three-quarter ton with Deal driving headed northeast to the mouth of the Perfume River, at what the U.S. referred to as Tan My Ramp and Dock. The remainder of the convoy headed south on QL1 toward Camp Eagle.

We arrived at Tam My Ramp and observed USNS LST 546 — the ship that had carried us to Tan My Ramp from Cam Ranh Bay in July — pull away from the dock and into the sea. The four cannons were parked near the dock. Seven soldiers from our gun sections stayed with the cannons to prepare them for a later shipment. At about 16:30 (4:30 pm), our FDC three-quarter ton and the 2½ ton departed Tan My Ramp. We were stopped on the outskirts of Hue by several U.S. Army Military Police (MP) who told us that they would escort us through the city, and that they only escorted groups of six or more vehicles.

For several months, Deal had been trying to get a replacement water pump for the FDC three-quarter ton truck. On our way back to Hue, the pump failed. The short-term solution was to have the three-quarter ton towed by the 2½ ton truck. After an hour or so, several other vehicles arrived, enabling a convoy through Hue. After we traveled through the city, we again found ourselves alone: a half dozen or so filthy U.S. troops traveling on a deuce and half, towing a three-quarter ton traveling down QL1, looking for Camp Eagle. We were told that Camp Eagle was only a few miles southeast of Hue. We did not have a map and did not know the precise location of Camp Eagle, but we assumed that it would be too big to miss. We were wrong. Eventually we were stopped at an MP checkpoint and informed that we had driven past the Eagle turnoff.

It was after 6:30 p.m., and the MPs informed us that QL1 was closed to U.S. military traffic at 18:30. Lieutenant Podkova eventually convinced the MP in charge to seek approval from someone in his chain of command to provide an MP escort for us back to Eagle. We finally got to Eagle. But rather than helping us locate the rest of our battery, the

Draftee

Military Police were more interested in threatening to arrest us for not wearing proper insignia, for not having polished boots, and for our unprofessional appearance. Indeed, we were filthy, but we had grounds for being so. Fortunately, somebody in authority agreed, and we were spared time in the brig.

From our perspective, Camp Eagle was huge. It contained facilities to house 15,000 troops.[2] After a delay, mostly exacerbated by concerns about our appearance, an MP with a jeep escorted us to our assigned location. We were driven several miles within Eagle, past rows of barracks, parked vehicles, crates of materials, and even a few buildings that appeared to be gymnasiums. It reminded me of an army base back in the States. We were not able to locate any Battery B personnel, but we did find several Battery B vehicles.

We found some C-rations in one of the trucks, sat down under night lights, and ate. We set up cots under a tent. The next morning, we were awakened at 6 a.m. I tried to shave. We then found a mess hall for breakfast. At 7 a.m., Captain Hunting called for a formation. We were not accustomed to such formalities. Hunting walked down the line.

Captain Hunting: "Epplin, did you shave this morning?"

Epplin: "I tried to, sir."

Captain Hunting: "Yes, I see that you tried. Have you got a sewing kit?"

Epplin: "Somewhere, sir."

Captain Hunting: "All right then, you'd better dig it out and put a few more stitches in your pants — and put a little black on your boots."

I didn't answer. I suspect that my facial expression betrayed my incredulity. He moved down the line.

Later in the day, we formed another convoy, sans cannon, left Camp Eagle, turned right on QL1, and headed south toward DaNang. The base at DaNang was about 90 kilometers (56 miles) southeast of Camp Eagle.

We arrived at the very large (by our standards) base at DaNang late in the day on September 23rd. As had been the case at Eagle, I was not comfortable at DaNang. Troops on these large bases wore insignia, clean fatigues, polished boots, and did not routinely carry an M16; I am not sure if all of them had M16s. They ate in mess halls that served real food, watched movies, and played basketball in gyms. Some appeared to be in a holding pattern with little purpose. I did not know who I could trust.

We were told that our job for the next few days was to clean, inventory, and turn in our FDC equipment. We did so. I was assigned to a barracks that housed troops from a number of units. Since most were in transition between units, there was no sense of security. When we were on isolated firebases, we depended on each other. We trusted our fellow soldiers to do their jobs. There was little opportunity for thievery, since there was no place to hide and nowhere to go. Things were different for us at DaNang. It seemed that every day, some new troops were arriving, and others were departing the barracks. Some of those leaving helped themselves to personal belongings of others prior to walking out the building and never returning. Within the barracks, there was a lack of leadership, resulting in anarchy. I grew to distrust everyone, except for the few remaining colleagues from Battery B.

We completed our battery equipment turn in (FADAC, generators, radios, antennas, maps, range deflection protractors, graphical firing tables, etc.) on September 30th. Fortunately for Sergeant Rodriguez, the official equipment list did not include a red three-gallon bucket.

Chapter 24

Albright's Forecast

"Whenever they want to."

As we were preparing to depart Camp Carroll on September 22nd, 1971, I glanced at fellow fire direction controller Albright and asked, as I then looked toward the north, "How long before you think they complete their road through the DMZ, hook up with QL1, and drive down to Saigon?" QL1 was the mostly two-lane, paved asphalt, north-south road connecting the old imperial capital Hue to Saigon, 650 miles south. Hue was about 60 miles southeast of the DMZ. Albright didn't hesitate; he gazed into the distance and replied, "Whenever they want to."

At the time, because those of us in FDC had access to maps and data, we knew that the NVA was in the process of constructing roads with modern road building equipment through the DMZ. We could deduce from our maps that one road was being designed to connect with QL1 south of the DMZ. We knew that the NVA had a number of serviceable cannons, including 130-mm towed Russian field guns that had a firing range of at least 17 miles. Neither of us expected that the ARVN soldiers that we observed at Carroll would provide much resistance.

During the "Easter offensive" of March 1972, NVA troops once again surrounded Carroll. On April 2nd, Ambassador Ellsworth Bunker cabled (National Security Advisor) Kissinger and Nixon that "ARVN forces are on the verge of collapse in I Corps..."[1]

On April 2nd, 1972, 194 days after we left, as we had expected, the ARVN at Camp Carroll surrendered.[2] According to Willbanks, the NVA attacked Carroll. "The NVA ... hit Camp Carroll with intense artillery and human-wave attacks supported by T-54 tanks ... Col. Pham Van Dinh, commander of the 56th regiment at Camp Carroll, informed (U.S. advisor) Camper that a "cabal" of his own officers had forced him to negotiate a surrender ... Dinh surrendered his entire regiment: 1,500 ARVN troops and 22 artillery pieces..."[3] However, Hastings reported that Dinh secured a vote from his officers for surrender after arguing that, rather than stand and fight and perhaps die, they "must take care of themselves." "Dinh was rewarded with a commission in the NVA..."[4]

The March 1972 offensive was a disaster for the ARVN. In ten days, ARVN units lost or abandoned 81 105-mm howitzers, 32 155-mm howitzers, and four 175-mm guns. "All the fire support bases north and west of Dong Ha were overrun and the artillery positioned there was captured or destroyed..."[5]

After the surrender at Carroll, President Nixon's team evidently realized that the South was on the verge of collapse. He did not want to lose the war prior to the November 1972 election. On April 4, two days after the Carroll surrender, Nixon ordered an intensive bombing campaign, including B-52 strikes against North Vietnam.[6] He said, "These bastards have never been bombed like they're going to be bombed this time..."[7] The Pentagon papers showed that "the prime motive of American presidents from Kennedy onward was to punt — to avoid being blamed for losing the war..."[8]

At U.S. military Pentagon East headquarters near Saigon, General Abrams expressed his dissatisfaction with the South Vietnamese. "The ARVN haven't lost their tanks because the enemy tanks knocked them out ... They abandoned them..."

He told President Thieu, "Equipment is not what you need. You need men that will fight. And you need officers that will fight and will lead men ... You've got all the equipment you need ... You lost most of your artillery because it was abandoned..."[9]

The April 4th, 1972, issue of the *New York Times* reported that "Camp Carroll ... was abandoned to the enemy yesterday..."[10] According to the *Times*, the Saigon administration was more upset by the *United Press International* for reporting the story than they were about the loss of the firebase to the NVA.

The infamous White House recordings include the following President Nixon dialogue from May 4, 1972: "The United States cannot lose ... Whatever happens to South Vietnam we are going to cream North Vietnam ... We got to use the maximum power of this country ... against this shit-ass little country..."[11]

Chapter 25

Leaving Vietnam

"Piss in the cup and set it on the table."

Some Battery B personnel were transferred to other units. Captain Hunting was reassigned as an advisor to an ARVN infantry unit. Hunting had no prior experience as an infantry officer. Those of us who were approaching one year in the country were told that we were going to be transferred to our battalion headquarters at Phan Rang.

On October 1st, a group of us, including myself and Albright, were flown from the DaNang air base, about 400 miles south to the Phan Rang air base on a C-130. Much of the base at Phan Rang, including rows of barracks, was deserted. On October 5th, 1971, I was one of a few from Battery B to participate in the stand-down ceremony for the 6th Battalion 32nd Artillery of the First Field Forces. The battalion was officially deactivated.

The following day, on October 6th, we were driven the 30 miles or so north to the large base at Cam Ranh Bay and assigned to the 22nd Replacement Battalion for transfer back to the U.S. In December, when we had arrived at Cam Ranh Bay, the stench was intense. Now, ten months later, we had become

Draftee

so accustomed to foul smells that it did not seem unusual. Albright noted that, "The fact that the stench of this place is tolerable is a clear indication that we have been in Vietnam too long."

One purpose of the 22nd Replacement Battalion was to assemble plane loads of troops for return flights to the U.S. However, prior to approving a soldier's departure, the battalion was charged with determining that the soldier was drug free. During our time near the DMZ, I doubt if many Battery B soldiers were addicted to drugs. We were too isolated to have easy access to drugs. Nonetheless, during our time at the 22nd, we were assembled and required to provide a urine sample on a daily basis. Evidently, someone in the chain of command did not want to return a group of drug addicts to the U.S. Word quickly disseminated to troops all over South Vietnam that if they tested positive for drugs, they would not be assigned to a flight home, but rather be sent to an in-country detox center. This threat was an attempt to incentivize sobriety. I did not envy the soldier whose job it was to hand a specimen cup to the next soldier in line. He greeted each soldier with the following statement: "Piss in the cup and set it on the table." He must have repeated that statement hundreds of times a week.

Every day, a flight manifest would be posted. We would check to see if our name was on the list. Finally, my name appeared. It was the last on a list for an October 14th, 1971, flight to McChord air force base in Washington. The flight had scheduled refueling stops at Okinawa and Honolulu. When we arrived at Okinawa, I was notified that I was being bumped from the flight by a local soldier who had been granted emergency leave. Since I was the last man on the list, I was the one to be bumped. I inquired about my duffle bag. I was told not to worry, that it would be flown to McChord, and that it would be available in baggage claim when I arrived.

Fortunately, someone at Okinawa notified someone at Cam Ranh Bay, and they left a seat open on the next flight scheduled to travel from Cam Ranh to Okinawa. Much to the surprise of the two senior officers who thought that they had an empty seat between them, I boarded the second plane, found the previously empty middle seat, and sat quietly for the flight from Okinawa to McChord.

The second plane did not stop in Honolulu. We flew without stops from Okinawa to McChord. When we arrived at McChord, I proceeded to the baggage claim and asked if they had an extra duffle bag from the prior flight. They told me that ours was the first arriving flight of the day. I then recalled that the first flight, in addition to the stop at Okinawa, had a scheduled stop at Honolulu.

Since I did not have a bag, I easily cleared the customs inspection line, found a chair in the post-inspection area, and waited for my duffle bag to arrive. The baggage claim area at McChord included a number of inspectors. Troops were told to find their bags; most were required to empty their bags. Inspectors paid special attention to containers of foot powder. Perhaps on some prior flight, someone had replaced foot powder with cocaine.

Eventually, the plane from which I had been bumped at Okinawa landed. Troops were held on the plane until the prior flight had been processed. Duffle bags began to flow into the inspection area. I saw my bag, reached over, grabbed it, and walked out. I did not care that no one bothered to inspect it.[1]

Chapter 26

Headed for Home

"We won the war... Just a couple of cleanup operations."

It was October 15th, 1971. I was dressed in an army uniform on a commercial flight from Seattle-Tacoma airport to Lambert International in St. Louis. I was going home on leave. The flight attendant permitted me to move to a window seat in an otherwise empty row. As I stared out the window at the "real world" below, I overheard a conversation across the aisle between an army major in uniform and a middle-aged civilian lady. She initiated the conversation.

Civilian: "Where are you headed?"

Major: "I am returning home from Vietnam."

Civilian: "My nephew just received orders to go over there. I am worried."

Major: "No need to worry. We won the war. The enemy was destroyed during the TET offensive in 1968. The fighting is all but over. Just a couple of cleanup operations."

Civilian: "That is good to hear."

I was stunned. Was the Major so ignorant that he believed this, or was he lying through his teeth? If the war was won in 1968, why are U.S. soldiers still dying more than three years later? He said it with such conviction. Should I enter the conversation and provide the lady a more truthful assessment? He was a Major. Not only did he outrank me, a lowly Spec-4, he outranked every officer that served in our Battery. What was I to do? What good could possibly come from me entering the conversation? None that I could think of. I kept silent, not because it was the prudent choice, but because I was paralyzed with disbelief at the Major's cavalier response. I was numb. But then, anything that I would say would certainly not allay her fears. What could I say?

I sat in silence for the remainder of the trip and continued to gaze out the window at the beautiful, peaceful country below us. I chose to ignore the Major. Fortunately, he did not complain when I did not salute. I came to realize that it would be a struggle to explain my experiences, as well as my expectations, regarding the short-term future of South Vietnam. Indeed, each of the approximately 2,594,000 U.S. servicemen that served "in country" had a unique experience. Their experience depended on when they served, where they served, and their specific military duties. Perhaps the Major was in the 80% that did not fight in combat and were not regularly exposed to enemy attack.[1] [2] I suppose that if my experience had been limited to one or more of the relatively large military bases that I observed during transit, such as those located near Cam Ranh Bay, Nha Trang, Phan Rang, and Da Nang, I might have come to the same conclusion as the Major.

I was reminded of an exchange from Remarque's *All Quiet on the Western Front*. After a year of fighting in the trenches of World War I, the narrator, fictional German infantryman Paul Baumer, returned home for leave and encountered an older civilian at a local beer garden who told him, "Smash through the Johnnies and then there will be peace..."

Paul tried to explain, "That ... a break-through may not be

possible. The enemy may have too many reserves. Besides, the war may be rather different from what people think..."

The civilian in the beer garden "dismisses the idea loftily and informs me (Paul) I know nothing about it..."[3] "It was different a year ago ... at that time, I (Paul) still knew nothing about the war, we had only been in quiet sectors..."[4] Perhaps the Major had spent a year or more in South Vietnam in "quiet sectors" and "knew nothing about the war." I, of course, knew nothing about his war, his experiences, or his observations, and my impression was he knew very little about mine.

Why, in 1971, would anyone believe that a lowly draftee knew more about the War than a Major who had "been there"? Of course, I knew what I knew. I knew that two months earlier on August 15th, 1971, the NVA had overrun the base at Baho (Nui Ba Ho) Mountain.[5] [6] I knew that our position at Carroll was next in line. I knew that several thousand NVA troops had been on the verge of a full-frontal attack on our battery at Carroll. I knew that we had been rescued by two back-to-back B-52 strikes. I knew that the NVA were in the process of constructing a road through the DMZ. It was obviously designed to connect with the existing coastal highway in South Vietnam, QL1, enabling them a fast lane to Saigon. I knew that precursors of the NVA had demonstrated their staying power. They had outlived the French, and they certainly were not going anywhere. (I also knew from history that in the late 1700s, a ragtag army [none of them draftees] of poorly equipped revolutionaries, with assistance from the French and Spaniards, had outlasted a very professional and powerful British military.)

Those of us in FDC joked about our secret clearances. It was not clear to us that we knew any information that the NVA did not know. But, perhaps, if the Major was being honest with the lady, we did know more than the Major. Perhaps he, and by extension other Americans, were the ones to whom we were not to reveal our secret information. Glancing down at the checkerboard pattern of the Great Plains, my mind drifted back to the FDC charting board and other maps in our bunker. I could visualize the NVA artillery positions, their bulldozers, their road building equipment, and deduce their intent. I was on my way home. I had survived. In a sense, the Major was correct. Relative to the 58,220 U.S. soldiers killed and 75,000 severely disabled, I had "won." Why was it that I felt numbness, sadness, and a sense of relief, rather than joy? During the remainder of the flight, and for many years, I could not find the words to succinctly and convincingly convey my feelings and concerns.

Chapter 27

Fort Hood

"Epplin, don't go to class."

I arrived at Lambert International in St. Louis, located a pay phone, and called home. A few hours later, my brother Arthur and my parents arrived. It was then that I wished I had written and told them about my missing front teeth. A good son would not have surprised his parents with missing front teeth. None of them asked what happened to my teeth. A good son would have explained it anyway.

I did tell them that my next assignment was to report to Fort Hood in Texas on November 18th. I explained that I could drive to Texas and would be permitted to have a car on base. Dad had stored my car in one of the sheds on the farm.

I spent most of the leave time sleeping. Mom did not seem to care; she prepared and served three delicious meals per day. In mid-November, I packed my duffle bag, placed it in the trunk of my car, told my parents goodbye, and left for Texas. Mom thought I should stay at home another week and celebrate Thanksgiving. I told her that it did not work that way. At Hood, I was assigned to Battery B, 1st Battalion, 78th Artillery, 2nd Armored Division.

Francis Epplin

My time at Hood was rather uneventful, except for the training that wasn't. I was the only Vietnam veteran in the FDC section of Battery B. Shortly after I arrived, the section was scheduled for FADAC training. We were marched to a classroom whereupon we met two noncommissioned officers, an E-6 (either a Specialist 6 or Staff Sergeant) and an E-7 (either a Specialist 7 or a Sergeant First Class). They mostly read from a lesson plan. They explained that their job was to teach us how to use the army's sophisticated modern Field Artillery Digital Automatic Computer (FADAC) to compute artillery firing data. They did not bother to ask if any of us had prior experience with a FADAC. Apparently, that question was not listed on their lesson plan.

They proceeded to click off the boxes on their lesson plan and finally arrived at the point where their next step was to start the computer. Of course, to do that, they needed to start the 3-phase, 4-wire, 400 hertz, gasoline-powered generator. They explained that the FDC section would include a troop trained as a tactical power generation specialist who would be in charge of the generator. I must have rolled my eyes; I had never heard of a tactical power generation specialist. They must be in a different army. I kept my mouth shut and tried to remain respectful. I should have known that eye rolling was not appropriate. Eventually, to their credit, they managed to start the computer without the assistance of a tactical power generation specialist, and were able to start the FADAC.

About mid-morning, when the computer did not do what they thought it should do, I raised my hand and tried to politely explain what they had done wrong. They were reluctant to try my suggestion and seemed surprised when it worked. They then moved on to the next item on the lesson plan.

After lunch, we returned to the classroom. After an hour or so, I did not have the self-control to keep my mouth shut. After

Draftee

they bungled methodically through an attempt to demonstrate a rather routine procedure, I raised my hand and was recognized. I explained: "What you are doing will work. But, in combat situations, it takes too long. That procedure will produce reasonable firing data, but, by the time the data are transferred to the guns, the target will have moved." I then attempted to explain what I had found to be a much less time-consuming procedure for arriving at the same firing data.

The E-7 was very polite. He looked at me and said, "We have just returned from training at Fort Sill. This is the way they told us to do it. This is the way we are going to teach it." I nodded and he continued with the lesson plan.

In hindsight, he was very kind. He did not raise his voice or belittle me. He did not send me to KP duty. I needed to learn that I was no longer in a battery where everyone did their job, no one wore rank insignia, and techniques for producing accurate firing data quickly were welcomed. For the remainder of the afternoon's session, I remained quiet and fought back involuntary eye rolls.

The following morning, the battery was assembled as usual. After a few standard formalities, I heard from the Sergeant in charge.

Sergeant: "Epplin."

I responded, "Present."

He paused the roll call, rolled his eyes, and looked at me.

Sergeant: "Epplin, don't go to class today."

I asked, "Where should I go?"

Sergeant: "You cain't stay in the barracks, and you cain't leave the base."

I inquired, "May I go to the base library?"

Sergeant: "No. You can go hang out in the motor pool."

Well, no FADAC class for me. No unwanted uncomfortable interruptions for the E-6 and E-7. It was probably for the best. It would have been painful for me to sit through more "training."

Albright, who had also been reassigned to Fort Hood, found himself in a similar situation. The battery to which he had been assigned was conducting war games. On his first day, he was assigned to a charting table. When the first target location was received, Albright plotted it, used his range deflection protractor and graphical firing table, and called out the firing data. Meanwhile, the instructors in his group were still trying to find the target coordinates on the map. Rather than have him share and teach his acquired skills, he was removed from the FDC and ordered to hold a sign that was used in the war games to designate the battery headquarters.

The Army could have sent those of us that had acquired FDC operational skills in Vietnam, and who had remaining service time, to the artillery training center at Fort Sill. We could have been debriefed and incorporated information from our experiences and improved the manuals. More importantly, we could have reduced the time required to compute accurate firing data for every battery in the army. Instead, I was sent to hide in the motor pool, and Albright was ordered to carry a sandwich board.

I walked to the motor pool and tried to act as if I was not out of place. There were several rows of vehicles, including several Armored Personnel Carriers (APC). APCs were fully tracked armored vehicles. I selected one parked near the center of the group, opened the door, crawled in, and closed the door. I sat and pulled out a paperback book that I had carried in my fatigues. At lunch time, I left the APC and met the rest of the battery at the mess hall. After lunch, I returned to my perch in the APC. After class time, I returned to the barracks. For the rest of my time on active duty, I was relegated to about eight hours a day of solitary confinement surrounded by the metal walls, metal ceiling, and metal floor of an APC.

I requested and was granted a leave of absence for the Christmas holiday. I drove 830 miles to my parent's home. From their perspective, the grandchildren were another year older, but not much had changed from prior Christmases. They chose to avoid discussing Vietnam, and I obliged. I enjoyed the holiday time with my family. On the return trip, after about 600 miles of driving, I saw a sign for a roadside hotel near Greenville, Texas. I stopped, walked in, and inquired as to the price of a room. It was $39. I pulled out my wallet, but only had $30. I looked up at the clerk and said, "I am sorry, I only have $30."

The clerk glanced at a gentleman in a back room who must have been the night manager. He looked at me and said, "Where are you headed?"

I replied, "Fort Hood."

He then said to her, "We only have one vacant room. $30 is fine. It's late. No need to wait and hope for another $9." I thanked them. She gave me the key and directed me to the room. The following day, I completed the return trip to Fort Hood.

During the week, I did the APC shuffle. On the weekends, I got into my car and drove. I visited President Johnson's boyhood home in Johnson City, drove by the LBJ ranch, and traveled through many miles of what Johnson referred to as Hill Country. I visited the Houston Space Center, the Astrodome, as well as the beach at Galveston. I visited Texas A&M and observed multitudes of students playing army. I visited the Johnson Presidential Library on the University of Texas campus.

One weekend, Furio from Chicago and Jones from Detroit suggested that we search for an authentic Texas dance hall. We drove through Killeen and north on Interstate 35 until we found what appeared to be a thriving nightclub. We parked in the lot, entered the facility, and found a table. It seemed that every eye was staring at us, but they were not friendly stares. Jones said, "Let's go." It was then that I realized that he was the only Black person in the facility. None of us wanted to pick a fight. Jones made it clear that we should leave. He could sense that we were not welcome. After a quick and uncomfortable beer, we left. We did not find an authentic Texas dance hall experience — or perhaps we had.

On January 7th, 1972, I received orders that January 17th would be my last day on active duty. I was transferred to the inactive army reserves beginning on January 18th. I placed my duffle bag in the trunk, drove home to Perry County, and that was that. I had completed my assigned active duty as a draftee. The war, the dying, and the destruction continued without me. My official terminal date of U.S. Army reserve obligation, that was fulfilled inactive, was July 7th, 1976.

Draftee

DEPARTMENT OF THE ARMY
HEADQUARTERS, III CORPS and FORT HOOD
Fort Hood, Texas   76544

SPECIAL ORDERS
NUMBER   5   7 January 1972
EXTRACT

47 TC 314. Following individual is relieved FROM ACTIVE DUTY not
by reason of physical disability and transferred to the United States
Army Reserve as indicated. TDN TPA

EPPLIN, FRANCIS M   SP4   13E20
AG Trf Pt USAG (WOVCTO) Fort Hood, Texas 76544 Fifth US Army

ADMINISTRATIVE ACCOUNTING DATA
Auth: Para 5-3 AR 635-200 & PART II DA MSG DAPE MPP 102035Z Dec 71
HOR: Rt 1, Box 57 Pinckneyville IL
Mail adrs: Rt 1, Pinckneyville IL 62274
PL EAD or OAD: St Louis MO (P1 Ind)
Last perm dy sta: Btry B 1st Bn 78th Arty 2d Armd Div
                   Ft Hood TX 76546
No yrs svc pay gr E-4: 1
SPN: 21L
PCS MDC: 7BE2
Eff date (REFRAD): 2400 hrs, 17 Jan 72   E-2-17

FOR THE INDIVIDUAL
Assigned to: USAR Control Group(Annual Training)USARCPAC Saint Louis MO 63132
Effective date of Reserve Assignment: 18 January 1972
UMTS obligation: 6 years
Special Instructions: NA

Transfer from Active Duty to Inactive Reserve

Election day was scheduled for November 7th, 1972. It was 223 months (more than 18 years) since Vice President Nixon declared that, if necessary, the United States was prepared to put "our boys in" Indo-China to "avoid further Communist expansion in Asia..."[1] It was 56 months since presidential candidate Nixon's March 1968 interview that gave rise to the interpretation that he had a secret plan to end the war.[2,3] It was 50 months since candidate Nixon proclaimed that "those who have had a chance for four years and could not produce peace should not be given another chance..."[4] It was 44 months since then-President Nixon on March 20th, 1969, told his cabinet, "The war will be over by next year..."[5]

The collapse of South Vietnam prior to the 1972 election was prevented by massive U.S. aerial bombardments. For the President, the bombing campaign was successful. President

Nixon did not preside over a lost war during his first term. One of his campaign slogans was "peace with honor." I was not sure about the honor, but I knew that peace had not come to South Vietnam.[6] Nixon was reelected, and the killing and destruction continued.

Part Two

*A War Fought by Draftees:
A Mess for the U.S.*

Chapter 28

Jesuits Following their Call

"Proclaim the gospel to every creature."

Perhaps the most difficult decision regarding formulating a story to explain how the sons of an Illinois farmer, a Pennsylvania steel worker, and an Indiana factory worker converged at a location in Southeast Asia for the purpose of calculating artillery firing data, is in deciding where to begin. We could start with the Big Bang, but that is probably not necessary. We could begin with the Old Testament book of Genesis, but that might be overkill. However, it is possible to hypothesize that the seeds for the mess can be traced to the New Testament. Jesus told his followers as reported in Mark 16:15-16 to "go into the whole world and proclaim the gospel to every creature. Whoever believes and is baptized will be saved..."[1]

By the 1500s, Christianity had spread into Europe. Members of religious societies were obligated to spread the Gospel across the world. Portuguese Dominican missionaries travelled to Vietnam in the 1500s. In 1615, French Jesuits established a mission in Hanoi. Over the next two centuries, a number of conflicts arose between local rulers and emperors, and foreign missionaries.² The French military became involved in Vietnam in the 19th century, ostensibly to protect French missionaries.³

In 1858, five years after my great-great grandfather Sebastian emigrated from France to Illinois (and thereby avoiding future service in the French military), the French navy, under orders of Napoleon III, attacked and occupied the Vietnamese city of DaNang.⁴ The military campaign that allegedly began as an effort to protect missionaries turned into a concerted effort to accumulate territory. George Carver wrote in a 1965 *Foreign Affairs* article that in the 1860s, non-Catholics concluded that "Vietnamese Catholics served as the claws which enabled the French crab to crawl across the land..."⁵ Over the years, the French military was involved in a number of campaigns, including the Sino-French war of 1884-85, that enhanced their control over the cities in the region. In 1887, the French colony of French Indochina — that eventually expanded to be composed of most of modern-day Vietnam, Laos, and Cambodia — was formed. Henry Norman wrote in 1893 that "every French priest abroad is a political agent, often in spite of himself..."⁶

As an anonymous author wrote in an 1893 British magazine: "The propagation of the Catholic faith, the promotion of commerce, and national glory pure and simple, may be taken as the concurrent motives of French policy in partibus..."⁷ A rough translation of "in partibus" is "in the lands of the unbelievers."

While the Jesuit priests may have been unknowing political agents, the French government established colonies in Africa and Asia, for the stated purpose of economic exploitation. French Indochina was designated as a colonie d'exploitation (colony of economic exploitation) by the French government.

They used taxes on locals and profits from government monopolies on selected consumer goods to fund government and military activities. Local people paid the costs the French incurred for governing Indochina. The region was a source of tea, rice, coffee, pepper, coal, zinc, and tin. Rubber plantations were established in French Indochina in the 20th century in response to the demand for rubber that coincided with the development of the automobile industry.[8]

French citizens were in charge. Consistent with their purpose of economic exploitation, they did not invest in educating indigenous peoples for self-governance and did not train locals for upper management positions. French administrators restricted Vietnamese travel, speech, and ability to assemble. Land was consolidated into large holdings enabling plantations. Over time, the number of landless peasants increased and the literacy rate declined.[9] French administrators and the French military facilitated the suppression of anticolonial movements. The French did not train the locals to flourish in the increasingly global marketplace and made no plans to transfer power. Perhaps the French expected to always be in charge, and they were, until World War II.[10]

The principal religion in French Indochina was Buddhism. However, over time, the Jesuit missionaries, under the protection of the French military, were successful in converting some members of the population to Catholicism. It is estimated that by the outbreak of World War II, approximately 10% of the population practiced Catholicism. Catholic missionary activity, and converts to Catholicism, became closely aligned with the French political encroachment.[11] There was a "cynical old French saying: 'Turn Catholic and have rice to eat.' Nguyen Van Thieu, later president, was among those who heeded this advice, converting from Buddhism in 1958..."[12]

In contrast, even though they were in the majority, Buddhist activities were restricted by law. Catholic Vietnamese worshiped alongside the French colonists. Non-Catholic Vietnamese perceived that Catholics were treated better by the French and covert hostility and distrust developed. The French created and perpetuated a class society.

Chapter 29

World War II Intervened

"France has milked it for one hundred years."

In 1940, Germany invaded France. The French government surrendered. The colonial administrators in French Indochina, having lost military power, enabled Germany's Axis power member Japan to allow thousands of Japanese troops to occupy Vietnam, ostensibly to guard the border with China. However, the French colonialists continued to govern the country. Japanese soldiers remained in Vietnam until the end of World War II in 1945.

At this point in the story, perhaps we should backtrack and explain one version of the pre-1945 history of Ho Chi Minh. The man who came to be known as Ho Chi Minh (a name that he adopted during the 1940s when he was in his fifties) was born around 1890 in central Vietnam, several years after the French officially formed French Indochina. He grew up under French rule in the implicit class system that existed. In his early 20s, Ho Chi Minh acquired a position as a cook on a French merchant ship. This enabled him to travel to Europe and to the U.S. He spent time in New York, London, Paris, and Moscow.

In the 1920s, Ho Chi Minh, while living in Paris, was among the founders of the French communist party.

During World War II, after the French government agreed to an armistice with Nazi Germany in 1940, and after Japanese troops began their occupation of Indochina, Ho Chi Minh saw World War II as an opportunity to take advantage of the French predicament, and to initiate the process for achieving independence for Vietnam. He returned home and founded the Viet Minh, a communist-dominated independence movement.

In 1943, during World War II, the U.S. and allies freed Ho Chi Minh from a Chinese prison. They facilitated his return to Indochina.[1] Ho Chi Minh and his Viet Minh collaborated with U.S. special forces in the region. They provided the U.S. with intelligence regarding Japanese troop numbers and locations and harassed the Japanese. Both groups were fighting the Japanese. Ho had studied the U.S. Declaration of Independence, and he may have hypothesized that the U.S. would be sympathetic to and support his objective of obtaining independence for Vietnam after the War.

President Roosevelt was aware of the plight of the Vietnamese people under French colonialism. Hastings wrote: "The peoples of Indochina were taxed to fund their own subjection, and by the 1930s, 70 percent of peasants were reduced to tenantry or smallholding. French planters — a few hundred families who accumulated colonial Indochina's great fortunes —adopted in the twentieth century an uncompromising attitude toward the Vietnamese, in the words of a British visitor 'identical with that of any of the old slave-owning aristocracies.' It is one of utter contempt; without which effective exploitation would probably be impossible..."[2]

During World War II, on January 24th, 1944, President Roosevelt sent a memo to his Secretary of State Cordell Hull

Draftee

that included the following: "Indo-China should not go back to France ... it should be administered by an international trusteeship. France has had the country ... for nearly one hundred years, and the people are worse off than they were at the beginning ... The case of Indo-China is perfectly clear. France has milked it for one hundred years. The people of Indo-China are entitled to something better than that..."[3]

President Roosevelt died on April 12th, 1945. Nazi Germany surrendered on May 2nd, 1945. Japan formally signed their terms of surrender on September 2nd, 1945.

After President Roosevelt died, Vice President Harry Truman ascended to the presidency. As World War II drew to a close, the U.S. was confronted with a number of concerns and the governance of Indochina was not high on the list.[4] At the end of World War II, the Viet Minh, under the leadership of Ho Chi Minh, declared Vietnamese independence. The August 18th, 1945, issue of the *New York Times* reported, "The Japanese puppet state of Viet Nam, created last March from the French Indo-China protectorate of Annam, has declared its independence and announced its intention to fight..."[5]

In the fall of 1945, Ho Chi Minh sent one or more letters to President Truman in which he requested that the U.S. recognize Vietnam as an independent nation. Ho argued that French colonial rule should not be restored because France had "sold Indochina to Japan and betrayed the allies..."[6] There is no record of a response to Ho Chi Minh from President Truman.

During several days of Congressional hearings in May of 1972, Abbot Moffat, who was a former U.S. state department chief of Southeast Asian Affairs, testified that by State Department policy, letters to the President from a chief of state engaged in a war with a U.S. ally were not acknowledged. Since France was a U.S. ally, and Ho Chi Minh was engaged in a War with France, letters from Ho, according to Moffat, would, by policy, not have been forwarded to the President.[7] Librarians at the Truman Library report that there are no letters from Ho Chi Minh in the Truman collection. The evidence suggests that President Truman did not receive, and was not made aware of, any letters from Ho Chi Minh, and thus did not respond.

French General Charles de Gaulle, who was head of the Provisional Government of the French Republic, insisted on the return of Indochina to its prewar status. Similarly, Britain wanted to restore its prewar status over its colonies, such as Hong Kong, Malaya, and Singapore. At the time, the U.S. was more interested in rebuilding a noncommunist Western Europe than in fighting a diplomatic war with allies over granting independence to their colonies. The August 17th, 1945, issue of the *New York Times* reported that Truman and Churchill "agreed on the advisability of re-establishing all French rights and prerogatives in the Indo-Chinese Union..."[8] Thus, the late President Roosevelt's proposal for an international trusteeship was not implemented. In his January 24th, 1944, memorandum to Cordell Hull, he had written, "I see no reason to play in with the British Foreign Office in this matter. The only reason they seem to oppose it is that they fear the effect it would have on their own possessions and those of the Dutch. They have never liked the idea of trusteeship because it is, in some instances, aimed at future independence. This is true in the case of Indo-China..."[9] But Roosevelt was dead, and Ho Chi Minh's dream of an independent Vietnam was delayed, in part, by Churchill's efforts to maintain British colonies, such as Hong Kong, Malaya, and Singapore.

While Churchill and de Gaulle were lobbying to maintain their colonies, the spread of communism was seen in the U.S. as a sinister movement orchestrated by the Soviet Union to take over the world. Albania, Bulgaria, and East Germany "fell" to the communists in 1945; Romania, Poland, and Hungary in 1947; and Czechoslovakia in 1948. The Soviets suffered more than 26 million casualties in World War II.[10] By comparison, the U.S. endured 418,500 casualties. If the spread of communism had been limited to countries proximal to the Soviet Union in Eastern Europe, the U.S. may have been more tolerant and interpreted the map as a Soviet strategy to build a protective moat. However, since North Korea "fell" to communism in 1948 and Mainland (we called it Red) China in 1949, many in the U.S. interpreted the spread of communism as a drive toward total world domination. Since Truman was President at the time, his political adversaries accused him of losing China to the communists. For some in the U.S., the choice seemed to be between enabling the French to reestablish colonial control or to relinquish de facto control of many of the former European colonies to the Soviets — the godless communists.

Harold Callender wrote in the March 30th, 1947, issue of the *New York Times* that a prevailing theory was that "Moscow wants an independent Viet Nam state in Indo-China, ruled by the Viet Minh communist movement there, to gain a zone of influence in Southeastern Asia adjoining Burma and not far from Singapore or the Netherlands Indies. Moscow is said to operate through Chinese communists scattered through Indo-China and beyond..."[11] Callender was describing what became known as the domino theory.

The U.S. was committed to stop the advance of communism. They needed British and French cooperation to reconstruct a democratic Western Europe. To maintain French cooperation, the U.S. ignored President Roosevelt's 1944 proposal to transition to independence for Vietnam. After World War II, and after the Viet Minh had declared independence for Vietnam in 1945, French military aligned forces were sent to Vietnam with the objective of defeating the Viet Minh and returning the area to its former status as a French colony. War between the Viet Minh and French aligned forces began in 1946. After the communists acquired control of mainland China in 1949, they formally recognized Ho Chi Minh's government in Vietnam. Given no response from his letters to President Truman, Ho Chi Minh requested and received military equipment and assistance from the Chinese.[12] The Chinese communists chose to provide funding, equipment, and military advice to Ho Chi Minh's forces. In the U.S., President Truman's advisors hypothesized that the French would need U.S. assistance to defeat the communists. Truman was already being accused of giving away China. He did not want to be accused of giving away more of the globe to communists. The U.S. provided military equipment and an estimated 80% of the cost of the French war effort against Ho Chi Minh's forces.[13]

In a March 17th, 1948, speech, during which he shared the podium with President Truman, Roman Catholic Cardinal Francis Joseph Spellman of New York "denounced communism and the Soviet Union in even stronger terms than the President ... He announced that as a private citizen, he would vote for universal military training..."

"We are permitting Soviet Russia to continue her policy of persecution and slaughter, dooming our neighbor-nations and ourselves to reap a rotted harvest of appeasement ... as Soviet Russia spews forth her Communist hordes over the face of the earth, adding whole empires to her orbit of power..."[14] For faithful Catholics, such as my parents, there was no ambiguity: communism was evil. Ho Chi Minh was a communist and, therefore, must be evil.

In the summer of 1950, President Truman was forced to face an international crisis that, at the time, was much more serious than that of saving Vietnam from communism. On June

25th, 1950, North Korean military forces (with economic and military assistance from their communist allies, the Soviet Union and China) moved across their southern border into South Korea, and thus, began the Korean War.

On July 19th, 1950, President Truman delivered a radio address to the nation: "On Sunday, June 25th, Communist forces attacked the Republic of Korea. This attack has made it clear, beyond all doubt, that the international Communist movement is willing to use armed invasion to conquer independent nations. An act of aggression such as this creates a very real danger to the security of all free nations..."[15]

"Communism was acting in Korea just as Hitler, Mussolini and the Japanese had ten, fifteen, and twenty years earlier," President Truman wrote, "I felt certain that if South Korea was allowed to fall, Communist leaders would be emboldened to override nations closer to our shores..."[16]

In the initial months of the war, North Korean forces were successful in occupying much of the South. However, the invasion resulted in a response from the United Nations. U.S. and other U.N. forces entered the conflict and managed to regain territory. Eventually, U.N. forces entered North Korea and approached the border with China. In October of 1950, the Chinese sent thousands of troops across the border into North Korea. The Soviet Union provided air support. The surprise ground intervention by the Chinese forced the U.N. and U.S. forces to retreat. Eventually, an armistice was achieved on July 27th, 1953, and the border between the North and the South, that was in place prior to the initiation of the war, was restored.

The Chinese response to the conflict in Korea had a profound influence on the policies pursued more than a decade later by U.S. politicians relative to Vietnam. When the Chinese military forces crossed into North Korea to confront U.S. and U.N. forces, the U.S. saw it as a precedent for potential future action in Vietnam. During the war in Vietnam, U.S. presidents were reticent of antagonizing China for fear of instigating the introduction of Chinese ground troops into the war.

The activities in Korea contributed to the Western narrative that the Soviet Union intended to dominate the planet. For example, French politician and political activist Jacques Soustelle wrote in 1950, "The United States has been fighting in Korea since June 26th, 1950 and France has been fighting in Indo-China since December 19th, 1946 ... They share a basic common factor. Each results from the expansion of Soviet power toward the sea, pushing its satellites ahead, and exploiting against the West the nationalism, even xenophobia, of the Asiatic masses..."[17]

Soustelle continued: "The Viet-Minh is the pawn which the Kremlin is moving up on the Indo-Chinese chessboard..."[18] "Through propaganda and sabotage of war material the Communist aim at bringing about the retreat of the French forces from Indo-China ... It would be an Asiatic Munich..."[19]

A common tactic used by U.S. political operatives against a political foe was to hammer the adversary or his/her political party for appeasing the enemy and thereby losing or giving away a country or region, especially to communists. British Prime Minister Neville Chamberlain was accused of giving away part of Czechoslovakia to appease Hitler with the Munich Pact of September 30th, 1938. Munich became a word to mean appeasement. President Roosevelt had been accused of giving away Poland to the Soviet Union at the February 1945 Yalta conference with Churchill and Stalin. During subsequent U.S. political campaigns, the words Yalta and Munich were invoked to paint the opponent as one who would appease communists and abandon the freedom of the U.S. and her allies to godless communists.

In an April 11th, 1951, radio address to the nation, President Truman reported, "I have another secret intelligence report here. This one tells what another Communist officer in the Far East told his men several months before the invasion of Korea. Here is what he said: 'In order to successfully undertake the long-awaited world revolution, we must first unify Asia ... Java, Indochina, Malaya, India, Tibet, Thailand, Philippines, and Japan are our ultimate targets ... The United States is the only obstacle on our road for the liberation of all the countries in southeast Asia. In other words, we must unify the people of Asia and crush the United States.' Again, liberation in commie language means conquest..."[20] If the U.S. did not take a firm stand and fight, the communists would not stop until they controlled the entire world.

Chapter 30

U.S. Leaders Discuss

"No military victory is possible in this theater."

President Eisenhower was inaugurated in January of 1953. On July 27th, 1953, the U.S., mainland China, North Korea, and South Korea agreed to an armistice, ending fighting on the Korean peninsula. Eisenhower did not want to get U.S. troops directly involved in another land war in Asia. He wrote in his diary, "I am convinced that no military victory is possible in this theater..."[1]

The War between French forces and Ho Chi Minh's Viet Minh had been ongoing since 1946. In the spring of 1954, a contingent of French forces found themselves in a very precarious situation in a valley about 250 miles west of Hanoi at a place called Dien Bien Phu. The French contingent occupied the low ground and were surrounded; the Viet Minh held the high ground. U.S. elected officials were deeply concerned. Some U.S. military officials proposed that U.S. forces intervene on the side of the French. Joint Chiefs Chairman Admiral Radford proposed that nuclear bombs be dropped on Viet Minh positions. Others proposed conventional air strikes by the U.S. Air Force.[2]

Draftee

Senator John Kennedy: "a hopeless situation"

The French military predicament in Vietnam triggered discussions regarding potential alternative U.S. responses. Members of the U.S. Senate understood that the U.S. was funding much of the French military effort in Vietnam. A rather remarkable (in hindsight) exchange occurred on the floor of the U.S. Senate on April 6, 1954.[3] The junior senator (and future President) from Massachusetts, John F. Kennedy, addressed the U.S. Senate: "The speeches of President Eisenhower, Secretary Dulles, and others have left too much unsaid ... if the American people are, for the fourth time in this century, to travel the long and tortuous road of war — particularly a war which we now realize would threaten the survival of civilization..." (This was a clear recognition of the possibility of a nuclear exchange between the U.S. and the Soviet Union or China or both.) "Then I believe we have a right ... to inquire in detail into the nature of the struggle in which we may become engaged..."

One alternative is "a negotiated peace, based either upon partition of the area between the forces of the Viet Minh and the French Union, possibly along the 16th parallel; or based upon a coalition government in which Ho Chi Minh is represented. Despite any wishful thinking to the contrary, it should be apparent that the popularity and prevalence of Ho Chi Minh and his following throughout Indochina would cause either partition or a coalition government to result in eventual domination by the Communists..." Kennedy's speech on the Senate floor was almost 21 years to the day prior to the eventual takeover of all of Vietnam, including South Vietnam, by communist forces on April 30th, 1975.

Senator Kennedy continued: "To pour money, materiel, and men into the jungles of Indochina without at least a remote prospect of victory would be dangerously futile and self-destructive. Of course, all discussion of 'united action' assumes that inevitability of such victory; but such assumptions are not unlike similar predictions of confidence which have lulled the American people for many years and which, if continued, would present an improper basis for determining the extent of American participation..."

"Permit me to review briefly some of the statements concerning the progress of the war in that area, and it will be understood why I say that either we have not frankly and fully faced the seriousness of the military situation, or our intelligence estimates and those of the French have been woefully defective..."

"In February of 1951 ... the late Brig. Gen. Francis G. Brink ... told us of the favorable turn of events in that area as a result of new tactics..."

"In the fall of [1951] ... [French] General De Lattre ... predicted victory...in 18 months to 2 years..."

"In June of 1952, American and French officials issued a joint communique in Washington expressing the two countries' joint determination to bring the battle to a successful end; [U.S.] Secretary of State Acheson stated during a 1952 press conference that: 'The military situation appears to be developing favorably ... Aggression has been checked and recent indications warrant the view that the tide is now moving in our favor ... We can anticipate continued favorable developments...'"

"In March 1953, the French officials again ... issued statements predicting ...their new goal of decisive military victory in 2 years..."

"In May of 1953, President Eisenhower ... told the Congress that our mutual security program for France and Indochina would help 'reduce this Communist pressure to manageable proportions...'"

Draftee

"In June [1953] an American military mission headed by [U.S.] General O'Daniel was sent to discuss with [French] General Navarre in Indochina the manner in which United States aid 'may best contribute to the advancement of the objective of defeating the Communist forces there...'"

"In the fall of [1953] ...General O'Daniel stated that he was 'confident that the French-trained Vietnam Army when fully organized would prevail over the rebels...'"

"In September of 1953, French and American officials ... in announcing a new program of extensive American aid, again issued a joint communique restating the objective of 'an early and victorious conclusion...'"

"On December 2, 1953, Assistant [U.S.] Secretary of State for Far Eastern Affairs Walter S. Robertson told the Women's National Republican Club in New York — in words almost identical with those of Secretary of State Acheson 18 months earlier — that 'In Indochina ... we believe the tide now is turning.' Later the same month Secretary of State Dulles stated that military setbacks in the area had been exaggerated; and that he did not 'believe that anything that has happened upsets appreciably the timetable of General Navarre's plan,' which anticipated decisive military results by about March 1955...'"

"In February [1954] ... Defense Secretary Wilson said that a French victory was 'both possible and probable' and that the war was going 'fully as well as we expected it to at this stage. I see no reason to think Indochina would be another Korea...'"

"In February [1954] Under Secretary of State Smith stated that: 'The military situation in Indochina is favorable ... Contrary to some reports, the recent advances made by the Viet Minh are largely 'real estate' operations ... Tactically, the French position is solid and the officers in the field seem confident of their ability to deal with the situation...'"

In March of 1954, "Admiral Radford, Chairman of the Joints Chief of Staff, stated that 'the French are going to win...'"

"Despite this series of optimistic reports about eventual victory, every Member of the Senate knows that such victory today appears to be desperately remote, to say the least, despite tremendous amounts of economic and material aid from the United States, and despite a deplorable loss of French Union manpower. The call for either negotiations or additional participation by other nations underscores the remoteness of such a final victory today, regardless of the outcome at Dien Bien Phu. It is, of course, for these reasons that many French are reluctant to continue the struggle without greater assistance; for to record the sapping effect which time and the enemy have had on their will and strength in that area is not to disparage their valor. If 'united action' can achieve the necessary victory over the forces of communism, and thus preserve the security and freedom of all southeast Asia, then such united action is clearly called for. But if, on the other hand, the increase in our aid and the utilization of our troops would only result in further statements of confidence without ultimate victory over aggression, then now is the time when we must evaluate the conditions under which that pledge is made..."

Senator Kennedy continued, "I am frankly of the belief that no amount of American military assistance in Indochina can conquer an enemy which is everywhere and at the same time nowhere, 'an enemy of the people' which has the sympathy and covert support of the people ... The apathy of the local population to the menace of the Viet Minh communism disguised as nationalism is the most discouraging aspect of the situation..." It is noteworthy that Senator Kennedy used the term "apathy" to describe the locals. Apathy persisted throughout the entire U.S. presence in Vietnam.

Kennedy continued, "With hordes of Chinese Communist

Draftee

troops poised just across the border in anticipation of our unilateral entry into their kind of battleground — such intervention, ... would be virtually impossible in the type of military situation which prevails in Indochina..." Kennedy and his fellow Senators were all familiar with the Chinese response when U.S. and U.N. soldiers approached their border with Korea. Thus, the referral to the "hordes of Chinese Communist troops poised just across the border." The discussion reflected a genuine concern based on experience from the Korean conflict, that direct U.S. military activity in Vietnam could be met with a response from the Chinese.

"The facts and alternatives before us are unpleasant ... in a nation such as ours, it is only through the fullest and frankest appreciation of such facts and alternatives that any foreign policy can be effectively maintained. In an era of supersonic attack and atomic retaliation, extended public debate and education are of no avail, once such a policy must be implemented. The time to study, to doubt, to review, and revise is now, for upon our decisions now may well rest the peace and security of the world, and, indeed, the very continued existence of mankind. And if we cannot entrust this decision to the people, then, as Thomas Jefferson once said: 'If we think them not enlightened enough to exercise their control with a wholesome discretion, the remedy is not to take it from them but to inform their discretion by education...'"[4]

Senator Kennedy was not alone in his concern. Several other Senators from both parties continued the discussion of the Indochina situation. Senate Majority Leader Republican William Knowland of California followed with: "There is much and probably the predominance, of what the Senator from Massachusetts has said with which I would fully agree..."

"Of course no one is wise enough at the present moment to know what the ultimate aim and objective of the Chinese

Communists may be — whether they will enter the war in Indochina in force, as they did in Korea, or whether they will continue to supply arms and equipment, as they are doing now. It seems to me that if they enter the war in force there will be a challenge to the free nations of the world and free men everywhere which they cannot ignore or sidestep..."

Senator Knowland continued, "The United States has expended billions of dollars in resources in order to rehabilitate the war-torn nations of Europe. It has expended billions of dollars in order to build up situations of strength so that more of the free world will not fall into the hands of the godless men in the Kremlin and the international conspiracy of communism..."

Washington Senator Henry "Scoop" Jackson added that, "I do not believe for one moment it follows that because the Chinese may not enter the conflict we can save Indochina..."

Senator Kennedy responded: "I do not think Indochina can be saved unless the other Asiatic nations which are now maintaining a policy of cold neutrality are willing to take their fair part in the struggle. After all, they are the ones who should do so. For the United States to intervene unilaterally and to send troops into the most difficult terrain in the world, with the Chinese able to pour in unlimited manpower, would mean that we would face a situation which would be far more difficult than even that we encountered in Korea. It seems to me it would be a hopeless situation..."

Montana Senator Mike Mansfield followed, "I wish to commend most highly the scholarly and statesmanlike address of the junior Senator from Massachusetts. I am glad he is facing realities as they are..."

Democrat Senator Stuart Symington from Missouri also commended Senator Kennedy. He explained the frustration that he and Republican Senator Henry Styles Bridges from New Hampshire encountered during a recent fact-finding trip to Paris at which they met with French officials: "We asked if they saw any military solution. The answer was, 'No.' We then asked if there was any political solution which could be seen. The answer was, 'No.' ... After extensive discussions, held over many hours, our feeling was one of frustration as to any definite, affirmative policy. At least at times, we became suspicious of the possibility there was no regret the matter was being held in such a state of flux, because it was a method to secure continued support [from the U.S. treasury] ... Apparently we are getting closer to entering into the war in Indochina ...We found no positive policy in Paris, which makes it more important, it would seem, to have a policy in this country ... considering the fact ... the United States is now paying 80 percent of the cost of the Indochina war..."

Senator Everett Dirksen, Republican of Illinois, entered the discussion. Dirksen indicated that he did not see the problem as serious as Kennedy but in many respects he concurred. He said, "Politically, in this situation we are at the short end of a very difficult administrative problem; namely, during all the years the French have failed to develop among the native people-and no one can condone this-a trained administrative talent to run their own affairs. The French set up at Saigon a miniature Paris, and the French administered the banking business and all the other businesses and arrangements, with the result that today, in the year of our Lord 1954, we pay the bill because there are no native administrators to handle their own affairs..."

"To develop effective fighting men among the natives, they must be given something for which to fight. At the present time they have no constitution, no bill of rights, no guaranties. That was the essence of the first report we made-namely, that it is necessary to set up a target of independence..."

"After 85 years of French tutelage and domination and

administration of the area, the natives are unable to administer their own affairs. Their capacity to administer them cannot be developed overnight. In solving that problem, we must summon some real restraint and patience..."

Senator John Stennis Democrat of Mississippi spoke as well. He said: "If there is not sufficient power and strength in Asia, or in some Asiatic country which is willing to take the chance, to stop communism, as we say, or give freedom, and work on the basis of freedom, with some support from the other free nations of the world, then it is a lost cause, as I see it. Unless those conditions are brought about we should not go in. To go in on a unilateral basis would be to go into a trap. It would be to send our men into a trap from which there could be no reasonable recovery and no chance for victory..."

Senators Clinton Anderson, Democrat of New Mexico, and Senator Warren Magnuson, Democrat of Washington, also spoke. In total, nine senators from across the country and across the political spectrum spoke. Although Senator Dirksen was less pessimistic than the others, the preponderance of assessment by the Senators was that unilateral involvement by the U.S. in Vietnam, if the French were defeated, would be, in the words of Senator Kennedy, a "disaster." Future President, Texas Senator Lyndon Johnson, was present, but did not engage in the Indochina discussion. The Congressional Record records that his effort during the day was devoted to achieving a vote on a road construction bill. Future President and Vice President Richard Nixon was serving as President of the Senate. The record indicates that he was present, but consistent with Senate policy, did not engage in the debate.[5]

The April 7th, 1954, issue of the *New York Times* reported a summary of the discussion under the headline: "Senate Weighs Indo-China; Bipartisan Stand Shapes Up: Knowland

Demands Allies Take Full Role if Asian War Comes — Kennedy Bids France Grant Liberty to People."[6]

The April 7th, 1954, issue of the *Wall Street Journal* "What's News" section contained a brief description of the Senate debate: "In the Senate, G.O.P. Leader Knowland declared the free nations 'cannot ignore or sidestep' any Chinese Communist entry in force into the war. Sen. Jackson (D., Wash.) asserted the fall of Indo-China 'means the fall of all southeast Asia.' And Sen. Kennedy (D. Mass.) demanded the Administration give out the 'blunt truth' about the situation..."[7] However, elsewhere in the "What's News" section, the editors of the *Wall Street Journal* devoted more lines to Senator Joseph McCarthy's claim that Communists had infiltrated the U.S. government and caused an 18-month delay in development of the hydrogen bomb.

President Eisenhower: "the 'falling domino' principle"

A day after the Senate debate, on April 7th, 1954, President Eisenhower was asked about Indochina. Mr. Robert Richards of the Copley Press asked, "Mr. President, would you mind commenting on the strategic importance of Indo-China to the free world?"

President Eisenhower responded, "The possibility that many human beings passed under a dictatorship that is inimical to the free world; and, finally, you have broader considerations that might follow what you might call the 'falling domino' principle. You have a row of dominoes set up, and you knock over the first one, and what would happen to the last one was the certainty that it would go over very quickly. So you could have a beginning of a disintegration that would have the most profound influences..."[8] [9]

The domino narrative followed from experience. The day after the news conference, the *New York Times* published an editorial in which they wrote: "The attack on Vietnam has a different background; but the central issue is the same, and the obligations of American leadership are not less now than then. The principle of falling dominoes still applies, as the President observed — push over the first and the last in line tumbles quickly..."[10]

The editorial continued: "We have seen this principle at work in Europe under Hitler and under Stalin. In almost every case these insatiable dictators relied on the fall of one country to open the way to the conquest of the next. In Asia the prospect is even more menacing, for whereas in Europe a bastion of free nations remains fairly firm and solid, in Asia the remaining independent states are directly threatened — Burma, Thailand and Indonesia first, and after that the defensive chain anchored to the Philippines, Japan and Formosa. When Mr. Eisenhower keeps on reiterating the strategic importance of the battle in Indo-China he is not thinking of that peninsula alone but of what a communist victory over the former French colonies would mean to all the non-communist peoples of the Far East..."[11]

The April 12th, 1954, issue of *Barron's National Business and Financial Weekly* included an opinion article titled "Cart and Horse: Freedom for Indo-China Depends Upon Security." The *Barron's* opinion writer expressed disagreement with Senator Kennedy's "thesis that all will be well in Asia and elsewhere if only dependent peoples are turned loose on their own." According to *Barron's*, granting independence will "play directly into the hands of Communist aggression."[12]

Vice President Richard Nixon: "Prepared to put 'our boys in' Indo-China"

A few days later, Vice President (and future President) Richard Nixon delivered a statement that confirmed that he also subscribed to the domino narrative: "It should be emphasized that if Indo-China went Communist, Red pressures would increase on Malaya, Thailand, Indonesia and other Asian nations. The main target of the Communists in Indo-China, as it was in Korea is Japan. Conquest of areas so vital to Japan's economy would reduce Japan to an economic satellite of the Soviet Union..."[13]

The article continued with, "On Friday Vice President Richard Nixon declared that, if necessary, the United States was prepared to put 'our boys in' Indo-China to 'avoid further Communist expansion in Asia.'"[14] Nixon may have been the first elected official to advocate direct U.S. military ground combat intervention in Vietnam.

Nixon was heard. The April 20th, 1954, issue of the *New York Times* reported that Senator Edwin Johnson of Colorado "made a brief, sharp attack on what he termed 'Mr. Nixon's war' in Indo-China."

"As a guest at a private party ... some weeks ago, I heard the Vice President, Mr. Nixon, whooping it up for war in Indo-China..."

Johnson continued, "I am against sending American G.I.s into the mud and muck of Indo-China on a blood-letting spree to perpetuate colonialism and white man's exploitation in Asia..."[15]

Chapter 31

1954 Geneva Accords

"Deliver us from evil."

In May of 1954, after eight years of war, the French military forces were surrounded and under siege at Dien Bien Phu. During the siege, representatives of the warring parties and the major powers met in Geneva to arrange a cease-fire agreement and an armistice. What became known as the Geneva Accords were formulated. The accords specified a temporary separation of Vietnam near the 17th parallel, along the Ben Hai River to the village of Bo Ho Su, and from there west to the Laotian border. Any remaining French forces were to leave the North and Viet Minh forces south of the artificial line were to relocate north of the line.

The July 25th, 1954, issue of the *New York Times* presented a summary of the agreement: "There will be a cease fire along roughly the 17th parallel with the French to the south and the Vietminh to the north. France will have an area of 50,000 square miles, including a population of 10,000,000 and the capital city of Saigon and large rice producing areas. In addition, the French have the right to stage their withdrawal from the Communist zone over a period of 300 days..."[1]

Draftee

"The Vietminh will have an area of 77,000 square miles including a population of 12,000,000, the cities of Hanoi and Haiphong and rich deposits of coal and non-ferrous metals. In addition, the Communists will be allowed to concentrate guerrillas in fixed areas below the line and withdraw them to the north over a period of 300 days. Beginning in July 1955, representatives of north and south Vietnam will meet to arrange for elections for an all-Vietnamese Government to be held before July 20, 1956..."[2]

Ho Chi Minh and his forces were to govern the North. The very popular Ho Chi Minh became president of North Vietnam. He was determined to reunite all of Vietnam into one country. Former emperor Bao Dai was appointed titular head of state of the South. Thus, by decree of diplomats — most of whom did not live in Indochina — the country was artificially split into a communist North and non-communist South.

The British chairman issued the final conference declaration that specified that an election be held by July of 1956 to create a unified Vietnamese state. Ho Chi Minh did not like the deal. His objective was to liberate the entire country from French colonialism. From his perspective, Bao Dai would simply be a figurehead for continuation of French colonial rule. But his allies at the conference, the Chinese and Soviets, pressured the Viet Minh representatives to sign the accords. Neither the U.S. nor the new state of South Vietnam signed. They understood that Ho Chi Minh was by far the most popular political figure in the region and that he was likely to win a fair election.[3] The U.S. did not want to see communism spread and did not permit a general election in 1956.

The 17th parallel in Vietnam became the de facto line provided to the U.S. for stemming the "red" tide of communism and to stop dominoes from falling in southeast Asia. Seventeen years later, in August of 1971, our battery was located on a hill about 12 miles south of the line established by the Geneva Accords and 9 miles south of the 6-mile-wide DMZ. We were doing our best to hold up a domino. The Geneva Accords enabled the French, British, and other western allies to transfer the responsibility for stemming the tide of communism in Southeast Asia almost entirely to the U.S.

The May 1954 Geneva Accords, which provided for the separation of Vietnam near the 17th parallel, also provided for a period of approximately ten months during which citizens on either side of the line would be free to move to the other side. At the time, it was estimated that the vast majority of the population (approximately 80%) were Buddhist. Approximately 10% were Catholic, and the remaining 10% included Cao-Dai, Hoa-Hao, Animists, and Protestants.[4]

During the period, from August 1954 through May 1955, the U.S. Navy conducted Operation Passage to Freedom, in which they assisted with the relocation of 800,000 from the North to the South.[5] Most who chose to move from the North to the South were Catholics who had fought on the side of the French against the Vietminh and feared retaliation if they stayed in the North.[6] This activity was described, some would say embellished, in a book titled *Deliver us from Evil*, by U.S. Navy physician Thomas A. Dooley.[7] In Dr. Dooley's version, Catholics in the North were persecuted (tortured) by the "godless communists" for practicing their religion. His story was described by Appy as a "Cold War parable of good versus evil."[8] The book was serialized in *Reader's Digest* and was a best seller.[9]

In 1954, 99% of Americans claimed to believe in God; "Under God" was added to the Pledge of Allegiance.[10] Thomas Dooley's description of the movement of Christian refugees from the North to the South during this period provided a narrative for political forces to support the South. If the South was permitted to "fall," the godless communists could be expected to persecute Christians in the South — including the 800,000 that had emigrated from the North to the South.

Most U.S. public officials were either ignorant of, or chose to ignore, the social or class situation that had developed over the decades of French rule in Indochina. From the perspective of non-Catholic Vietnamese, the French had created a class society that provided privileges to Catholics. From the standpoint of the majority of those who lived in the South, the 800,000 who moved from the North, who were mostly Catholic, were viewed to be closely aligned with the old French colonialists. "The Catholic religion bore the taint of foreign ownership..."[11]

What President Roosevelt's January 24th, 1944, memo to his Secretary of State Cordell Hull did not say was that over the decades of "milking" Vietnam, the French had propagated a class society within the indigenous population.[12] The French were in charge and restricted management and leadership roles for locals. The limited advancement opportunities for locals were often awarded to Catholics. Catholics were more likely to have spent time in French Jesuit Catholic schools, on average more fluent in French, and more in sync with the French overlords.

Some in the U.S. were well aware of the difficulty that the U.S. was likely to encounter in attempting to transform South Vietnam into a democratic capitalist system. For example, World War II veteran, University of Chicago economist, and U.S. Senator Paul Douglas wrote in a 1955 *Foreign Affairs* issue that "The oppression of the colonial administrators of the European Powers has been experienced directly and in the very recent past ... is keenly remembered and deeply resented. Thus the uncommitted third of the world tends to be much more angry at Western than at Communist imperialism, and since we are a Western Power and part of the white race we are included in the general dislike..."[13] Perhaps, unfortunately, many more U.S. citizens and church officials read Dr. Dooley's "Deliver Us From Evil" excerpts in *Reader's Digest* than Senator Douglas' assessment in *Foreign Affairs*.

Chapter 32

Bao Dai and Ngo Dinh Diem

"Whimsical and indolent young puppet emperor."

The U.S. was not dealt a good hand. The North was to be governed with Ho Chi Minh as President. Ho Chi Minh had organized and led the Viet Minh's battle against the French since 1946. His team had defeated the French. Ho Chi Minh was a national hero: he had widespread support, not only in the North, but also in the South. An arbitrary line at the 17th parallel would not diminish the knowledge of what he had accomplished and the respect that he carried. If it were a neighborhood game of pickup basketball, the North was starting with a player with talent analogous to that of Michael Jordan.

The South began with a huge disadvantage. French policies over the years had been very successful in ensuring that indigenous citizens did not attain leadership skills that might challenge French rule. Someone had to be in charge of the South. Unfortunately for the U.S., former emperor Bao Dai was appointed. Bao Dai had been the emperor of the Nguyen dynasty whose ancestors had ruled part of the territory prior to French colonization. While the French were in command, the frills of the politically powerless reign continued. Bao Dai was the last in a line of figurehead emperors.

The appointment of Bao Dai as nominal head was not a wise choice for the long-term viability of South Vietnam. As a young prince at the age of nine, he left Vietnam to attend school in France. Bao Dai had lived most of his life on the French Riviera and had virtually no popular support in Vietnam. He was closely aligned with the French. Hastings described Bao Dai as a "whimsical and indolent young puppet emperor..."[1]

"The emperor, indolent and spoiled, was soon preoccupied with currency racketeering in partnership with French politicians. Bereft of both moral and political authority, his interests were girls, hunting, and yachts..."[2]

The game was set. The North had a seasoned team that included their charismatic leader, Ho Chi Minh. The South was to be led by an anointed spoiled brat who had previously never played the game and had little interest in doing so. Indeed, the team intended to support democracy was dealt a terrible hand. In July 1954, the Eisenhower administration attempted to improve their chances by convincing the French to have Bao Dai appoint Ngo Dinh Diem as prime minister.

It was 1954, and back in the U.S., Wisconsin Senator Joseph McCarthy was ranting and raving about communists.[3] The Eisenhower administration needed a staunch anticommunist, and Ngo Dinh Diem was selected. Diem grew up in Vietnam in a Catholic family with five brothers and three sisters. He was educated in the French system to the extent that the French would permit. He entered a career as a mandarin — that is, a bureaucrat in the French colonial system, and in some respects, the highest economic rung for an indigenous Vietnamese. Diem lost favor with the French when he attempted to lobby for independence.

Draftee

In 1951, Ngo Dinh Diem traveled to the U.S. with the aid of one of his five brothers, Ngo Dinh Thuc. Thuc was a Catholic bishop in Vietnam, and he later became the highest-ranking Catholic official in South Vietnam. He had studied religion with Francis Spellman in Rome in the 1930s, and the two were friends.[4] Bishop Thuc introduced Diem to Spellman, who in 1951 was a Catholic Cardinal, head of the New York diocese, strongly anti-communist, and politically astute. Yes, the same Cardinal Spellman who, in a March 17th, 1948, speech, during which he shared the podium with President Truman, had said that "we are permitting Soviet Russia to continue her policy of persecution and slaughter, dooming our neighbor-nations and ourselves to reap a rotted harvest of appeasement ... as Soviet Russia spews forth her Communist hordes over the face of the earth, adding whole empires to her orbit of power..."[5]

Cardinal Spellman used his political connections to assist Diem in order to gain support of U.S. government officials. Their lobbying efforts were successful to the extent that in July 1954, the Eisenhower administration facilitated the appointment of Ngo Dinh Diem as prime minister of South Vietnam. In January of 1955, after he had returned to South Vietnam as Premier, Ngo Dinh Diem announced that the U.S. had been requested to assume full responsibility for assisting South Vietnam to organize and train its armed forces.[6] In April of 1955, a photo of South Vietnam's prime minister Ngo Dinh Diem was featured on the cover of *Time* magazine.[7] The U.S. had their staunch anti-communist ally, or perhaps, he had them.

Hastings wrote that, "The gravest handicap burdening the Saigon regime was that scarcely any of its standard-bearers and officials had participated in the independence struggle; many, indeed, were former servants of the French ... within the tiny circle of Saigon's educated elite, [the Americans] ... could identify no more plausible noncommunist candidate to rule..."[8]

In October of 1955, a referendum was held in the South. Diem defeated Bao Dai and became the President.[9] Diem's regime left no room for any legal opposition, carried elections with 98% majorities, and had no competing legislative candidates.[10]

Diem, his brothers, and other close relatives proceeded to develop a very undemocratic system that favored Catholics.[11] Their role model was French colonialism, not U.S. democracy. In January of 1956, the regime issued an ordinance designed to eliminate opposition.[12] Later, in 1956, Diem issued decrees to replace elected village councils with officials appointed by his loyalists. Political and military positions were filled predominately with Catholics loyal to Diem. His army implemented a series of oppressive laws that resulted in over 150,000 political prisoners by the late 1950s. He failed to implement promised land reforms. His policies drove many to sympathize with the North.[13]

The overt discrimination against non-Catholics established by the French continued under Diem. Ngo Dinh Diem promoted Catholicism as an important safeguard against communism. Under Diem, Catholics enjoyed an advantage over non-Catholics in commerce, the professions, education, and the government. This was not a good strategy for winning the "hearts and minds" among the 90% who were not Catholic.

For decades, the French had required peasant farmers who remained outside the French plantation system to work for no pay up to 30 days per year on French government projects, such as government buildings, roads, dams, and other infrastructure. Diem continued these "corvee" labor requirements "whereby people were obliged to give five days' free service a year to government projects."[14] However, when Diem wielded the power, most Catholics were exempt.[15]

When they were in charge, the French required Buddhists (but not Catholics) to obtain official permission to conduct public Buddhist activities. Diem did not repeal the requirement. Buddhists were required to obtain permits in advance for activity that had to be authorized by provincial officials. To gain favor with Diem, some local officials enhanced the red tape imposed on the non-Catholics.[16] As Wulff reported in 1963, "During those same years of increasing harassment of the Buddhists, the Catholic Church kept acquiring more privileges..."

Hastings wrote that: "Unfortunately, [Diem] was ... a Catholic religious zealot imbued with messianic faith in his own rightness, blindly devoted to a greedy and unscrupulous family, nostalgic for a nonexistent past, and insensitive to the needs and aspirations of his people. Life under Diem seemed to most Vietnamese a mere continuation of colonialism..."[17]

The *Pentagon Papers,* published in several U.S. newspapers in 1971, summarized the policies of the Diem regime and confirmed that U.S. officials were well aware of the policies: "As of 1960, 45% of the land remained concentrated in the hands of 2% of landowners, and 15% of the landlords owned 75% of all the land. Those relatively few farmers who did benefit from the program were more often than not northerners, refugees, Catholics, or Annamese-so that land reform added to the [Government of South Vietnam] GVN's aura of favoritism which deepened peasant alienation ... Farmer-GVN tensions were further aggravated by rumors of corruption, and the widespread allegation that the Diem family itself had become enriched through the manipulation of land transfers..."[18]

"The GVN appointees to village office were outsiders —

northerners, Catholics, or other 'dependable' persons — and their alien presence in the midst of the close-knit rural communities encouraged revival of the conspiratorial, underground politics to which the villages had become accustomed during the resistance against the French..."[19]

In July of 1962, Homer Bigart, who had spent six months in Vietnam, wrote, "Victory is remote. The issue remains in doubt because the Vietnamese President [Diem] seems incapable of winning the loyalty of his people..."[20]

"Forced labor on hamlet defenses is not the way to win the affection of the peasants ... workers are not even fed but must provide their own food..."[21]

"One rarely sees a uniformed Vietcong guerrilla; generally the Communist rebels are indistinguishable from peasants ... many of the 'enemy' dead reported by the South Vietnam Government were ordinary peasants shot down because they had fled from villages as the troops entered. Some may have been Vietcong sympathizers, but others were running away because they did not want to be rounded up for military conscription or forced labor ... No one who has seen conditions of combat in South Vietnam would expect conventionally trained United States forces to fight any better against Communist guerrillas than did the French in their seven years of costly and futile warfare..."[22]

In May of 1963, the American embassy in Saigon sent a telegram to State Department officials in Washington that included: "Buddhist leaders met with President Diem to present series of demands ... Give Buddhists rights with Catholics. Buddhists pointed out GVN Ordinance Number 10 does not cover Catholic organizations, which still enjoy privileges originally granted by French. Buddhist organizations on other hand considered foreign by Property Registration Office so that presidential permit required to allow them to buy prop-

Draftee

erty. Diem stated inconsistencies resulted from administrative errors and that he would have matter investigated..."[23]

On September 2nd, 1963, the CBS television network expanded their evening national news broadcast from 15 to 30 minutes. News anchor Walter Cronkite conducted an interview with President Kennedy at Kennedy's Hyannis Port, Massachusetts home. President Kennedy used the opportunity to send a very public message to Diem and his family. He made it clear that Diem's Buddhist repression policies and attacks on Buddhist shrines and places of worship were very unwise. Kennedy told Cronkite, "I don't think that the war can be won unless the people support the effort, and in my opinion ... the Government has gotten out of touch with the people ... it's their war. They're the ones who have to win it or lose it. We can help them, give them equipment, we can send our men out there as advisers, but they have to win it, the people of Vietnam, against the Communists..."[24]

Diem and his family ruled until November 2nd, 1963, when he was removed and killed by a military coup.[25] President Kennedy was assassinated 20 days later on November 22nd, 1963 — 81 days after the CBS interview.

Chapter 33

Pawn in a Cold War

"We will bury you."

Given that President Eisenhower, as early as July of 1953, was "convinced that no military victory is possible in this theater,"[1] why did he continue to support the effort with money and advisors throughout his presidency that ended in January of 1961? Why did President Kennedy, starting in 1961, increase the number of U.S. advisors until his assassination in 1963 if he considered the situation "hopeless" as early as 1954? Why did President Lyndon Johnson, who was in the Senate during the 1954 discussion, and who, in a speech on October 21, 1964, at Akron University say that "We are not about to send American boys 9 or 10,000 miles away from home to do what Asian boys ought to be doing for themselves,"[2] send thousands of U.S. soldiers into the war during his presidency?

Given that it had been labeled "Mr. Nixon's war"[3] in April of 1954, it is understandable why President Nixon, who was Vice President at the time of the 1954 Senate discussion, continued to support the war throughout his entire presidency from 1969 until his resignation in August of 1974. Years later, the infamous White House tapes recorded President Nixon saying on May 4th, 1972: "The United States cannot lose ... Whatever happens to South Vietnam we are going to cream North Vietnam ... we got to use the maximum power of this country ... against this shit-ass little country..."[4] Why did President Ford, who was in the U.S. House of Representatives in 1954, continue to seek funding for the war until South Vietnam collapsed in 1975? What was so important about supporting a very unstable and not-all-that-democratic domino?

Two issues explain the response of U.S. presidents. One was the overall concern felt across the economic and political spectrum that the Soviet Union's goal was to dominate the world and subject all caught in their web to godless communism and servitude to the state. The second was the nature of the two-term limit and the timing of the four-year U.S. presidential election cycle. The *Pentagon Papers* concluded that "the prime motive of American presidents from Kennedy onward was to punt — to avoid being blamed for losing the war..."[5]

Reason One for U.S. Involvement: Fear of Communist (Soviet Union) Expansion

In a March 1947 speech, President Truman described the struggle between the U.S. and Soviet Union: "At the present moment in world history nearly every nation must choose between alternative ways of life. The choice is too often not a free one. One way of life is based upon the will of the majority, and is distinguished by free institutions, representative government, free elections, guarantees of individual liberty, freedom of speech and religion, and freedom from political oppression. The second way of life is based upon the will of a minority forcibly imposed upon the majority. It relies upon terror and oppression, a controlled press and radio; fixed elections, and the suppression of personal freedoms..."[6]

On October 22nd, 1947, Russian General and member of

the Soviet Union Politburo Zhdanov "called upon Communists and their sympathizers everywhere in the world to join in a battle against ... attempts by the United States to achieve world domination..."[7] The genuine fear among American policy makers was greatly enhanced when the Soviet Union exploded their first atomic bomb on August 29th, 1949. The North Vietnamese communists were viewed in the U.S. as proxies for the Soviet Union.

On November 22nd, 1955, the Soviet Union detonated its first hydrogen bomb.

On November 18th, 1956, Soviet Union Premier Khrushchev told Western ambassadors at a reception in Moscow that "we will bury you."[8]

On October 4th, 1957, the Soviet Union successfully launched Sputnik I, the world's first manmade earth orbiting satellite. Several years later, in 1960, U.S. television evening news programs, that in 1960 included ABC, CBS, and NBC, showed as Premier Khrushchev removed a shoe and pounded it on a delegate desk at the United Nations.[9] Clearly, communism as practiced in the Soviet Union was on a roll. The fear in the U.S. was genuine. If communism was not stopped, it would continue to roll, and it would eventually capture and enslave the entire world, including the U.S.

The 17th parallel in Vietnam became a line at which successive U.S. administrations (some reluctantly) decided, or perhaps thought they had no choice other than, to take a stand. While the U.S. was taking a stand, it is not clear if the vast majority of people that occupied the area referred to as South Vietnam had any say in the matter, or if indeed they had any interest in taking a stand against the spread of communism. The apathy that Senator Kennedy referred to in his April 6th, 1954, address on the floor of the U.S. Senate persisted. It is likely that those occupants of the area, especially the area around Saigon that controlled most of the wealth of the South, were pleased that they could count on the U.S. to protect, and perhaps enhance, their wealth. However, it was not clear that they would be willing to sacrifice sons and daughters to fight a war to protect it.

McNamara wrote that "the danger of Vietnam's loss and, through falling dominoes, the loss of all Southeast Asia made it seem reasonable to consider expanding the U.S. effort in Vietnam..."

"Our government lacked experts for us to consult to compensate for our ignorance..." This gap "existed largely because the top East Asian and China experts in the State Department ... had been purged during the McCarthy hysteria of the 1950s..."[10]

The widespread concern among U.S. officials was, that if not stopped, communism would continue to spread. That was expected to be very bad. From my mother's perspective, it was bad because it was godless. From the perspective of civil libertarians, it was bad because communism enslaved people. From the perspective of business entities, it was bad because trade between communist bloc countries and U.S. allies was restricted, thus limiting potential economic growth and wellbeing. It had to be stopped if the American way of life was to be preserved and individual liberties maintained.[11] No American president wanted to risk the loss of another country to communism during his reign.

Reason Two for U.S. Involvement: Fear of Losing a U.S. Presidential Election

A second factor to explain why successive administrations engaged and continued to invest in Vietnam is related to the nature of the presidency. Presidents are elected to a four-year term. Most presidents enter office with multiple goals. However, the goal with the highest priority is to conduct activities during their first term in a manner consistent with enhancing their likelihood of reelection to a second four-year term.[12] Presidents who lose wars during their first term are expected to reduce their chances of being reelected. Certainly, presidents that served from 1954 through 1975 were of the opinion that given the amount of time, talent, and treasure that the U.S. had invested in Vietnam, losing a war to a "shit-ass little country," as President Nixon described North Vietnam, and enabling communism to spread would reduce their chances for reelection.

A common tactic used by opposition candidates against an incumbent candidate was to hammer the incumbent or his/her political party for appeasing the enemy and thereby losing or giving away a country or region, especially to Communists. British Prime Minister Neville Chamberlain was accused of giving away Czechoslovakia to appease Hitler with the Munich Pact of September 30th, 1938.[13] President Roosevelt had been accused of giving away Poland to the Soviet Union at the February 1945 Yalta Conference with Churchill and Stalin. During subsequent U.S. political campaigns, the words Yalta and Munich were invoked to paint the opponent as one who would appease communists and abandon the freedom of allies to godless communists.

President Truman and his administration was accused of losing China (that is, mainland [Red] China) to the Communists. The 1952 Republican Platform included the following: "By the [Truman] Administration's appeasement of Communism at home and abroad it has permitted Communists and their fellow travelers to serve in many key agencies and to infiltrate our American life." The platform statement also included: "There are no Communists in the Republican Party. We have always recognized Communism to be a world conspiracy against freedom and religion. We never compromised with

Communism and we have fought to expose it and to eliminate it in government and American life..."[14]

The 1952 Republican platform alleged that the Truman administration, "in seven years, has squandered the unprecedented power and prestige which were ours at the close of World War II. In that time, more than 500 million non-Russian people of fifteen different countries have been absorbed into the power sphere of Communist Russia, which proceeds confidently with its plan for world conquest ... They abandoned friendly nations such as Latvia, Lithuania, Estonia, Poland and Czechoslovakia to fend for themselves against the Communist aggression which soon swallowed them. They required the National Government of China to surrender Manchuria with its strategic ports and railroads to the control of Communist Russia. They urged that Communists be taken into the Chinese Government and its military forces. And finally they denied the military aid that had been authorized by Congress and which was crucially needed if China were to be saved. Thus they substituted on our Pacific flank a murderous enemy for an ally and friend..."[15]

The Republican strategy was successful. World War II hero General Dwight Eisenhower was elected in 1952. He was the first Republican to be elected president since Herbert Hoover in 1928. Eisenhower continued the Truman policy of funding the French effort. However, during the siege at Dien Bien Phu, Eisenhower did not take the advice of his Vice President, Nixon, and "put 'our boys in' Indo-China..."[16]

The U.S. did not sign the Geneva Accords. The Eisenhower administration did not permit a general election in Vietnam in 1956 as called for by the Accords. They understood that Ho Chi Minh was, by far, the most popular political figure in the region and that he was likely to win a fair election.[17] President Eisenhower poured aid funds into South Vietnam and prevented a collapse of the government during his administration.

The 1956 Republican platform declared victory. It included: "The advance of Communism has been checked, and, at key points, thrown back. The once-monolithic structure of International Communism, denied the stimulant of successive conquests, has shown hesitancy both internally and abroad," and "in Indochina, the Republics of Vietnam and Cambodia and Laos are now free and independent nations. The Republic of [South] Vietnam, with the United States assistance, has denied the Communists the gains which they expected from the withdrawal of French forces..."[18] President Eisenhower was reelected in 1956. My mother voted for him because, as she said, "He kept us out of war." My mother would have found it difficult to vote for Eisenhower's Democratic opponent, Adlai Stevenson, given that Stevenson was divorced.

In 1957, communist guerrillas assassinated several hundred South Vietnamese officials and detonated bombs in Saigon. In July of 1959, Scripps-Howard newspapers published a series of articles by Albert M. Colegrove titled: "Fiasco in Vietnam-Our Hidden Scandal We Put Out $1 Million a Day, But We Have No Say in Where it Goes."

"In less than five years, U.S. taxpayers have spent roughly $2 billion to help this newborn anti-Communist nation, about half the size of New Mexico and with a population roughly equal to that of the metropolitan New York City area ... We have wasted many millions of dollars, and still are. Following a reckless, foolish, made-in Washington policy of 'noninterference,' we've forked over bundles of American cash to the fledgling, inexperienced Vietnam Government, and then looked piously at the ceiling while the money melted away..."[19]

President Eisenhower continued to support the South with financial aid and advice, even though his administration was aware of the corruption facilitated by South Vietnamese president Ngo Dinh Diem, who, along with his cronies, from 1955 until his assassination in 1963, appeared to be more interested in maintaining power and building personal wealth than in constructing a well-functioning government. Even though only approximately 10% of the population was Catholic (with approximately 80% Buddhist) during Ngo Dinh Diem's regime, high public offices were reserved for members of Diem's family and other Catholics.[20][21] The Catholic Church was the largest landowner in the country. The Diem government continued the old French policy that required Buddhists to obtain government permission to conduct public Buddhist activities.

The Soviet Union and the Chinese continued to support the North. President Eisenhower, who had inherited the mess after the French defeat and withdrawal from the South, managed to complete his second term with maps showing that the domino, South Vietnam, was still standing.

Vice President Nixon was the Republican candidate for president in 1960. His Democratic opponent was Senator John Kennedy, who, in the April 6th, 1954, speech on the Senate floor, opined that unilateral U.S. involvement in Vietnam would be a "disaster." Neither the Republican nor Democratic 1960 platforms included the word Vietnam.[22][23] Perhaps it was best to let sleeping dogs or smoldering embers lie, especially since the Republicans had already declared victory in their 1956 platform: "The Republic of [South] Vietnam, with the United States assistance, has denied the Communists the gains which they expected from the withdrawal of French forces..."[24]

Kennedy was elected and inherited the mess, or using his term, the "disaster." He and his team expected that his chances for reelection in 1964 would be reduced if the domino fell. Their strategy was to continue to support the South with financial aid and advice, including military advisors, at least until after the 1964 election, at which time they could reevaluate.

President Kennedy is reported to have said to "senator and Vietnam skeptic Mike Mansfield after the Cuban Missile Crisis, if I tried to pull out completely now from Vietnam, we would have another Red scare on our hands." In July 1963, he is said to have told reporters at an off-the-record news conference: "We don't have a prayer of staying in Vietnam ... But I can't give up a piece of territory like that to the Communists and get the American people to reelect me..."[25] Six weeks prior to his assassination, President Kennedy approved a plan to withdraw U.S. military advisors from Vietnam.[26]

On November 22nd, 1963, Lee Harvey Oswald assassinated President Kennedy. Lyndon Johnson became President, inherited the mess, and the mess became more complicated. In May of 1955, then-Democratic leader of the Senate, Lyndon Johnson said that "power rests ultimately with the people ... unless we win them to our side ... we are lost..."[27] Unfortunately, in South Vietnam, the U.S. was supporting a government that either did not know how to win citizen support, did not have sufficient time to do so, or had more interest in building personal wealth than in building a country.

If Kennedy had lived and been reelected in 1964, he could have declared victory (as the Republicans had done in 1956 prior to Eisenhower's reelection) and removed U.S. advisors from Vietnam. He would then not have to worry about accusations of giving away Vietnam costing him future elections. Instead of President Kennedy seeking reelection, and if elected, having more options relative to South Vietnam, President Johnson had to run for election in 1964. And, if elected in 1964, he could legally run for reelection in 1968.

Kennedy's defense secretary Robert McNamara wrote that: "Throughout the Kennedy years, we operated on two premises that ultimately proved contradictory. One was that the fall of South Vietnam to Communism would threaten the security of the United States and the Western world. The other was that only the South Vietnamese could defend their nation, and that America should limit its role to providing training and logistical support. In line with that latter view, we actually began planning for the phased withdrawal of U.S. forces in 1963, a step adamantly opposed by those who believed it could lead to the loss of South Vietnam and, very likely, all of Asia..."[28] Of course, after the fact, it is costless to argue that if President Kennedy had lived and been reelected in 1964, he would have withdrawn U.S advisors and permitted South Vietnam to either clean up its corruption and defend itself, or to fall to the communists. It is not known if he would have been willing to accept the likelihood of a legacy of giving away, or losing, Vietnam.[29]

Chapter 34

President Johnson
"North Vietnam has attacked."

President Johnson retained many of the key personnel of Kennedy's cabinet, including Defense Secretary McNamara, who wrote that when Johnson became President, South Vietnam "was besieged by religious animosities, political factionalism, corrupt police, and ... a growing guerrilla insurgency supported by its northern neighbor..."[1] He went on to write that "Johnson was convinced that the Soviet Union and China were bent on achieving hegemony ... He saw the takeover of South Vietnam as a step toward that objective ... He failed to see the fundamentally political nature of the war..."[2]

McNamara wrote that "the danger of Vietnam's loss and, through falling dominoes, the loss of all Southeast Asia made it seem reasonable to consider expanding the U.S. effort in Vietnam..."

"Our government lacked experts for us to consult to compensate for our ignorance..." This gap "existed largely because the top East Asian and China experts in the State Department ... had been purged during the McCarthy hysteria of the 1950s..."[3]

Draftee

If Johnson was to be elected in 1964, after completing 12 months of President Kennedy's term, he would have to face consequences of actions regarding Vietnam in the 1968 election. In hindsight, it is not unreasonable to argue that Lee Harvey Oswald complicated the mess by reducing U.S. political options, and he may have been responsible for many more premature deaths than the one to which he is credited.

In August of 1964, the U.S. Navy reported that North Vietnamese Patrol, Torpedo (PT) boats fired torpedoes at the USS Maddox, a U.S. Navy destroyer located in the international waters of the Tonkin Gulf. This reported activity resulted in legislation that became known as the Gulf of Tonkin Resolution. It was approved unanimously in the House, and by a margin of 82–2 in the Senate. The legislation authorized President Johnson to "take all necessary measures to repel any armed attack against forces of the United States and to prevent further aggression..." Article 1, Section 8, of the U.S. Constitution grants Congress the power to declare war. However, Johnson chose to construe the Gulf of Tonkin Resolution as permission for the U.S. to wage war against North Vietnam without securing a formal declaration of war from Congress.[4][5]

Johnson was facing an election in November of 1964. His Republican opponent was Arizona Senator Barry Goldwater. In 1963, Senator Goldwater, had been quoted as saying that "I'd drop a low-yield atomic bomb on the Chinese supply lines in North Vietnam," and perhaps support "defoliation of the forests by low-yield atomic weapons..."[6] On September 7th, 1964, the Johnson campaign aired a one-minute political ad on the NBC television network. The video began by showing a small girl in an idyllic pasture picking daisies. A voiceover countdown was followed by a nuclear blast. As the mushroom cloud lingered, the announcer spoke: "Vote for President

Johnson on November third. The stakes are too high for you to stay home."[7] The "daisy" ad became known as the "mother of all attack ads."

On October 21st, 1964, President Johnson, in a speech at Akron University said that "we are not about to send American boys 9 or 10,000 miles away from home to do what Asian boys ought to be doing for themselves..."[8]

Several weeks later, in November 1964, several days before the election, Senator Goldwater said, "We are not down there instructing and advising. We are down there at war, and I think it is high time that the President tells the people we are and tells the people what he plans to do..."[9] Johnson won the election, and the four-year clock was reset. He was now confronted with how to manage the situation in Vietnam, preferably — from his perspective — in a manner that would not reduce his likelihood of reelection in 1968.

My brother James had been drafted and was inducted into the U.S. Army on February 27th, 1964. It was normal; young men his age were drafted. My parents were not overly concerned. The U.S. was not at war. Vietnam was not part of our vocabulary. After basic training at Fort Leonard Wood, Missouri, he served the remainder of his two years of active duty at Fort Richardson near Anchorage, Alaska.

President Johnson was inaugurated and began his elected term in January of 1965. On February 7th, eight U.S. soldiers (advisors) were killed at Pleiku; on February 10th, 23 were killed at Quinhon. The U.S. retaliated by bombing targets north of the DMZ.[10] The communists responded by detonating a car bomb adjacent to the U.S. embassy in Saigon, killing 22 and injuring more than 180. The U.S. countered by sending more Marines to guard air bases against attacks.[11] It was becoming clear that if an independent noncommunist South

Vietnam was to be preserved for another four years, enhancing President Johnson's chances for reelection in 1968, changes were necessary.

President Johnson was frustrated. He explained his decision to send Marines in a speech on April 7th, 1965: "Since 1954 every American President has offered support to the people of South Vietnam. We have helped to build, and we have helped to defend. Thus, over many years we have made a national pledge to help South Vietnam defend its independence. And I intend to keep that promise..."[12]

Johnson continued: "North Vietnam has attacked the independent nation of South Vietnam: its object is total conquest ... Over this war and all Asia is another reality: the deepening shadow of Communist China. The rulers in Hanoi are urged on by Peking..." (In 1965, the U.S. referred to the capital of China as Peking rather than Beijing.) "This is a regime which has destroyed freedom in Tibet, which has attacked India and has been condemned by the United Nations for aggression in Korea ... The contest in Vietnam is part of a wider pattern of aggressive purposes..."[13] Chinese intervention in Korea was a recent memory. President Johnson and his advisors wanted to avoid direct military confrontation with the Chinese. Between 1965 and 1968, more than 300,000 Chinese — mostly engineers and logisticians — served in Vietnam.[14] The Chinese wore NVA uniforms. By 1974, the Chinese had provided 170 planes, 176 gunboats, 552 tanks, 320 armored vehicles, 16,000 trucks, 2.14 million rifles, and 70,000 artillery pieces.[15]

President Johnson went on to explain that if the North Vietnamese would agree to a settlement and permit the existence of South Vietnam as an independent country, the U.S. would be willing to invest millions of dollars in infrastructure, schools, electrification, and modernization of agriculture. He said that to start the aid program he would ask Congress for one billion dollars. If the communists did not accept the offer, he said he had little choice other than to escalate "to slow down aggression. We do this to increase the confidence of the brave people of South Vietnam who have bravely born this brutal battle for so many years with so many casualties. And we do this to convince the leaders of North Vietnam — and all who seek to share their conquest — of a simple fact: We will not be defeated. We will not grow tired. We will not withdraw either openly or under the cloak of a meaningless agreement..."[16]

President Johnson had inherited a much bigger mess in Vietnam than any of his predecessors. The election cycle was not in his favor. He did not have their option of kicking the can down the road. Based on the advice he was given, if he did not escalate, South Vietnam would soon cease to exist as an independent noncommunist country. His military advisors assured him they were confident that with a sufficient number of ground troops and air strikes, they could defeat the Communists. If South Vietnam fell, his chances of being reelected in 1968 would be jeopardized. If, on the other hand, the military option was not successful and U.S. casualties continued to increase, his reelection chances would still be reduced. From his perspective, he had only bad options.

In May of 1965, President Johnson spoke to a meeting of Texas Electric Cooperatives. He explained that he had sent a Rural Electric Association team to South Vietnam. They had been assigned to plan and work with local officials "to find ways to bring the healing miracle of electricity to that poor, war-torn countryside..."

He continued, "We must be ready to fight in Viet-Nam, but the ultimate victory will depend upon the hearts and the minds of the people who actually live out there..."[17] Consistent with his political career, Johnson preferred a carrot approach, rather than a stick approach, to win hearts and minds.

Ho Chi Minh and the North Vietnamese rejected Johnson's offer to invest millions of U.S. dollars in infrastructure, schools, electrification, and modernization of agriculture. On July 27th, 1965, President Johnson made what McNamara described as "the fateful decision to embark on a major ground war in Southeast Asia..."[18] At the time, the majority of U.S. citizens supported the President's "fateful decision." In August 1965, a nationwide Gallup poll (institution.gallup.com) contained the following question: "In view of the developments since we entered the fighting in Vietnam, do you think the U.S. made a mistake sending troops to fight in Vietnam?" Only 24% responded "yes."

After President Diem was killed by a military coup in 1963, military officials assumed leadership positions. Nguyen Cao Ky, who had been in charge of the South Vietnamese air force, served as the prime minister of South Vietnam in a military junta from 1965 to 1967. On February 18th, 1967, two leading Buddhist monks, Thich Tri Quang and Thich Quang Do, sent an open letter to the American people in which they said: "The longer the war goes on, the stronger communism becomes; Americans become colonialists, and our people are destroyed..." On March 29th, 1967, Thich Tri Quang addressed a similar letter to the religious leaders in the U.S. He said in part: "The situation in Vietnam, which the U.S. authorities report to the American public as favorable, is in fact a tragic carnage of the Vietnamese people, and the present situation in South Vietnam has deteriorated to a point where it is comparable with, if not worse than, a communist domination..."[19]

In an attempt to display a semblance of democracy, a presidential election was scheduled for September 1967. Nguyen

Cao Ky was expected to run for the presidency. However, after interventions by senior military officials in the existing junta, he was persuaded to run as a candidate for Vice President on a ticket with Nguyen Van Thieu for President and Ky for Vice President.[20] The Thieu-Ky ticket won the election with a reported 35% of the vote. Ky was bitter about the arrangement and openly critical of Thieu, but nonetheless, he agreed to the arrangement. In March 1968, while serving as Vice President, Ky said, "The elections ... were a joke. They have served to install a regime that has nothing in common with the people — a useless corrupt regime. We need a revolution. The laws we have protect the rich. We must make new laws that will give power to the poor..."[21]

"Nine out of ten of the leaders on our side are corrupt," he complained to the Italian journalist Oriana Fallaci. Ky continued, "We need a revolution." After Ky's diatribe, Fallaci is reported to have responded, "That is what Ho Chi Minh says."[22] There is no report of Vice President Ky's response.

On January 31st, 1968, communist forces initiated the TET offensive. They attacked 36 of 64 provincial capitals, 5 of the 6 major cities, all 64 district capitals, and 50 hamlets.[23] An estimated 4,000 attacked prominent facilities in Saigon, including the U.S. embassy. Thousands of communist troops were killed. High-ranking U.S. military officials regarded the campaign as a failure for the communists, and thus, a military victory for the ARVN forces and their U.S. allies.[24] Communist military officials in the North had assumed that the citizens of the South would be emboldened by the attacks and assist their Vietnamese comrades with fighting against the U.S. invaders. They were wrong. On the other hand, U.S. military officials, while publicly claiming success, were surprised that the local population did not provide any warnings prior to the attack. Apathy worked both ways.

Both sides were surprised. A *New York Times* editorial published on February 8th, 1968, surmised that: "What this suggests is that the South Vietnam's towns and cities are characterized neither by a Marxist 'revolutionary situation' that would favor the Vietcong nor by widespread support for the Saigon regime which normally governs them. The two-armed factions ... probably both represent minorities in a population whose majority is war weary and apathetic..."[25] This was 14 years after Senator Kennedy's April 6th, 1954, speech on the floor of the U.S. Senate that included: "The apathy of the local population to the menace of the Viet Minh communism disguised as nationalism is the most discouraging aspect of the situation..."[26]

In a *Foreign Affairs* article published in April 1968, Hamilton Fish Armstrong posited that the U.S. military "are fighting under handicaps that are not military in nature. One is the apathy of the population around them; after years of colonialist exploitation and confused struggle, and lacking dynamic leadership like that of the North Vietnamese, the people of South Viet Nam are understandably weary, numb and uninterested. Another handicap is the inadequacy of the governments in Saigon which we have been fighting to maintain; these have been flagrantly and persistently corrupt, have shown little concern with principles and do not exercise effective influence over great sections of the population..."[27]

Junior officer Marine Corps Captain H.L. Preston penned a letter to the editor of the *Marine Corps Gazette* that was published in August 1968: "The March issue of the *Gazette* sounds like all official reports of the progress of the war in general, and of pacification in particular: that everything is going well and great progress is being made. From a description of specific projects and a consideration of statistics, this would indeed seem to be the case. However, the continuing ineffectiveness of all levels of Vietnamese government, the apathy or open hostility of the population, and the dramatic success of the TET offensive indicate quite clearly that pacification and civic action throughout Vietnam, but especially in I Corps, have been dismal failures..."[28]

Among some U.S. military and government officials, the story that the TET offensive resulted in U.S./ARVN military victory persisted for many years. The U.S. and the ARVN had killed more; they had destroyed more. Indeed, by these metrics, the Vietcong and NVA had lost. Thus, on my October 15th, 1971, flight from Seattle-Tacoma airport to Lambert International in St. Louis, more than three and half years later, I overheard an army Major say with great confidence that "We won the war. The enemy was destroyed during the TET offensive in 1968." However, there was much more to the story. In hindsight, TET highlighted two problems for the U.S. military that became insurmountable. One was that the government of South Vietnam was corrupt, ineffective, lacked widespread support, and was not winning the battle for the hearts and minds of the majority who lived in the country. The second problem was that many citizens, especially in rural areas, were apathetic for several reasons. They had been provided no evidence that their lives would be improved by victory from either side. And, the lack of a free press in the North enabled the communists to shield their atrocities from public scrutiny. Both sides were corrupt, but the North was much more successful at hiding their corruption and carnage. Wealth concentration was a visible issue in the South, and religious liberty was an issue for both sides.

The timing of the TET offensive, 40 days prior to the New Hampshire presidential primary election, was not good for President Johnson. Clark Clifford replaced Robert McNamara as Secretary of Defense in March of 1968. Clifford traveled to South Vietnam and reported back to President Johnson "that South Vietnamese leaders ... did not want the war to end — not while they were protected by over 500,000 American troops and a 'golden flow of money.'"[29] U.S. officials understood that the corrupt regime in power in South Vietnam was wholly dependent on the flow of funds from U.S. taxpayers and the flow of blood from U.S., allied, and ARVN soldiers. Unfortunately, U.S. dollars were being used to kill and destroy, rather than to invest in infrastructure, schools, electrification, and modernization of agriculture, as President Johnson had offered in April of 1965.[30]

President Johnson presided over the passage and initial implementation of a portfolio of legislation that addressed domestic issues. Examples include the Civil Rights Act of 1964, Food Stamp Act of 1964, Voting Rights Act of 1965, Immigration and Nationality Act of 1965, Economic Opportunity Act of 1964 (that established the Head Start program), and the Social Security Amendments of 1965 (that created Medicare and Medicaid).[31] However, many citizens, especially those subject to the draft, and those who had lost children and siblings in the war, were very unsatisfied with the inability of the U.S. military to bring the war to a successful conclusion. They remembered that on October 21st, 1964, candidate Johnson had said "we are not about to send American boys 9 or 10,000 miles away from home to do what Asian boys ought to be doing for themselves..."[32]

The TET offensive had consequences. On March 31st, 1968, President Johnson announced that he would not seek reelection. He said that he would spend his limited time remaining in office to attempt to bring an honorable settlement to the war, rather than to use his limited time to campaign for reelection. In an April 1968 nationwide Gallup poll, 48% responded "yes" to the question: "Do you think the US made a mistake sending troops to fight in Vietnam?" (institution.-gallup.com). After President Johnson announced that he would not seek reelection, the North Vietnamese agreed to meet for discussions that were to begin in Paris in mid-May 1968.

Chapter 35

Nixon Elected

"Throw a 'monkey wrench' into the peace talks."

Based on the U.S. Senate debate and President Eisenhower's statements in April of 1954, the expert opinion of many leading U.S. government officials was that U.S. military involvement in Vietnam was likely to end in a disaster. One notable exception was Vice President Nixon.

For the 1968 presidential election, the Democrats nominated Vice President Humphrey and the Republicans nominated former Vice President Nixon. George Wallace, former Alabama Governor and staunch racial segregationist, ran on the American Independent Party ticket. Candidate Nixon pledged on March 9th, 1968, that he had a plan to end the war. Candidate Nixon proclaimed that "I will deal with it in within six months..."[1]

On August 1st, 1968, Nixon issued a statement to the Republican National Convention Committee on Resolutions in which he wrote: "The present Administration's emissaries in Paris must be able to speak with the full force and authority of the United States. Nothing should be offered in the political arena that might undercut their hand..."[2] His statement followed his March 1968 pledge that he would "end the war," but when asked about his plan to do so, he responded, "Let me tell you why I won't tell you that. No one with this responsibility who is seeking office should give away any of his bargaining positions in advance..."[3] These statements formed the basis for what was interpreted as an affirmation that Nixon had a secret plan to end the war. He would keep his plan secret, as to not interfere with the Johnson administration's peace negotiations.

During the campaign, Nixon repeatedly told his audience that the U.S. policy under Humphrey would be the same as that of President Johnson, and that "those who have had a chance for four years and could not produce peace should not be given another chance..."[4]

Discussions between U.S. and North Vietnamese representatives continued in Paris. During the presidential election campaign, candidate Nixon had been concerned that an agreement in Paris to transition to peace in South Vietnam would result in more votes for Vice President Humphrey. In public, Nixon issued statements proclaiming that nothing should be offered in the political arena that might undercut the peace talks. In private, Nixon requested that his aides throw a monkey wrench into the peace talks by encouraging the South Vietnamese to not participate.[5] His campaign officials secured the services of Anna Chennault, who arranged a channel of communication with the South Vietnamese. Chennault was a Chinese-born Republican fund-raiser, anti-Communist lobbyist, and the widow of a highly-regarded American general. She was an informal diplomat and well known in the Asian diplomatic community.[6]

Nixon's campaign manager, John Mitchell, who later served as the U.S. attorney general, communicated with Chennault every day during the last week of the campaign to confirm

Draftee

that South Vietnamese President Thieu was on board with Nixon, and that South Vietnam would not participate in the Paris talks until after the election.[7] (In 1975, Mitchell was found guilty of conspiracy, obstruction of justice, and perjury for his role in the Watergate break-in and cover-up. He served 19 months in a federal prison.)

Chennault, at Nixon's request, promised South Vietnamese President Thieu that if he refused to participate in the talks prior to the election, that, as U.S. President, Nixon would give Thieu a better deal than President Johnson's team.[8] President Thieu did boycott the Paris talks. For him, it was an easy decision. If the peace talks failed, he would continue to be protected by thousands of U.S. troops and funded by billions of U.S. dollars. If the peace talks succeeded, his future was less certain. Candidate Nixon was successful in undercutting the negotiations by encouraging the South Vietnamese not to participate as long as Johnson was President. After Nixon was elected, Thieu agreed to send a representative to the Paris talks.[9]

President Johnson, whose team had illegally bugged the Nixon 1968 campaign, was aware of the Chennault Affair. However, since some of the tactics used to confirm the information had been obtained by illegal means, he chose not to reveal it. Later, Nixon, as President, contacted then-former President Johnson and asked him to tell Democrats in Congress to discontinue the Watergate investigations, or he might reveal the illegal Johnson wiretaps. But, Johnson responded by threatening to release the Chennault files showing that candidate Nixon had illegally interfered with the Paris talks.[10] Johnson was of the opinion that Nixon had committed treason, a violation of the 1799 Logan Act that prohibits private citizens (including presidential candidates) from engaging in unauthorized negotiations between the U.S. and foreign governments.[11]

Both parties held illegally obtained secrets that they could not disclose.

Nixon won a narrow victory — by less than one percent of the popular vote — in part because he convinced a sufficient number of voters that he had a plan to end the war, in part because he had interfered with the Paris talks by convincing President Thieu of South Vietnam not to participate, in part because Humphrey was tied to the policies of Johnson, and in part due to the candidacy of third party racial segregationist candidate Wallace. Wallace obtained 13.5% of the popular vote and won the electoral votes of five states: Alabama, Arkansas, Georgia, Louisiana, and Mississippi.

Fourteen years earlier, in April 1954, Senator Edwin Johnson of Colorado had termed it "Mr. Nixon's war." He reported that he had "heard the Vice President, Mr. Nixon, whooping it up for war in Indo-China..."[12] On January 20th, 1969, President Nixon was inaugurated. Fourteen years had passed, but he was now the Commander in Chief of the U.S. forces who were engaged in the war for which he had "whooped it up."

Chapter 36

President Nixon

"The war will be over by next year."

The war, along with assistance from President Thieu, contributed to Nixon's election success. But, as the sitting first-term President, he had a problem. If he withdrew U.S. troops from Vietnam and the communists prevailed, his likelihood of reelection in 1972 would be diminished. He could be accused of giving away South Vietnam to the communists. Additionally, he was on record as saying that "Those who have had a chance for four years and could not produce peace should not be given another chance..."[1] The clock was ticking.

President Nixon and his National Security Adviser Henry Kissinger were very optimistic about their chances of negotiating a favorable settlement. In March of 1968, candidate Nixon had said, "I will deal with it in within six months."[2] On March 20th, 1969, President Nixon told his cabinet, "The war will be over by next year."[3] In May of 1969, Kissinger told a visiting group, "Give us six months, and if we haven't ended the war by then, you can come back and tear down the White House fence."[4]

Charismatic Henry Kissinger seemed to enjoy the limelight, and he had an uncanny ability to appear calm and professorial in every interview. Kissinger's heavy German accent and propensity to speak and write in long monotonous sentences provided the impression of being the smartest person in the room. However, some who knew him well questioned his honesty and motives. Kissinger's close assistant and adviser, Helmut Sonnenfeldt, who was a senior staff member of the National Security Council from 1969–1974, was quoted as saying, "Kissinger doesn't lie because it's in his interest. He lies because it's his nature."[5] Nixon's press secretary, Ron Nessen, reported that the "Kissinger trait that troubled me most was his lack of commitment to the truth as a matter of morality..."[6] Others who knew Kissinger described his tendency to lie.[7,8]

Candidate Nixon may have sincerely believed if he, as President, via diplomatic channels, threatened to escalate the bombing of the North to the point of total annihilation, the North would agree to withdraw all of their troops from the South, discontinue supplying the Vietcong, and release U.S. prisoners of war.[9] In other words, if his implied threat had been fully executed, little other than a barren landscape and corpses would have been left to win.

If the North Vietnamese chose to ignore Nixon's threat to bomb to total annihilation, then President Nixon had no plan other than to tweak policies that had been attempted by the Johnson administration. President Nixon had been elected, in part, because of his pledged plan to end the war. However, 35% (20,309) of the total number of U.S. soldiers who lost their lives in Vietnam during the war were killed after President Nixon was inaugurated in January of 1969.

Given the intransigence of the North Vietnamese, President Nixon continued three strategies that were in process during the Johnson administration. First, he continued the negotiations that had been started in Paris and that he had successfully monkey wrenched while a candidate. Second, he continued the policy attributed to President Johnson's defense secretaries, McNamara and Clifford, of training and transferring combat responsibilities from U.S. to South Vietnamese forces.[10] Nixon's team did rebrand the policy. His Defense Secretary Melvin Laird proposed the word "Vietnamization" because it sounded better than Johnson's "de-Americanizing."[11] The term was good for U.S. politics.[12] But, to the South Vietnamese, it implied that they had not been fighting and dying.[13] It was a political coup for the North, adding credence to their propaganda of the U.S. as invaders. It was not good for ARVN morale. Third, President Nixon continued with the implementation of the draft lottery system that had been proposed by the National Advisory Commission on Selective Service that President Johnson had established.[14]

After McNamara quit or was fired, the Johnson team did not want to announce reductions in U.S. troop numbers that might reduce their leverage during the peace talks. But Nixon sabotaged the talks, and later, announced reductions in numbers of U.S. troops with no corresponding concessions from the North. The unilateral troop reductions reduced Nixon's leverage in the negotiations.

Chapter 37

Fair and Impartial Random (FAIR) Draft Lottery

"I could blame the defeat...on him."

President Johnson understood that since draft boards were organized at the local level, children of wealthy and powerful citizens were gaming the system and avoiding service.[1] The draft was prone to favoritism and corruption. He sought to improve the fairness of the Selective Service System. On July 2nd, 1966, President Johnson "appointed a National Advisory Commission on Selective Service, composed of 20 citizens, distinguished and diverse in their representation of important elements of our national life." Johnson had instructed the "Director of Selective Service, working in collaboration with the Secretary of Defense, to develop a Fair and Impartial Random (FAIR) system of selection to become fully operational before January 1, 1969..."[2] [3]

Based on the findings of the Commission, President Johnson recommended on March 6th, 1967, that "a fair and impartial random (FAIR) system of selection be established to determine the order of call for all men eligible and available for the draft..."[4] Johnson's Commission recommended a draft lottery — however, he was not successful in implementing a lottery.[5] On June 30th, 1967, President Johnson signed a four-year extension of the draft, known as the Military Selective Service Act of 1967, and an executive order to implement it. In a major setback for President Johnson's plan to reform the draft, the 1967 law prohibited a draft lottery without Congressional approval in the form of new legislation.[6]

In June of 1967, a sufficient number of Representatives and Senators did not support a lottery.[7] [8] They understood that quick implementation of a fairer system would make it more difficult for their sons, nephews, and the sons of their donors to avoid service. They needed more time for their favored constituents to plan for dodging in the event that they were randomly selected. For example, they might be able to negotiate a slot in the National Guard; at the time, National Guard units were not sent to Vietnam. The 1967 law specifically permitted enlistment in the National Guard any time up to the day of induction, thereby providing an honorable alternative for favored constituents. Prior draft legislation did not permit enlistment in the National Guard after receiving notice of induction.[9]

Draft law reform was delayed until November 19th, 1969, when Congress passed, and President Nixon signed, a one-sentence bill that repealed the 1967 law that had prohibited President Johnson from using a random selection system for drafting men into the armed services.[10] The first Vietnam-era draft lottery was held on December 1st, 1969.[11] [12]

We waited — especially those of us who were of draft age — for President Nixon to reveal and implement his secret plan to end the war. It is not clear when President Nixon and Kissinger came to the realization that they did not have superior powers of diplomacy and that the secret plan was evidently unknown to them, as well as to the rest of us. A year after the 1968 election, on November 3rd, 1969, President Nixon addressed the nation. His speech was part of his reelection campaign. Evidently, he realized that to imply the notion of a secret plan to end the war in Vietnam would not be a successful stump speech for the 1972 campaign. He pivoted his sales pitch to blaming the mess on President Johnson and the failure of peace talks during his time in office on any Americans who were not in support of his policies.

He began by saying that "we became involved in the war while my predecessor was in office ... I could blame the defeat ... on him." In other words, don't blame President Nixon. He did not mention that 15 years earlier, in April of 1954, while serving as Vice President, he may have been the first high-ranking elected U.S. official to advocate direct military combat intervention in Vietnam when he proclaimed that "the United States was prepared to put 'our boys in' Indo-China to 'avoid further Communist expansion in Asia.'"[13] He also failed to mention in the November 1969 speech that the conflict had been termed "Mr. Nixon's war" beginning in 1954, and that he had been overheard "whooping it up for war in Indo-China..."[14] He also did not reveal he had ordered his campaign officials to throw a monkey wrench into the peace talks attempted during the Johnson administration. Mainline U.S. news media, such as the *New York Times* and the television network news programs, also failed to mention Nixon's early advocacy for introducing U.S. soldiers into a ground war in Indochina.

He said, "For the future of peace, precipitate withdrawal would be a disaster of immense magnitude..."[15] He did not say that the biggest disaster, from his perspective, was that if he withdrew, South Vietnam would collapse, and he would reduce his chances for reelection in 1972. He also said, "In the previous Administration, we Americanized the war in Vietnam. In this Administration, we are Vietnamizing the search

Draftee

for peace." He didn't explain that his team had simply rebranded the policy attributed to President Johnson's defense secretary McNamara, of training and transferring combat responsibilities from U.S. to South Vietnamese forces.[16]

Near the end of the speech, President Nixon explained that if he did not achieve peace with honor (prior to the 1972 election) for President Johnson's war, it would be the fault of those Americans who chose to exercise their free speech and protest the war. He said, "To you, the great silent majority of my fellow Americans, I ask for your support. I pledged in my campaign ... to end the war ... The more support I can have from the American people, the sooner that pledge can be redeemed. For the more divided we are at home, the less likely the enemy is to negotiate in Paris..." [17] [18]

I was serving as an apprentice teacher in the Fall of 1969 and did not listen to or read the November 3rd, 1969, speech. I was more concerned about how to teach a class of high school sophomores to effectively weld two pieces of metal with arc and oxyacetylene welders.

Based on responses to pollsters, the majority of U.S. citizens and the majority of Congress supported the War even after the TET offensive. "By November 12, (1969) 300 members of the House of Representatives-119 Democrats and 181 Republicans-had cosponsored a resolution of support for Nixon's Vietnam policies, and 58 senators — 21 Democrats and 37 Republicans — had signed letters expressing similar sentiments..."[19] This was 10 months after the TET offensive. This strong show of bipartisan Congressional support was six months after the May 1969 Kissinger proclamation: "Give us six months, and if we haven't ended the war by then, you can come back and tear down the White House fence..."[20]

On November 19th, 1969, Congress passed a bill permitting the draft lottery.[21] It was the first major piece of new legislation that the Nixon Administration obtained during his first 10 months in office. The bill contained one sentence that repealed the 1967 law that had prohibited President Johnson from using a random selection system to decide draft order. On November 26th, 1969, President Nixon signed the legislation that enabled the lottery, as had been recommended by President Johnson's 1966 National Advisory Commission on Selective Service.[22]

Chapter 38

No Secret Plan Only Secret Bombing

"You see these bums, you know, blowing up campuses."

In the spring of 1970, President Nixon publicly authorized the use of U.S. forces in Cambodia. Previously, "between March 1969 and May 1970, the president had personally mandated 4,308 B-52 sorties against (NVA) targets in Cambodia, which were undisclosed even to USAF chief Gen. John Ryan. Before flying missions over Cambodia and Laos, navigators were required to sign a nondisclosure agreement..."[1] The communists could not complain about the bombing, since they denied they had any troops in Cambodia. U.S. "Strategic Air Command kept two sets of after-action reports: one for very limited circulation, identifying real targets; the other recording fictional attacks inside South Vietnam..."[2]

The plan was to destroy NVA supplies and disrupt their logistics. Many saw expansion of the war into Cambodia as inconsistent with President Nixon's campaign rhetoric. University students on campuses across the country protested.

On Monday, May 4th, 1970, Ohio National Guardsmen fired live rounds into a group of students, killing four Kent

State University students and wounding nine others. A group of Kent State students had assembled to protest the bombing of Cambodia by U.S. forces. The Ohio National Guard had been activated to maintain order. The killings at Kent State instigated protests on campuses all across the U.S. President Nixon referred to the students as "bums."

President Nixon's response to the Kent State killings — in effect blaming the students, two of whom had been killed, who were walking between classes and not protesting — served to further divide public opinion. However, Nixon's "support the troops" as opposed to the "bums" was a successful narrative. After the Kent State killings in May of 1970, one poll found that 50% supported the Cambodian invasion, while 39% opposed.[3,4]

On September 21st, 1970, U.S. officials in Saigon reported that 92.8% of South Vietnam's population was under government control. Only 184,700 of 16,722,100 were under Vietcong control, with 996,600 living in regions where neither the Vietcong nor the government had decisive control.[5]

The news media seemed to have forgotten that more than a year had passed since Nixon told his cabinet on March 20th, 1969, that "the war will be over by next year..."[6] They also failed to report that more than a year had passed since Kissinger told a visiting group in May of 1969, "Give us six months, and if we haven't ended the war by then, you can come back and tear down the White House fence..."[7] Given Kissinger's failure to achieve any type of settlement that would not appear to be a U.S. failure, the two realized that they would need to continue the war until after the election in November 1972. Nixon developed a divide-and-conquer political strategy by promoting a narrative of hard-working citizens, supporting the troops, supporting the flag, and supporting the struggle against godless communism — in short, the moral silent majority versus the privileged draft dodging college students and flag burning bums. The rallying cry was not "support the war" but rather "support those who have been killed and the prisoners of war." The Nixon administration painted anyone who questioned his war tactics as anti-U.S. soldier, even though some of the protestors were veterans of the war, some had siblings or children or cousins serving in the war, and most knew someone from their community who had been injured or killed in the war.

The NVA Easter offensive of March 1972 provided a major test of Nixon and Kissinger's Vietnam strategy. All South Vietnamese bases in the area immediately south of the DMZ were either overrun by the NVA or abandoned or surrendered to the NVA. Almost all of the area that had been in our 20.5 miles circular firing radius during our time in military region I in 1971 was now controlled by the NVA. The South was on the verge of collapse. President Nixon sensed that he was near the edge of presiding over a lost war and close to being subject to accusations by political opponents of the abandonment of millions to godless communists.

In April 1972, it should have been obvious to unbiased observers that regular NVA troops were defeating the ARVN and that there was a chance that the South would collapse prior to the November 7th, 1972, election. The infamous White House recordings include the following President Nixon diatribe from May 4th, 1972: "The United States cannot lose ... Whatever happens to South Vietnam we are going to cream North Vietnam ... we got to use the maximum power of this country ... against this shit-ass little country..."[8]

On May 29th, 1971, the recordings include:

Kissinger: "So we get through '72. I'm being perfectly cynical about this, Mr. President."

Nixon: "Yes."

Kissinger: "If we can, in October of '72 go around the country saying we ended the war and the Democrats wanted to turn it over to the Communists..."

Nixon: "That's right."

Kissinger: "Then we're in great shape ... If it's got to go to the Communists, it'd be better to have it happen in the first six months of the new term than have it go on and on and on."

Nixon: "Sure."

Kissinger: "I'm being very cold-blooded about it."

Nixon: "I know exactly what we're up to."[9]

Nixon authorized increased bombing of suspected NVA-held areas in South Vietnam and B-52 strikes against North Vietnam. He said, "These bastards have never been bombed like they're going to be bombed this time." [10] In the spring of 1972, for the first time since November 1967, U.S. B-52s bombed North Vietnam, including sites in Hanoi and Haiphong.[11]

Election day was scheduled for November 7th, 1972. It was 223 months (more than 18 years) since Vice President Nixon declared that, if necessary, the United States was prepared to put "our boys in" Indo-China to "avoid further Communist expansion in Asia." It was 56 months since presidential candidate Nixon implied on March 9th, 1968, that he had a secret plan to end the war. It was 50 months since candidate Nixon proclaimed that "Those who have had a chance for four years and could not produce peace should not be given another chance." It was 44 months since then-President Nixon on March 20th, 1969, told his cabinet, "The war will be over by next year..."

Massive U.S. aerial bombardments prevented the collapse of South Vietnam prior to the 1972 election. Knowledge that both North Vietnam and the U.S. obtained from the Easter offensive of 1972 affected peace talk negotiations. As Hastings

Draftee

writes, "Nixon's heinous offense, in which Kissinger served as his instrument, was to sacrifice twenty-one thousand American lives, and vastly more Vietnamese ones, in military and diplomatic maneuvers designed not to benefit anyone in Indochina but only the president's political interests..."[12]

Chapter 39

Official Paris Talks and Unofficial Kissinger-Le Duc Tho Meetings

"A long stall that aimed at dividing the U.S. from Saigon."

After the TET offensive in 1968, and prior to the 1968 U.S. presidential election, President Johnson attempted to initiate negotiations and transition to a diplomatic solution to end the killing, and perhaps enhance Vice President Humphrey's chances in the upcoming presidential election. At the behest of candidate Nixon, South Vietnamese President Thieu refused to participate in talks with his adversaries until after the 1968 election. In January of 1969, after President Nixon was inaugurated, formal meetings were initiated in Paris. I was a junior in college, and to the extent possible, ignored happenings concerning Vietnam.

Arranging meetings among the warring parties was complicated. The U.S. recognized the area south of the 17th parallel as an independent country known as South Vietnam (Republic of Vietnam, RVN). The U.S. recognized the President Thieu administration as the legitimately-elected, governing authority of South Vietnam. North Vietnam (Democratic Republic of Vietnam, DRVN) chose to not recognize the Thieu government, but rather to refer to it as a U.S. puppet. North Vietnam

Draftee

contended that the Provisional Revolutionary Group (PRG) — which was a revised name for the National Liberation Front (NLF), which was known in the U.S. as the Vietcong (VC) — spoke for the people south of the 17th parallel. The Thieu government did not recognize the PRG as a legitimate entity, but rather as an extension of the NVA, composed of illegal rebels. Eventually, North Vietnam was successful in using the PRG to occupy another chair in the room (spot at the table), as well as to further agitate South Vietnam. Months were spent arguing over who was permitted at the table and the shape of the table.[1] It should have been obvious from any educated observer that the North Vietnamese could, and would, use these meetings to effectively stall. Time was on their side. Threats from the U.S. to bomb North Vietnam back into the stone age did not seem to bother them.

The objectives of the various parties were relatively clear. Publicly, the U.S. wanted out of the war, U.S. and allied prisoners of war (POWs) to be returned, and a noncommunist, independent South Vietnam that could survive and thrive on its own. Privately, they wanted this to happen prior to the 1972 election. President Nixon did not want the domino to fall while he was in charge. He wanted to declare victory and be reelected to a second term. The U.S. election deadline provided an advantage for the North's negotiators. Time was clearly an ally of the North Vietnamese.

The North Vietnamese wanted the war to end with a reunited North and South into one Vietnam. This is what Ho Chi Minh thought he had won prior to the 1954 Geneva Accords that separated what he saw as one country at the 17th parallel. They wanted the U.S. to leave and for South Vietnam to no longer exist. In other words, they wanted to unite the North and South and declare victory. They did not care how many years it would take. They had been at war for years and knew that they could outlast the U.S. Stalling enabled them, with the assistance of Russia and China, to build up air defense systems and to continue to drain U.S. resources. "All along, their [the North Vietnamese] plan was a long stall that aimed at dividing the U.S. from Saigon [South Vietnam] and world opinion against the U.S. It succeeded brilliantly..."[2] Stalling was a winning strategy for North Vietnam. From 1969 through most of 1972, the Paris meetings consisted of each side politely restating their position with zero compromise.

The negotiating position of the North Vietnamese was much stronger than that of the U.S. Previously, the Johnson administration deliberately chose to not publicly discuss their de-Americanization plans and did not announce reductions and planned reductions in U.S. troop numbers. They realized that doing so would reduce their leverage in seeking a diplomatic solution. President Nixon, on the other hand, chose to promote Vietnamization and routinely announced reductions in the number of U.S. troops in South Vietnam. It enhanced his political situation in the U.S. but reduced his leverage with the North Vietnamese. During most of Nixon's time as President, monthly replacement ratios for U.S. troops completing their typical one-year assignment was less than one — less than one replacement for each homebound U.S. soldier. U.S. military personnel in South Vietnam were reduced from more than 500,000 in 1968 to 25,000 by December of 1972.

The only remaining U.S. bargaining chip was the threat of bombing. Because of the nature of the North's military and mostly agrarian economy, bombing had limited effect. Isolated, stationary military targets were rare. Most were bombed multiple times.

After a few months, President Nixon determined that the formal Paris talks were unlikely to result in a timely justification for the U.S. to withdraw while maintaining a noncommunist independent South Vietnam. He needed an alternative, especially if he was going to fulfill his March 9th, 1968, commitment to "deal with it within six months."

In August 1969, Nixon, a big fan of secrets, and his National Security Advisor Henry Kissinger, initiated secret discussions with North Vietnamese official representative Le Duc Tho. For the first three years, these secret meetings were no more productive than the official Paris meetings. Even though in the U.S., we were told that the war was about South Vietnam defending itself against local (Vietcong) as well as foreign (North Vietnam) godless communist fighters, neither the South Vietnamese official government nor the Vietcong participated in the secret meetings.

The clandestine Kissinger-Le Duc Tho meetings began in August of 1969, the summer prior to my senior year in college. They continued during my senior year, my entire time in the Army, and into my first year after completion of active duty.

The NVA Easter offensive of March 1972 demonstrated to objective military observers, and to the NVA, that many of the ARVN units lacked sufficient motivation to stand and fight. It was that old apathy problem. It was also evident that the South Vietnamese government of President Thieu would have collapsed in the spring of 1972 had it not been for the intensive U.S. bombing of NVA targets in the South. It was that old corruption problem. After the Easter offensive, much of military region I was controlled by the NVA. More than 150,000 NVA troops remained in companies dispersed all across South Vietnam. Some units were relatively close to Saigon.

In response to the Easter offensive, President Nixon relaxed many of the restrictions relative to the bombing campaign. Military leaders were given permission "to wage the air war as they want in Indochina — sealing off North Vietnam's coast and harbors with mines, followed by the systematic and relatively unrestricted destruction of military and industrial targets throughout the country."³ However, a 25-mile buffer zone was designated along the Chinese border.

"The only military target in Haiphong to remain generally off limits is the dock area where foreign ships are trapped..."⁴ The bombing in the North was another attempt to destroy the North's ability to continue the war and to counter criticisms from U.S. military hawks who had criticized previous efforts at limited war. Bombs were intended to destroy antiaircraft batteries, railroad links to China, petroleum supplies, power plants, industrial sites, citizen morale, and to incent Le Duc Tho to compromise with Kissinger. The U.S. used "an armada of 800 American fighter-bombers, as many as seven aircraft carriers, 35 destroyers and cruisers, and more than 150 B-52 strategic bombers to halt the North Vietnamese advance..."⁵ Nuclear weapons may have been the only tools in the U.S. kit that were not used.

The Easter offensive provided information for both Le Duc Tho and Kissinger. Le Duc Tho gained confidence that, in the absence of U.S. air support, the NVA could win battles against the ARVN. For the first time in the negotiations, he elected to compromise on what had been a major sticking point in achieving a ceasefire. The North would agree to return the U.S. POWs and permit President Thieu to remain in office if the U.S. would agree to a ceasefire in place, meaning that the NVA troops that were in the South would not be required to return to the North.

As the Presidential election of 1972 neared, Nixon and Kissinger — perhaps recalling that four years earlier, in October 1968, candidate Nixon proclaimed, "Those who have had a chance for four years and could not produce peace should not be given another chance." — elected to give up one of their major demands. They elected to permit a ceasefire in place that would, in effect, permit North Vietnam to maintain NVA troops, estimated to be more than 150,000 well-trained and well-equipped experienced fighters, in South Vietnam.[6] These NVA troops that remained in place after the NVA's 1972 spring offensive were not concentrated, but rather scattered in units throughout the country. In spite of the intensive U.S. bombing, the NVA had, during the Easter offensive, won the areas that they occupied. Kissinger desperately wanted a success story that included the return of the U.S. POWs that were held by the North. He sought a story that he could present to the American people prior to the November 1972 election. Kissinger accepted the offer. He and Le Duc Tho prepared a draft agreement that he then had to sell to South Vietnamese President Thieu.

When President Thieu learned the details of the proposed agreement that Kissinger had achieved with Le Duc Tho, he was incensed. President Thieu understood that conditions laid out in the draft document would not bring the war to an end. The South Vietnamese were of the opinion that Kissinger had agreed to terms with Le Duc Tho that Kissinger had previously told the South Vietnamese he would not accept. In their opinion, Kissinger was so eager to obtain an agreement prior to the U.S. election that he compromised on several issues that would result in their ultimate defeat. Thieu recognized that permitting the 150,000 NVA troops to remain in the South was, in effect, ceding vast chunks of what he thought was his country to the North.

From Thieu's perspective, these well-trained, seasoned NVA troops would enable the North to rather easily continue the fighting after the U.S. fully withdrew. Based on the performance of his troops relative to the NVA during the Easter offensive, Thieu also knew that even with massive U.S. air assistance, his ARVN troops failed to defend vast areas. There was no evidence to suggest that the ARVN would be able to reclaim the lost areas and drive the NVA out of the South.

If the U.S. was successful in getting their POWs returned from the North, Thieu reasoned that it would be a matter of time until the U.S. no longer provided protection for his government and the level of funds transferred from U.S. taxpayers would not be maintained. Thieu's response was a clear indication that his government was almost totally dependent on the U.S. Chances were high that implementation of the details described in the draft document would very likely result in the demise of his government. He told Kissinger that he would not sign the agreement.

Kissinger was facing the same President Thieu that U.S. Defense Secretary Clark Clifford encountered four years earlier, in March 1968. Clifford reported to President Johnson that Thieu "did not want the war to end — not while he was protected by over 500,000 American troops and a 'golden flow of money.'"[7] One difference was that Kissinger was aware of Thieu's assistance to Nixon during the 1968 campaign. Now it seemed that Thieu expected it was time for Nixon to assist him.

Chapter 40

Kissinger's October Surprise

"Peace is at hand."

On October 26th, 1972, 12 days before the November 7th, 1972, U.S. presidential election, Kissinger held a press conference to report on his secret meetings with Le Duc Tho. He proclaimed that "peace is at hand."[1] [2] Kissinger did not reveal the whole truth; he did not disclose that South Vietnamese President Thieu had told him that he would not sign the document. Kissinger's problem with Thieu was compounded when the North Vietnamese announced that an agreement to end the hostilities had been achieved.

South Vietnam had several major objections to the "peace is at hand" document. The agreement would permit 150,000 NVA troops to remain, after the ceasefire, in what had been South Vietnam. On November 11th, in a meeting with one of President Nixon's representatives, Thieu asked, "Have you ever seen any peace accord in the history of the world in which the invaders had been permitted to stay in the territories they had invaded?"[3]

Thieu knew that if his ARVN troops could not rid the South of the NVA when they had the assistance of U.S. air power during the Easter offensive, it was highly unlikely that, even with U.S. air power, they would be able to defeat the NVA. In other words, Kissinger's draft ceasefire agreement was ceding vast areas in what had been South Vietnam to the communists. It also failed to recognize the existence of a border and a DMZ near the 17th parallel.

South Vietnamese President Thieu insisted on the withdrawal of all NVA troops back to North Vietnam. He wanted Kissinger to win through negotiations what he had failed to achieve through good government and had clearly lost during the years of war, including the Easter offensive. Thieu wanted the re-establishment of the DMZ and a clear, internationally-recognized border near the 17th parallel. Thieu objected to the recognition of the Vietcong as a legitimate entity. A further source of agitation for Thieu was that Kissinger had agreed to a new entity: the National Council of Reconciliation. Thieu feared that introducing a Council that included both the North Vietnamese and the Vietcong would leave his government with only 1/3 representation of what he considered to be his country. From Thieu's perspective, Kissinger had negotiated to not only permit 150,000 NVA troops to remain in the South, but he had permitted Le Duc Tho to stack the deck so that there was no way Thieu's government could prevail in future negotiations or future military battles. However, Kissinger said that the North had "dropped their demand for a coalition government which would absorb all existing authority..."[4]

Four and a half years earlier, on March 10th, 1968, then-candidate Nixon said, "A settlement could not under any circumstances indicate that aggression pays — that is why, in my view, a coalition government or another partition would end the war but lose the peace..."[5] In the speech 12 days before the 1972 election, Kissinger did not explain that in the ambiguous peace plan that he was describing, South Vietnam was interpreting the proposed National Council of Reconciliation as a precursor to a coalition government.

Kissinger was well aware of these issues, but he did not mention these problems in the October 26th "peace is at hand" press conference. He did say a few small details remained, but that he expected the final issues would be resolved in one more meeting with Le Duc Tho.[6] Kissinger proclaimed that the timing of the decision was not related to the upcoming election, but rather to the breakthrough in that the North was willing to separate the military from the political questions. He did not specify what he considered to be political versus military issues.

I was skeptical of the "peace is at hand" statement. I assumed that the timing of Kissinger's very cleverly-worded, ambiguous statements was orchestrated to further enhance Nixon's vote totals in the upcoming election. Senator George McGovern of South Dakota was Nixon's opponent in the 1972 election. McGovern was a decorated Distinguished Flying Cross World War II veteran, having flown 35 B-24 bomber missions over enemy-occupied Europe. McGovern had voted in favor of the Gulf of Tonkin Resolution, and, through 1968, voted in favor of Vietnam military appropriations he thought necessary to support the troops. McGovern was not in the Senate in 1954 when Senator John F. Kennedy described the potential disaster. However, as early as 1963, McGovern publicly challenged U.S. military involvement in Vietnam.

The 1972 Democratic Party Platform that was officially approved on July 10th, 1972 (three months prior to the "peace is at hand" speech), included the following: "Elected with a secret plan to end this war, Nixon's plan is still secret, and we — and the Vietnamese — have had four more years of fighting and death..."[7]

The platform statement included: "The Saigon Government, despite massive U.S. support, is still not viable. It is militarily ineffective, politically corrupt, and economically near collapse. Yet it is for this regime that Americans still die, and American prisoners still rot in Indo-China camps..."

The Republican Party Platform of August 1972 included the following: "We stand unequivocally at the side of the President in his effort to negotiate honorable terms, and in his refusal to accept terms which would dishonor this country..."[8] President Nixon's campaign included an organized program run by White House aide Charles Colson to subversively discredit opponents. (Colson later served time in federal prison for obstruction of justice in the Watergate affair.) McGovern was an easy target for Colson's team. McGovern was painted as being for peace at any price. His plan, as characterized by Colson's team, was to give up and let the godless communists win. Under McGovern, the U.S. would admit defeat and lose. More than 50,000 U.S. soldiers would have died in vain. McGovern stood for retreat and defeat; he was a salesman of surrender, he was for amnesty, abortion, and acid. Even though he was a decorated World War II veteran, McGovern was characterized by Nixon's team as not supporting the troops.

Nixon, on the other hand, was for peace with honor. He was against those godless communists. He was supporting the troops. He was protecting the wonderful people of South Vietnam, and indeed people all over the world, from the encroachment of godless communism.

Even in the absence of issues relative to Vietnam, and in the absence of Colson's dirty tricks team, President Nixon would very likely have been reelected in 1972. During his first term, he was credited with initiating efforts to bring China into the family of nations, helping to create the Environmental Protection Agency, signing Title IX legislation that requires girls' sports teams to receive equal funding with boys' teams, implementing President Johnson's draft lottery, creating the

Draftee

Office of Management and Budget and the Office of Energy Policy, signing the Clean Air Act of 1970, and for reducing the number of U.S. military personnel in South Vietnam from more than 500,000 in 1968 to fewer than 30,000 by election day. Kissinger's "peace is at hand" October surprise was icing on the cake.

Nixon referred to the "peace is at hand" agreement as fulfilling his stated goal to achieve peace with honor. Nixon, with Kissinger's help, used the "peace is at hand" press conference to imply that the war was effectively over and that Nixon's policies had worked. McGovern's fate was sealed. The one issue that had propelled McGovern to be nominated as the Democratic candidate was no longer an issue. According to Kissinger, an agreement had been achieved that would end the war. Nixon won 61% of the popular vote and a 520 to 17 count in the Electoral College.

Meanwhile, Kissinger had a problem. The North Vietnamese announced that they were willing to sign the draft peace document. But South Vietnamese President Thieu insisted that Kissinger return to the negotiations, and he gave him more than 60 proposed text changes for the draft document.[9] Kissinger was not happy and did not want to ask for 60 changes. He described Thieu's demands as "verging on insanity."[10] However, Nixon, perhaps still indebted to Thieu for his assistance with the 1968 election, instructed Kissinger to introduce the proposed changes in his next scheduled meeting with Le Duc Tho. After the election, Kissinger met with Le Duc Tho on November 20th. Kissinger presented Thieu's list of more than 60 changes, proposed by Thieu and approved by Nixon. The North Vietnamese refused the proposed changes. On December 16th, the talks stalled with no plans to reconvene. In spite of Kissinger's and Nixon's pre-election "peace is at hand" rhetoric, the war, the killing, and the destruction continued.

Nixon was desperate to have the POWs returned. He wanted to bring the North Vietnamese back to the negotiating table. He had won reelection by a massive landslide and no longer needed to fear political consequences of his decisions regarding Vietnam. On December 18th, he ordered the initiation of what the U.S. military labeled Linebacker II. It was a 12-day bombing operation that became known as the Christmas Bombing. Nixon wanted to incentivize the North Vietnamese to return the POWs and to also convey a strong message to South Vietnamese President Thieu that the U.S. had not abandoned South Vietnam. During the 12 days, the U.S. lost 13 tactical aircraft and 16 B-52s. Four other B-52s suffered heavy damage and five B-52s suffered medium damage. 43 U.S. airmen were killed, and 49 more were taken prisoner. During the entire war prior to Linebacker II, only one B-52 had been lost.[11] [12] [13]

After the bombing was halted, Kissinger and Le Duc Tho met in Paris. They initialed an agreement on January 27th, 1973, that was very similar to the October 1972 draft.[14] South Vietnamese President Thieu agreed to the treaty after President Nixon pledged (privately) that the U.S. would use bombing to punish North Vietnam if they broke the terms of the agreement, and by Nixon's threat, that U.S. economic support would end if Thieu refused to sign. Some speculate that "in the end, Kissinger arrived at an agreement that was essentially the same as the one the Communists presented to him in May 1969..."[15] But he had secured what became known as a "decent interval," between the signing of the agreement and the eventual collapse of South Vietnam.[16] He also enabled President Nixon to proclaim that he had achieved "peace with honor." Of course, the consequences of achieving what may

Draftee

have been a similar agreement in 1969 (almost four years earlier) remain unknown.

The U.S. agreed to withdraw all combat troops and the North Vietnamese agreed to return all U.S. prisoners of war. The 150,000 NVA troops were permitted to remain in the South. Both the Vietcong and President Thieu's South Vietnamese government structures were retained, and at the time, in control of noncontiguous regions in the South. President Nixon had privately assured Thieu that if the North broke the agreement, U.S. air power would be at his disposal. Upon his return to Hanoi, Le Duc Tho described the agreement as a "great victory for the Vietnamese people."[17] Nixon described it as "peace with honor." By April of 1973, 591 American POWs were released.

Hastings contends that "the war was almost certainly beyond winning before Nixon entered the White House. President Thieu and his associates had done little to serve the interests of the society they governed, and only experience would show that the communists did less. Nixon's heinous offense, in which Kissinger served as his instrument, was to sacrifice twenty-one thousand American lives and vastly more Vietnamese ones in military and diplomatic maneuvers designed not to benefit anyone in Indochina but only the president's political interest..."[18] 35% of the total number of U.S. soldiers who lost their lives as a result of the war were killed after President Nixon was inaugurated in January of 1969.

Hasting writes that "Kissinger and Nixon's skill in manipulating the war and U.S. public opinion prior to the 1972 election was rather remarkable. No doubt, the lack of scruples was beneficial. On October 23rd, 1972, two weeks prior to the November 7th, 1972 election, Kissinger met with Thieu and told him 'The U.S. will never sacrifice a trusted friend.' Two days later when back in Washington he told Commerce Secretary Pete Peterson, 'I have only one desire — to turn the Vietnamese loose on each other in the hope the maximum will kill each other off.'"[19]

After most of the U.S. personnel left, the level of corruption among South Vietnamese officials increased. Some officers embezzled from the payrolls of their own soldiers. Some military supply officials extracted bribes for delivering food and equipment to their own troops. Thieu's wife made a fortune in illegal real estate deals. One of Thieu's cousins, who had been appointed province chief, taxed almost everything sold in his province. Thousands of U.S.-provided artillery rounds were fired at faux targets so that the brass shell casings could be sold on the black market. Thieu then complained that his soldiers were short of ammunition and expected the U.S. to provide more.[20] [21]

Meanwhile, corruption was not limited to South Vietnam. After the U.S. Justice Department uncovered widespread evidence of his political corruption, Nixon's Vice President Spiro Agnew resigned on October 10th, 1973. Gerald Ford was sworn in as Vice President on December 6th, 1973. Less than a year later, on August 9th, 1974, President Nixon resigned after the revelation of an audio recording of Nixon discussing plans to obstruct justice proceedings relative to the Watergate break-in and cover-up. Ford became President; he was the only person to serve as U.S. President without having been previously voted into either the presidential or vice-presidential office.

President Ford, who, with his eye on the 1976 election, shied away from greater assistance to South Vietnam for fear of "making it his war instead of Nixon's."[22] Publicly, Ford proclaimed support for South Vietnam and made perfunctory requests to Congress for additional military aid.[23] But Ford, who, prior to being appointed Vice President, had served in

Congress from 1949, was well aware that the Congress, given that the POWs had been returned, was in no mood to provide more funds to what many in Congress were finally willing to acknowledge was a corrupt Thieu administration. For Ford, the decision was not too difficult. He could express support for the South and request funds that he knew would not be provided, and then after the South collapsed, blame the loss on the U.S. Congress.

President Thieu resigned on April 21st, 1975. He, along with 15 tons of luggage, was flown out of the country to Taiwan by the CIA. According to some reports, the luggage included $15 million in gold. Thieu denied that he absconded with any gold.[24] However, it was not for lack of trying. *Time* magazine reported that a West German Red Cross plane that delivered medical supplies to Saigon received a request to fly out some personal belongings of the presidential family. When the Germans learned that the intended cargo consisted of 16 tons of gold, they refused.[25] [26] Thieu settled in Foxborough, Massachusetts, and died a natural death in 2001.[27]

U.S. soldiers continued to die in Vietnam until the war formally ended, when NVA forces captured Saigon and South Vietnamese President Duong Van Minh surrendered on April 30th, 1975. Charles McMahon and Darwin Lee Judge were killed in a rocket attack on April 29th, 1975, one day before the official surrender and almost four years after Albright had learned that "we were not there." They are considered to be the last two U.S. soldiers killed in Vietnam during the War.

South Vietnam ceased to exist on April 30th, 1975. Nixon and Kissinger had achieved a decent interval between the settlement that resulted in the return of POWs on January 27th, 1973, and the unconditional surrender on April 30th, 1975. They claimed that they had won the peace and, along with President Ford, blamed the loss on the U.S. Congress (for reducing the level of funds transferred from U.S. taxpayers to the Thieu government). More than 21 years had passed since "Vice President Richard Nixon declared that, if necessary, the United States was prepared to put 'our boys in' Indo-China to 'avoid further Communist expansion in Asia.'"[28]

New York Times reporter Fox Butterfield, who witnessed the collapse of the country, wrote a few days after the collapse: "In the end, the collapse was the product not so much of the Communists' plans or prowess in battle as of the inherent weaknesses of the South Vietnamese Army and South Vietnamese society — poor leadership, corruption, a system of promotion based on personal loyalty rather than ability, and, above all, the lack of any unifying goal or ideology beyond the old Confucian ideal of the family. When the crunch came, there was nothing to bind officers to their men or men to their officers. All those years of American aid had never touched the heart of the matter..."[29] After Saigon fell, Butterfield interviewed a South Vietnamese on one of the U.S. evacuation ships who told him that: "We beat ourselves ...We are a country that destroyed itself..."[30]

Another assessment was provided by historian Christian Appy. The U.S. "military demonstrated its capacity to maintain control of South Vietnam as long as the United States was willing to incur the cost. But the U.S. goal was not to fight forever; it was to bolster a non-communist South Vietnamese government that could survive on its own. Achieving that end depended on gaining what the United States could never secure — the broad political support of the people. Military power could not persuade; it could only destroy..."[31]

The U.S. could use military might to kill and to destroy. The U.S. military could claim victory when the winner was determined by the side that killed and destroyed the most. By this measure, and by these rules, the U.S. could claim victory in

Draftee

every battle. We were trained to kill and destroy. We were good. When funded with the almost-blank checks provided to the U.S. military industrial complex for delivering lethal tools, it was easy to destroy. It is hard to build.

A decade earlier, in May of 1965, President Johnson said that "the ultimate victory will depend upon the hearts and the minds of the people who actually live out there."[32] Johnson offered millions of dollars for infrastructure, schools, electrification, and modernization of agriculture.[33] His offer to help build, to improve living standards, and thereby winning "hearts and minds" to prefer democracy was not accepted by Ho Chi Minh. It is easier to instill fear and distrust than it is to win "hearts and minds."[34] It is wrong to argue that the U.S. and her allies won every battle in Vietnam. Their ally, the South Vietnamese government, failed to win what turned out to be the most important battle: that for the "hearts and minds" of the majority of those who lived in what we called South Vietnam.

Chapter 41

Rationalizing a Loss

"Denied permission to win."

South Vietnam ceased to exist when South Vietnamese President Duong Van Minh surrendered on April 30th, 1975. The U.S. objective of an independent, noncommunist South Vietnam was not achieved. However, for many in the U.S., for supporters of the U.S. military industrial complex, for some who profited from the military industrial complex, for many who had served, and for many families that had been directly affected by the war, it was not conceivable that the U.S. military lost. It was unthinkable that 58,220 U.S. (plus 5,100 South Korean, 500 Australian, 40 New Zealand, and 9 Philippine) soldiers had died, that 300,000 had been wounded and 75,000 severely disabled, that billions had been collected from U.S. taxpayers and spent, and that the U.S. military had not been successful. Defenders of the U.S. military industrial complex needed a palatable narrative that would exonerate the U.S. military. One was provided by the great communicator, Ronald Reagan.

In 1964, while Governor of California, Reagan was one of the strongest agitators for the buildup of U.S. involvement. In

1964, he said, "We are at war with the most dangerous enemy that has ever faced mankind in his long climb from the swamp to the stars, and it has been said if we lose that war, and in so doing lose this way of freedom of ours, history will record with the greatest astonishment that those who had the most to lose did the least to prevent its happening."[1]

In 1967, a few months before the TET offensive, Reagan opined: "I have a feeling we're doing better in the war than we're being told, that the corner has been turned."[2] After the collapse of South Vietnam, in 1975, Reagan concluded that "the U.S. gave up in Vietnam and abandoned an ally."[3] In a speech delivered by then-President Reagan at the Pentagon on February 24th, 1981, he said, "They came home without a victory, not because they'd been defeated, but because they'd been denied permission to win."[4]

Reagan's rhetoric reminded me of a passage from Remarque's *All Quiet on the Western Front*. While on leave at home after fighting in the trenches of World War I, the narrator, fictional German infantryman Paul Baumer, was frustrated with the ignorance of several older gentlemen he encountered in the local beer garden: "They are quite confident they know all about it; they often say so with their air of comprehension, so there is no point in discussing it. They make up a picture of it for themselves..."[5] Few, if any, politicians were alive who could say "it" with more confidence and conviction than professional actor Ronald Reagan. He was an exceptional orator; he was convincing. He told many — perhaps the majority — of U.S. citizens what they wanted to hear. The U.S. military DID NOT LOSE. The _____ (Fill in the blank with one or more: "media," "peaceniks," "Congress," "Vietnam Veterans Against the War," "Walter Cronkite," "Jane Fonda," "George McGovern," "Smothers Brothers," "protestors," "demonstrators," "privileged college students," "hippies," "flag burners," "television news," "lazy freeloading unpatriotic bums.") _____ denied the U.S. military permission to win.

President Reagan's "denied permission to win" rhetoric facilitated acquittal of those who condoned the transfer of billions of dollars from U.S. taxpayers to corrupt South Vietnamese military officials and politicians. Based on Reagan's oratory, the only military personnel he found culpable was that relatively small group of outspoken, brave, courageous Vietnam veterans who returned from the war and dared to articulate the war's waste, corruption, carnage, and the failure of the South Vietnamese government to address and win the "hearts and minds" battle. Many veterans, perhaps the majority, agreed with Reagan's assessment. No veteran wanted to be thought of as a loser.

It should not be surprising that not all veterans agreed. Each veteran had a unique experience depending on when they were there, where they were, and what they were doing. If my experience had been limited to one or more of the relatively large military bases that I observed during transit, if I had not observed ARVN draftees, if I had not been aware of NVA activities in and around the DMZ, if I had not been a fire direction controller, if I had not observed B52 bombing, or if I had not witnessed the results of munitions, I might have come to the same conclusion as President Reagan.

The vast majority of U.S. military personnel spent most of their time in country on secure bases, on which it was easy to assume that the U.S. was on the winning side. Across South Vietnam on the large bases, tens of thousands of highly paid (by Vietnamese standards) South Vietnamese catered to the Americans' needs.[6][7] Vietnamese cooks prepared their meals. Vietnamese maids and laundresses tidied up their barracks and made sure their uniforms were clean and crisply ironed. Vietnamese processed the human waste.

Draftee

After a year of fighting in the trenches of World War I, fictional German infantryman Paul Baumer, in Remarque's *All Quiet on the Western Front,* explained that his assessment of Germany's chances changed over time. "It was different a year ago ... at that time, I [Paul] still knew nothing about the war, we had only been in quiet sectors..."[8] Many U.S. soldiers spent a year or more in South Vietnam in relatively quiet sectors and had little opportunity to observe ARVN draftees in combat. Fictional Paul Baumer continued, "The war may be rather different from what people think..."

Blame for the U.S. failure to achieve her objectives was ascribed to any individual or group who had the audacity to question U.S. official policies. Special culpability was assigned to war correspondents who occasionally reported more than that included in military press releases, and who had the nerve to show and to describe the consequences of the war.

President Reagan was convincing. His message was much more palatable than the alternative. There was no market for a narrative for the failure of South Vietnam to survive as a thriving democracy, other than the U.S. and her allies were "denied permission to win." To do so would be to acknowledge that even though thousands had died, and billions of dollars had been collected from U.S. taxpayers and spent, the U.S. military had not been successful.

Reagan's narrative failed to address the real issues that we had encountered and observed in Vietnam. The U.S. military, into which I had been drafted, was woefully unprepared to conduct operations that would have resulted in the survival of an independent flourishing noncommunist South Vietnam. Reagan's statements illustrated a profound ignorance of the situation that we had faced. However, similar to those in Baumer's local beer garden, he said it with an "air of comprehension, so there is [was] no point in discussing it..."[9]

From my perspective, many U.S. senior officers thought that they could conduct business in Vietnam in a manner similar to what they had done during World War II and win another victory. The Japanese military had attacked U.S. territory in 1941. More than 2,400 Americans were killed at Pearl Harbor. War was declared by Congress and the U.S. military chose to consider every citizen of Japan to be the enemy. During World War II, in the spring of 1945, U.S. bombers dropped incendiary bombs over the city of Tokyo. More than 100,000 people are estimated to have died. The fires did not discriminate among soldiers, men, women, and children. An area approximately four miles square was destroyed.[10] In August 1945, the U.S. military exploded two atomic bombs over Japanese cities. The bombs did not discriminate between civilians and soldiers, between children and adults, and immediately killed an estimated 120,000. Over time, radiation exposure killed thousands more. 90% of Hiroshima was obliterated.[11]

During World War II, Japanese soldiers demonstrated their willingness to refuse to surrender, even when their predicaments were hopeless. U.S. officials expected that if they did not use the atom bombs, the War would require an invasion of Japan that was expected to result in many thousands of casualties. The nuclear attacks on Japan were justified as a means to win the war with the fewest casualties possible. As Senator Henry Bellmon, whose platoon of 32 suffered 21 causalities at Iwo Jima, wrote: "Many are critical of President Harry Truman and his decision to use atomic weapons at Hiroshima and Nagasaki, but Marines who were survivors of other Pacific battles and who were facing the necessity to fight on Japanese home islands were not among Truman's critics..."[12]

The U.S. military that arrived in Vietnam was designed to use overwhelming force to kill and destroy an obvious and visible enemy. In the war to which I was assigned, the enemy was not obvious. The ambiguity made it impossible to restrict the killing to enemy combatants. People other than soldiers were killed. Any structure could be rationalized as providing enemy support. The U.S. military was not prepared to fight the type of war in which we were engaged. This should not have been a surprise. On July 27th, 1953, President Eisenhower wrote in his diary, "I am convinced that no military victory is possible in this theater..."[13]

In April of 1954, Senator Kennedy explained to his fellow Senators: "I am frankly of the belief that no amount of American military assistance in Indochina can conquer an enemy which is everywhere and at the same time nowhere ... an enemy of the people which has the sympathy and covert support of the people..."[14] In May of 1965, President Johnson said that "the ultimate victory will depend upon the hearts and the minds of the people who actually live out there..."[15]

President Roosevelt noted in 1944, "France has had the country ... for nearly one hundred years, and the people are worse off than they were at the beginning ... France has milked it for one hundred years..."[16] What President Roosevelt's January 24th, 1944 memo to his Secretary of State Cordell Hull did not say was that over the decades of milking Vietnam, the French had propagated a class society within the indigenous population.[17] When the French were in charge, the vast majority of the population, approximately 80%, were Buddhist. Approximately 10% were Catholic, and the remaining 10% included Cao-Dai, Hoa-Hao, Animists, and Protestants.[18] However, Catholics were more likely to have spent time in (French Jesuit) Catholic schools, were on average more fluent in French, and were more in sync with the French overlords. Thus, the limited advancement opportunities for locals were often awarded to Catholics.

For the vast majority of Vietnamese, Ho Chi Minh was a hero. He defeated the French. He was their George Washington. Unfortunately, for Vietnam and for the U.S., he was a communist. South Vietnam began with a huge disadvantage in that no noncommunist, competent political leaders approaching the popularity of Ho Chi Minh could be found. The U.S. had several added constraints in that the only obvious, staunchly noncommunists were Catholics. Many of the South Vietnamese political and military officials had supported the French during the war with Ho Chi Minh. An additional problem was that many South Vietnamese government officials emulated what they had observed while under French rule. They maintained the class society and operated as if it was appropriate for special benefits to accrue to those in charge.

The net effect was that the majority of those who lived in South Vietnam had little allegiance to the South Vietnamese government that the U.S. fought to maintain. Unfortunately, South Vietnamese governments invested insufficient effort in gaining support of those they ostensibly governed. Enabling widespread draft evasion for the sons of the upper class was not helpful. ARVN draftees from poor families understood that wealthier upper class Vietnamese families were able to buy draft exemptions for their male members.[19] Consequently, most ARVN draftees, who came from families that were treated as second class citizens, could be expected to have little interest in fighting to support a government that, if successful, would treat them no better than the French had treated them and their families in prior decades.

Another impediment to success was that the Vietnamese in charge of the South Vietnamese government were more interested in acquiring personal wealth and power than in winning the "hearts and minds" of the vast majority of those that they ostensibly governed. They clearly did not win the battle for the

Draftee

"hearts and minds." It was the battle that ultimately decided the outcome.

The "denied permission to win" rhetoric was part of a winning strategy for Reagan in the 1980 campaign and for the military industrial complex. President Reagan was reelected in 1984. From 1981 to 1988, national annual defense outlays for major, public, direct physical capital investment increase by more than 220%, from $39 billion to $86 billion.[20]

Many years have passed, but supporters of the U.S. military industrial complex continue to exploit the "claim, championed by President Reagan, that the United States had lost the war only because soldiers had been 'denied permission to win.'"[21] A few military officials and historians have tried to explain why the assertion in not correct. For example, Appy asserts that "If all your information about the Vietnam War came via the POW films of the 1980s (such as *Uncommon Valor, Missing in Action,* and *Rambo*) you would have to conclude that there had been a massive conspiracy to betray American soldiers by ensuring their defeat..."[22] For many U.S. citizens, the notion that the U.S. lost because soldiers were required to fight with one hand tied behind their back was the more palatable narrative.

Retired Air Force Lieutenant Colonel and National War College and U.S. Air Force Academy professor Mark Clodfelter conducted an extensive study of the effectiveness of the air war. He explains that multiple air forces supported South Vietnam: these included U.S. Marine helicopters and jets; U.S. army helicopters, transports, and spotter planes; U.S. Navy fighters; U.S. air force fighters and bombers; and South Vietnamese fighters, helicopters, and transports.[23] [24] Clodfelter concluded that no amount of bombing could stop the small quantity of supplies that were required to be shipped from the North to the South to sustain the communists' guerrilla war.

He found that during many years of the war, the communists averaged fighting only one day out of 30. Meanwhile, the U.S. dropped four million tons of bombs on South Vietnam — more than one quarter of a ton of bombs (500 pounds) per person on the country the U.S. was trying to save. "Not exactly the best way to win so-called hearts and minds..."[25]

Clodfelter notes that there were few industrial targets in North Vietnam. When the bombing campaigns began, the North had one cement factory, one steel mill, and seven electrical power plants. All were bombed multiple times. The effects of bombing a country back to the stone age are limited when it is only a few bricks short of being in the stone age. Bombing could not be used to address the fundamental problem: the corrupt, out of touch, and ineffective South Vietnamese governments. Clodfelter concludes that "No amount of American airpower could sustain such regimes..."[26]

Colonel Herbert Y. Schandler graduated from West Point and served two tours as an infantry commander in Vietnam between 1966 and 1970. After the war, he served as a Pentagon policymaker and a scholar who taught at West Point and the National Defense University. In addition to his familiarity with U.S. and ARVN issues, more than 20 years after the war, he returned to Vietnam and conducted extensive personal interviews with North Vietnamese who had served in the NVA during the war. Schandler wrote in 1999 that: "Now, nearly 25 years after the end of the war, and nearly a half-century after the United States first became involved, the evidence points to the conclusion that to believe that the US military was denied a victory it could have and should have won in Vietnam is an illusion — a dangerous illusion if acted upon in future U.S. conflicts..."[27]

Colonel Schandler continued, "The claim most often made by military analysts and historians since 1975 is that the military was denied victory because of constraints placed on U.S. military power by political leaders in Washington..."[28]

Colonel Schandler continued, "The following are some of the unmistakable conclusions to be drawn from a comprehensive analysis of the data on military aspects of the war, conclusions that are incompatible with the illusion of a U.S. military victory in Vietnam. The heart of the illusion is the failure of U.S. military and civilian leaders alike to understand the nature of the war in which they became involved in Vietnam: It was a *people's war* — a civil war. Fundamentally, therefore, it was not simply a war of North Vietnamese aggression, as we viewed it at the time ... The U.S. military responded in a conventional manner, attempting to follow doctrine and strategy that derive from its World War II experience. That is to say, they prepared to fight a conventional war based on doctrine designed for fighting on the plains of Western Europe in an all-out war ... American attention to social programs in community organization in South Vietnam was trifling. This was a mistake that the Communist fighting a people's war did not make. Indeed, their understanding of a people's war suggested that it was first a *political* struggle; only secondarily, after proper political and social preparation, did it become an *armed* struggle..."[29] "The North Vietnamese and their southern allies, the National Liberation Front, understood the nature of the war in Vietnam far better than we did..."[30]

"The Nixon administration fell victim to its own illusion, which it called 'Vietnamization' — the idea that the United States could withdraw completely and that the South Vietnamese government would successfully defend itself against the NLF and North Vietnamese forces ... Nixon administration officials blamed the U.S. Congress for refusing to grant it adequate funds to successfully pursue Vietnamization..."[31]

"There is no evidence that the South Vietnamese would

ever have been able to accomplish on their own what they failed to achieve with massive American assistance. The level of congressional funding was irrelevant to the final outcome. The Nixon administration, like the Johnson administration before it, could not give the South Vietnamese the essential ingredient for success: genuine indigenous political legitimacy..."[32]

"525,000 American soldiers — however courageous, however well-trained, equipped, and supplied were not the answer to South Vietnam's political problems; the civil war — the Vietnamese 'people's war' — could not be won by any external military force, no matter how powerful. From 1964 to 1973 ... South Vietnam existed only because of the willingness of the United States to send soldiers to fire on its behalf. When U.S. support was removed, the inevitable results could have been predicted, whether in 1964, 1968, or 1973..."[33]

In spite of the scholarly work by Lieutenant Colonel Clodfelter, Colonel Schandler, and others that has debunked the "one hand tied behind their back — denied permission to win" narrative, it has persisted. The military industrial complex has been successful in placing the blame for their failures on civilian leaders. Appy reported that "about two weeks after the [1991] Gulf War began ... 79% of poll respondents supported the statement that 'the current war would not be like the one in Vietnam because U.S. troops would not have to fight with one hand tied behind their back.'"

The same poll asked respondents to estimate the number of Vietnamese killed in the Vietnam war. "The median answer was 100,000. The Vietnamese government estimates that 3.4 million Vietnamese died in the war..."[34] [35]

The inability to debunk the "denied permission to win" should not be surprising. Defense contractors spend millions on lobbying efforts and have contributed millions to politicians and political action committees.[36] [37] Between 1990 and 2012, individuals and political action committees associated with the defense sector contributed a total of nearly $200 million to politicians and their campaigns.[38] In addition, the defense sector annual lobbying expenditures exceeds $100 million.[39] Since the end of the military draft, there has been no power in the U.S. political system to countervail the influence of the defense sector. One consequence is that an extended war in Afghanistan cost U.S. taxpayers an estimated $1.5 trillion and thousands of lost lives on all sides. Horton posits that: "The parallels between the war in Afghanistan and the Vietnam War are striking. In the Afghanistan Papers that were acquired by the *Washington Post*, the senselessness of the war is laid bare by U.S. government officials. The papers are reminiscent of the Vietnam-era Pentagon Papers and show that for years, the U.S. government has known that the war in Afghanistan is a costly and deadly exercise in futility..."[40] Unlike the Vietnam War and the publication of the Pentagon Papers that were met with collective national outrage and public demonstrations, the war in Afghanistan and the publication of the Afghanistan Papers barely elicited a yawn. No U.S. draftees were sent to Afghanistan.

Part Three

Opportunity to Change America: Freedom to Choose

Chapter 42

Family Tradition

"Any Frenchman is a soldier and owes himself to the defense of the nation."

Family legend has it that one of my 16 great-great-great-grandfathers, a French citizen named Sebastien Epplin, and two of his brothers (my great-great-great-uncles) were conscripted (drafted) to serve in Napoleon Bonaparte's "Grande Armee" (Great Army). Napoleon acquired fame prior to, and power during, the French Revolution of 1789–1799. The 1798 Jourdan Law established universal conscription for all young French men. The law included the clause that: "Any Frenchman is a soldier and owes himself to the defense of the nation..." France was the first modern country to enact a universal draft. All able-bodied young men 20 to 25 years of age were expected to serve or risk losing citizenship. France was in chaos when Napoleon seized political power in a 1799 coup and became First Consul (military dictator) of France. His team eventually created a state with relatively more stable finances, and relatively more stable government services, than the regime that they ousted.[1]

The Jourdan universal draft law enabled Napoleon to assemble a large number of soldiers into the Great Army. Most of the men drafted into Napoleon's Great Army were sons of peasant farmers. According to family lore, two of my great-great-great-uncles were with Napoleon's army of 600,000 men that invaded Russia in the fall of 1812. The Russians employed a wise strategy. They retreated and waited for winter. More than 300,000 of Napoleon's soldiers (including both of my great-great-great-uncles) perished from either battle wounds, disease, or inclement weather during Napoleon's attempt to conquer Russia.

My great-great-great-grandfather Sebastien was spared from the French attempt to conquer Russia. He served as a junior infantry officer during one of Napoleon's campaigns and was once ordered by a General, who was on horseback, to storm a building. Sebastien knew that there were many enemy soldiers in the building and that he and his men were greatly outnumbered. An assault on the building would be a suicide mission. Sebastien was contemplating the order when the General turned his horse to depart. At that instant, an enemy sniper fired from the building and, as fate would have it, the bullet killed the General. Sebastien was then free to choose an alternative. He chose to not implement the fallen General's order. Family lore is silent on Sebastien's subsequent military activities. We do not know if he participated in the 1815 battle at Waterloo. But we do know that he returned to Soultzmatt, Alsace-Lorraine, France and that his son, Sebastian (spelled with an a-n rather than e-n) junior, my great-great-grandfather, was born in 1817.

Sebastian (junior) was in his late twenties and early thirties during the time France was involved with a war in Morocco in 1844–1847, Tahiti in 1848, and the second French Revolution in 1848. Perhaps he was not drafted, or he may have fulfilled service requirements during more peaceful times. According to family lore, Sebastian married. However, his (first) wife and

Draftee

baby died. He was distraught, and in 1853, at the age of 36, gathered a few meager personal belongings that he could carry, left Europe and what remained of his extended family, and purchased passage to New York. However, rather than New York, the ship traveled to New Orleans. Sebastian traveled from New Orleans, up the Mississippi River to French Village, Illinois, near St. Louis, Missouri, where he found employment at a livery stable. The area known as French Village in 1853 is now located within the city of Fairview Heights. In 1855, Sebastian married a widow who had four children. Their first child together, Victor, my great grandfather, was born in 1857 in French Village.

In 1858, the year of the Lincoln–Douglas debates, also known as The Great Debates of 1858, Sebastian moved his family from French Village in St. Clair County to near Du Quoin in Perry County, Illinois. He rented a farm, and the family began their farming career.

Sebastian was 43 when the Confederate forces in Charleston began a bombardment of Fort Sumter on April 12th, 1861. Sebastian did not serve in the U.S. Civil War. His son, my great grandfather Victor Epplin, was three at the beginning of the Civil War.

Chapter 43

Military Drafts in the United States

"Those who expect to reap the blessing of freedom must...undergo the fatigue of supporting it."

Prior to the establishment of the United States, English colonial governments in North America required that able-bodied free men (not slaves) participate in local colonial militias. The colonialists were responsible for providing their own equipment, including their personal firearms that most had available for hunting wildlife. These early militias were established, called upon, and used to protect villages from external marauders.[1]

European immigrants provided few objections to the public service of providing for village defense. After the United States was established, President Washington, in a May 2nd, 1783, letter to Alexander Hamilton, wrote: "It may be laid down as a primary position, and the basis of our system, that every citizen who enjoys the protection of a free government, owes not only a portion of his property, but even of his personal services to the defense of it..."[2] [3] Thomas Paine wrote: "Those who expect to reap the blessing of freedom must, like men, undergo the fatigue of supporting it..."[4] The country was able to survive without implementing a federal system of conscription for military service until the Civil War.

Civil War Draft

In 1863, President Lincoln explained, "The principle of the draft ... has been practiced in all ages of the world. It was well known to the framers of our constitution as one of the modes of raising armies ... Shall we shrink from the necessary means to maintain our free government? ... I do think every patriot should willingly take his chance under a law made with great care in order to secure entire fairness..."[5]

On March 3rd, 1863, President Lincoln signed into law The Enrollment Act of 1863 that enabled a federal military draft to be used in the U.S. for the first time.[6] The law was based on the "raise and support armies" clause in Article 1, Section 8 of the U.S. Constitution. It was passed by Congress in response to a series of battle defeats that the U.S. had suffered. Federal agents assigned a quota to each congressional district. A lottery system was developed to randomly draw a sufficient number of names to fulfill the quota. The states preferred to fulfill their quotas with volunteers rather than draftees. Federal bounties of $100 and more were paid to incentivize men between the ages of 20 and 45 to voluntarily enlist. In some districts, the combined federal, state, and local monetary incentives exceeded $500 and were sufficient to encourage unscrupulous men to enlist, take the money, relocate, re-enlist, and collect another bounty in another place, perhaps under another name.

The Enrollment Act of 1863 also enabled individuals whose names were selected by the lottery process to purchase an exemption for $300 or to hire a substitute. That is, wealthy citizens were given the legal option of paying for their sons to avoid the draft. $300 was more than most laborers earned in a year. Thus, the 1863 act established the precedent for legal draft avoidance (dodging) and sowed the seeds for civil unrest. Poor residents and recent immigrants who had left Europe to avoid the divine right of kings were in no mood to accept a legislated privilege of wealth. As could be expected, the draft was seen as blatantly unfair, especially among the working class.

The legal right granted to purchase an exemption was based on a modification of French law. In France, a man selected for military service could legally hire a substitute. However, in France, the draftee was required to find and pay a substitute, who was then required to serve in the draftee's place.[7] The U.S. law permitted a draftee to avoid service for a fee of $300 and did not require a substitute.

Residents across the country assembled to protest. A draft office in New York City was set on fire. After several days of civil unrest, Union soldiers were mobilized to assist the police to regain control. More than 100 people were killed, several thousand were injured, and property damage was estimated to be in the millions of dollars.[8][9] The following headlines were included in the July 16th, 1863, issue of the *New York Times*: "Facts and Incidents of the Riot: The Murder of Colored People in Thompson and Sullivan Streets. The Sacking of Buildings in Avenues B and A. A Colored Man Beaten to Death in Leroy Street. The Rioters in The Seventh Precinct. The Draft. The Riot in the Tenth Precinct. The Plundering of Stores in the Eleventh Precinct. Another Station House Burned. Other Outrages. The Body of Col. O'Brien. Warehouses Guarded. Some of the Killed and Wounded. Policemen Shot. The Riot at Harlem. Riotous Demonstrations on Staten Island. Defenses of the Times Office. Reinforcements for The Mob. Arrival of Troops. The Common Council on the Draft..."[10]

The following description was included in an unsigned article titled The Great Riot.[11] "On Monday, the 13th day of July, 1863, the national conscription was proceeding in two districts of New York City. By Monday night the buildings and the blocks in which the provost marshals had their respective offices had been burned to the ground by a furious rabble, whose onset the police had in vain attempted to stay, and the great metropolis of North America was at the mercy of a raging mob, which roamed through the streets, robbing, beating, burning, murdering where they would..."

"By Tuesday the police had thoroughly organized, and the trial of strength between mob-law and authority began. Night closed over a still unconquered, defiant, law-contemning insurrection. On Wednesday the public conveyances of the city were stopped, the places of business mostly closed, while the rioters alternated between hanging negroes, burning their houses, and plundering generally, on the one hand, and fighting the military on the other. Thursday the final struggle ensued, and when Friday dawned, though not until then, was the city fairly delivered from the hands of the insurgents, and restored to its wonted order. Now all is tranquil, and save the occasional ruins, the groans of the wounded in the hospitals, the agony of those who have lost friends or homes in the struggle, and the diminished number of the blacks, little remains to attest the scenes of terror through which New York has passed..."[12]

As economist Robert Frank has documented, many people care more about their income relative to that of others in their community than they do about the absolute level of their income. Government intervention — in this case, a successful Civil War — was expected to change the economic position of poor, recently-arrived European immigrants relative to that of freed slaves. A group that expected to be worse off relatively, could be expected to, and in some cases did, fight the intervention.[13]

There was resistance to the draft elsewhere, including my home state of Illinois. An August 14th, 1862, article in the *New*

York Times reported that Illinois "dailies have much to say about sneaks leaving for Canada to avoid the draft..."[14] The August 9th, 1863, issue of the *New York Times* reported that "on the evening of [July] 29th a courier came riding into Olney, [Illinois] the headquarters of the Deputy Provost-Marshal, with intelligence that an armed mob was advancing from the neighboring counties for the purpose of destroying the enrollment papers. The citizens immediately armed with whatever weapons were within reach, determined to defend the enrolling lists, which were in the Court-house. The Commissioner took the papers in a buggy, and escaped into the country, and finally to Springfield. The mob lingered in the vicinity all the next day, but a force of from 600 to 800 had assembled to oppose them and so they made no hostile demonstrations..."[15] There were organized objections to the draft in other Illinois counties.[16]

The following excerpts from the September 1863 issue of *The Continental Monthly* provide several hypotheses regarding the motivation for the New York City riots. "The insurrection had not, therefore, in its largest proportions, one single distinctive purpose, and was not the work of one set of men. It was a rising against the draft, but not wholly so. It was a blow in aid of the South, though not this only. It was a thieves' tumult, but that was not all. It was all of these, with some other ingredients, previously mentioned, the whole clustering and crystallizing around a nucleus of crude, ignorant, hard-working, passionate, rough, turbulent men, deceived by the adroit misrepresentations of interested persons, until, driven to madness by a sense of supposed injustice, they believed themselves justified in securing redress by the only means they knew..."[17]

"The prevailing complaint among the first active insurgents, and their sympathizers among the poor, was that they were about to be forced away from home to fight for the freedom of the blacks, who when free would become their competitors for the little they now earn. In listening to the knots gathered at the corners, to the conversation among the inhabitants of the most violently riotous districts, the words which fell oftenest upon the ear were those of bitter, burning, blasting denunciation against the apathy of the rich, who, while enjoying the comforts of a competency, are forgetful of the continuous, persistent, hopeless, never-to-berelieved, and crushing poverty of the poor, with its inevitable accompaniments. The writer does not hesitate to affirm, that but for this sense of the insecurity of their means of living, and the mistaken notions which had been instilled into them in regard to the negroes and the object of this war, as increasing still further this insecurity-a deception to which their ignorance, the necessary result of their present pecuniary conditions, even were there no other causes for it, renders them at all times liable-they could not have been incited to the recent sedition..."[18]

The majority of congressional districts successfully used the bounty system to assist in fulfilling their quota via enlistments. The following is from the July 27th, 1863, issue of the *New York Times*: "There has been very little excitement about the draft for some days past, it being generally understood that the Common Council will make a sufficient appropriation to release all such as who do not wish to go by procuring substitutes. It is thought that the quota of Kings County can be raised by paying $300 bounty to each man..."[19] Thus, in some districts, local public funds were used to pay bounties. By defining one who accepted a bounty as an enlistee, it is estimated that a very small percentage of the Union soldiers — perhaps no more than 2% — were draftees.

Medical Deferments

Perceived differences in awarding medical deferments also existed during the Civil War. The following is from an article titled "From Chicago: The Labors of Logan and McLennan General News," published August 9th, 1863: "But when the draft comes [to Illinois], we suppose it [Camp Douglas] will be filled ... unless our Surgeons do, as those in Massachusetts have done, exempt nine-tenths of the conscripts. By the way isn't that scoundrelism? It is a sneaking way to defeat the draft meaner than your New York riots..."[20]

Conscientious Objection

The 1863 Enrollment Act did not include a provision for conscientious objection. The following is from the July 18th, 1863, issue of a Quaker sponsored publication *The Friend, A Religious and Literary Journal*. "As arrangements are now being made by the United States Government to carry into effect the Conscription Law, passed at the last session of Congress, it may be desirable to Friends to know something about the provisions of the law, and the course which it may be proper to take in claiming exemption from military service, on account of our long settled and well-known conscientious scruples against all war and fighting. The law requires the enrolment of all citizens, between 20 and 45 years of age; from among whom the draft is to be made. Exemption is granted to the only son of a widow, or of aged and infirm parents, dependent on him for support; the only brother of children not twelve years old, having no parents, and who are dependent on the brother for support; and the father of motherless children, dependent on him for their living..."[21]

The Quaker publication continued, "Where a Friend receives notice that he has been drafted ... he should appear before the provost marshal or board of enrolment ... state his conscientious scruple against all wars, and respectfully ask exemption ... It would seem a judicious and brotherly course for some suitable, prudent Friends to accompany the person thus appearing before the board..."[22]

Deserters

The May 28th, 1894, issue of the *New York Times*, published 29 years after the Civil War ended, reported that "one-third of the Union army deserted," and that some of them enlisted in the Confederate army. They argued that "the large bounties paid to recruits from 1863 to 1865, inclusive both encouraged and facilitated desertion..."[23]

"The States which gave the highest local bounties were marked by the largest proportion of deserters. The bounty was meant to be an inducement to enlistment, but it became, in fact, an inducement to desertion and fraudulent re-enlistment ... The number of drafted men actually held to service was only 52,068, but there were 75,429 conscripts who sent substitutes. Besides the substitutes there were 42,581 men who enlisted as substitutes for men who, although not drafted, were enrolled under the Conscription act, and were liable to future drafts, but who secured exemption there from by sending men to the field in their place. There were also 86,724 drafted men who received exemption upon the payment of $300 each in commutation..."[24]

World War I Draft

In April of 1917, the U.S. declared war on Germany. Efforts to convince U.S. residents to voluntarily join the war effort resulted in an insufficient number of volunteers to meet the planned requirements. To solve this, Congress passed, and President Wilson signed, the Selective Service Act of 1917. The Act contained three provisions included to avoid problems associated with the Enrollment Act of 1863. First, substitutes were not permitted. Second, potential draftees were not permitted to purchase an exemption. Third, the 1917 Act included a provision for conscientious objectors that said, if deemed credible upon being drafted, they were permitted to serve in non-combat positions.

In June of 1917, men aged 21 to 30 were required to register in their district.[25] My mother's father, who was born in Germany, was 36. My father's father, who was born in the U.S., was 35. Both exceeded the maximum age and thus, by the 1917 legislation, were not required to register. Each registrant was assigned a number by their local district office. On July 20th, 1917, a lottery was held in Washington. 10,500 numbers were drawn (selected), which exceeded the number registered in any one district. Orders to report were then based on the outcome of the lottery and the registrant's number. More than 5,000 local draft boards were established and given the authority to determine if the young man whose number had been drawn would be drafted or exempted.[26]

Military officials found that the age limit in the 1917 legislation restricted the number of young men that they could draft to less than the planned quantity of conscripts. In the summer of 1918, new legislation was prepared, and on August 31st, 1918, President Wilson signed a new military manpower bill that required registration of all men between the ages of 18 and 45.[27] Records indicate that my grandfather Henry Bruns registered on September 6th, 1918, and my grandfather John Epplin registered on September 12th, 1918.

Draftee

Henry T. Bruns Draft Registration Card, September 6, 1918

John Epplin Draft Registration Card, September 12, 1918

There were three rounds of draft registrations for World War I. The first began on June 5th, 1917, the second on June 5th, 1918, and the third on September 12th, 1918. Those whose religious views were contrary to violence were permitted to seek exclusion. Approximately 4,000 men were classified as conscientious objectors, though the number who applied for this status was much greater.

The draft was not met with universal support. For example, in August 1917, hundreds of poor Oklahomans, including whites, African Americans, and Native Americans, objected to the draft, which they characterized as conscripting the poor to fight to preserve the rich. They planned to display their objection by marching to Washington and eating roasted green corn along the march. Thus, the protest became known as the Green Corn Rebellion. Prior to the planned march, some members of the group were accused of burning bridges and cutting telegraph lines. The planned Green Corn Rebellion march was thwarted by local officials. At least three were killed and hundreds arrested with 150 sentenced to federal prison terms of up to 10 years.[28] [29] In 1935, William Cunningham published a fictionalized description of the revolt.[30]

Of the 4.8 million U.S. men who served during World War I, 2.8 million had been drafted. Over two million troops were transported to Europe. "The typical soldier was a drafted man between the ages of twenty-one and twenty-three; he was white, single, and poorly educated. 400,000 soldiers were black and roughly 18 percent of the soldiers were foreign-born..."[31]

Over 300,000 men illegally dodged the World War I draft. About 10,000 were prosecuted. Their appeals were consolidated into one case that was heard before the Supreme Court on January 7th, 1918 (Arver versus United States, No. 663).[32] The defendants argued that conscription was akin to slavery and that the federal government did not have the authority to force them to fight. The Court sided with President Wilson and found that the draft was legal. This was not the last time that the Supreme Court would have the opportunity to rule on Selective Service issues.

World War II Draft

After World War II began in Europe in 1939, a small group of influential private citizens, led by Grenville Clark, constructed a case for implementing a military draft in the U.S.[33] They feared that the U.S. military was not prepared to defend the country against a potential attack by Germany. In the absence of an attack and a declared war, President Roosevelt was reluctant to support draft legislation. He was more inclined to support a compulsory vocational training program to prepare young men to work in defense industries that could then produce war goods to be used by U.S. allies. He was also an astute politician, was facing an election in 1940, and understood that many of his supporters were isolationists.

Congressional support for a military draft was enhanced when the Republicans nominated Wendell Willkie to run against Roosevelt. Willkie affirmed his support for the Selective Service Act during his Republican nomination acceptance speech. He said, "I cannot ask the American people to put their faith in me without recording my conviction that some form of selective service is the only democratic way in which to secure the trained and competent manpower we need for national defense ... We must honestly face our relationship with Great Britain. We must admit that the loss of the British fleet would greatly weaken our defense. The Atlantic might be dominated by Germany. This would be a calamity for us. Also our foreign trade, vital to prosperity, would be profoundly affected..."[34]

The Selective Training and Service Act of 1940 was introduced by Democratic Senator Burke from Nebraska and Republican Congressman Wadsworth of New York. It was described as the nation's first peacetime draft. The legislation had bipartisan support. However, there was also bipartisan opposition, and the vote was not unanimous. Congressman Fish of New York proclaimed, "If peacetime conscription is adopted, we will have by a vote of Congress imported the very essence of Nazism and Hilterism into the United States."[35] During the congressional debate, the gallery was packed.

Citizen William Keneally of New York was removed from the gallery by officials after he shouted, "American conscription is American fascism."[36] In the Senate, 50 Democrats and 8 Republicans voted "aye," and 17 Democrats, 10 Republicans, 2 Farmer-Laborites, 1 Progressive and 1 Independent voted "nay."[37]

The debate was also lively and passionate in the House. Congressman Martin Sweeney, Democrat of Ohio, was seated next to Congressman Beverly Vincent, Democrat of Kentucky. Sweeney spoke against the bill and also condemned President Wilson for entering World War I. Vincent, who had served in World War I, remarked that he refused to continue to "sit by a traitor." Sweeny was incensed and threw a punch at Vincent. Vincent responded with a right to the jaw that was described as the best punch landed in the House in at least 50 years.[38] After order was restored, the vote was 263 for and 149 against: 211 Democrats and 52 Republicans voted "aye," 33 Democrats, 112 Republicans, 2 Progressives, 1 Farmer-Laborite and 1 American Laborite voted "no."[39]

The first peacetime draft legislation was approved by both houses of Congress more than 14 months prior to the Japanese attack on Pearl Harbor and signed into law by President Roosevelt on September 16th, 1940, 50 days before the U.S. presidential election, held on November 5th, 1940. Burke had lost his primary and was not up for reelection in 1940.

Draftee

Wadsworth was reelected to the House and served until his death in 1952.

During the campaign, in September 1940, Roosevelt's eldest son Elliot volunteered for service in the Army Air Corps and immediately received a captain's commission. Some draft-age Willkie supporters acquired and wore campaign buttons with the caption "I want to be a captain too."[40] President Roosevelt was reelected to an unprecedented third term.

My father, Michael Epplin, was 31 when he registered on October 16th, 1940. President Roosevelt addressed the nation on October 29th, 1940, the day prior to the first World War II Selective Service draft lottery as specified in the legislation: "Members of your government are gathered here in this Federal building in Washington to witness the drawing of numbers as provided for in the Selective Service Act of 1940. This is a most solemn ceremony. It is accompanied by no fanfare, no blowing of bugles or beating of drums, and there should be none. We are mustering all our resources, manhood and industry and wealth to make our nation strong in defense, for recent history proves all too clearly, I am sorry to say, that only the strong may continue to live in freedom and in peace. We are well aware of the circumstances, the tragic circumstances, in lands across the sea which have forced upon our nation the need to take measures of total defense..."[41]

Michael Epplin Draft Registration Card, October 16, 1940

President Roosevelt continued, "In the considered opinion of the Congress of the United States, this selective service

Draftee

provides the most democratic as well as the most efficient means for the mustering of our manpower. On October 16th, more than 16,000,000 young Americans registered for service. Today begins that selection from this huge number, the selection of 800,000 [5%] who will go into training for one year. Reports from all over the country attest the quality and the general spirit of the young men who registered for service. The young men of America today have thought this thing through. They have not been stimulated by or misled by militarist propaganda. They fully understand the necessity for national defense and are ready, as all citizens of our country must be, to play their part in it..."[42] Some young men did not agree with the President, some refused to register, and some were arrested for violating the Selective Service Act.[43]

Roosevelt continued: "I have here three letters. Because I believe that a great deal of the spiritual part of our natures is affected today, three letters from representatives of the three great faiths, Protestant and Jewish and Catholic. They were written to me in solemn recognition of this occasion and I want to read you brief excerpts from them..."[44] This speech was delivered one week prior to the 1940 election; President Roosevelt was running for his third term. He read letters from Dr. Buttrick, the president of the Federal Council of the Churches of Christ in America; Dr. Edward L. Israel, president of the Synagogue Council of America; and Catholic Bishop Francis J. Spellman.

Roosevelt continued, "I do believe it is better to have protection not needed than to need protection and not have it. I do believe that Americans want peace, but that we must be prepared to demand it. There are other people who have wanted peace and the peace they received was the peace of death. I do feel that our good-will and the sincerity of our desire for peace have been demonstrated by our action in sinking many battleships and that no more sincere demonstration of a willingness to lead the way toward universal disarmament could have been given by any people. But we really cannot longer afford to be moles, moles who cannot see or ostriches who will not see. For some solemn agreements are no longer sacred and vices have become virtues, and truth a synonym of falsehood. We Americans want peace and we shall prepare for a peace. But not for a peace whose definition is slavery or death..."[45]

The 1940 legislation required all men between 21 and 35 to register. If drafted and found to be qualified for service, the legislation specified 12 months of service. Service was limited to the Western Hemisphere, except for U.S. territories located elsewhere.

The 1940 act included a clause to account for and manage conscientious objection: "Nothing in this act shall be construed to require any person to be subject to combatant training and service in the land or naval forces of the United States, who, by reason of religious training and belief, is conscientiously opposed to participation in war in any form..."[46] Registrants could indicate their objection on the registration form. Local draft boards were assigned the task of determining the legitimacy of their claim. If the claim was adjudicated to be legitimate, depending on the type of objection, the claimant could be drafted and assigned to either a noncombat job in an unarmed unit or a medical unit. Some objectors were assigned to and served in civilian public service camps.[47]

The volunteer members of local draft boards were assigned the responsibility of classifying each registrant based on less-than-precise criteria provided by federal authorities. Lobbying for exemptions was intense. University presidents lobbied for exemptions for students. Farm organizations argued for exemptions for farmers and farm workers. Businesses lobbied for exemptions for workers in critical industries. Many groups, and perhaps most members of local boards, were inclined to defer married men.[48] [49] Marriage rates per thousand population increased from 10.7 in 1939, to 12.1 in 1940 and 13.2 in 1942.[50]

Less than two weeks after the Japanese bombed Pearl Harbor, the Draft Act of 1942 was signed on December 20th, 1941. It amended the Selective Service Act of 1940 by requiring that all men from 18 to 64 register.[51] Those between the ages of 20 and 44 were liable for military service. The 12-month and Western Hemisphere limits that were included in the 1940 Act were removed.

My grandfather John Epplin was 60 and my grandfather Henry Bruns was 61 when they registered on April 27th, 1942. They were included in the group of more than 13 million men between the ages of 45 and 64 who registered on April 25th, 26th, and 27th in 1942.[52] The purpose of the 1942 registration was to provide the government with an inventory of skills and experience. These 45–64 year old men were not liable under the law to provide combat service.

Francis Epplin

John Epplin Draft Registration Card, April 27, 1942

Draftee

Henry T. Bruns Draft Registration Card, April 27, 1942

Post World War II Draft

The Selective Service Act of 1948 served as the base legislation for drafting men after World War II. "The President is authorized from time to time, whether or not a state of war exists, to select and induct into the armed forces of the United States for training and service ... such number of persons as may be required to provide and maintain the personnel strengths ... of the respective armed forces..."[53]

The 1948 Act was originally intended to remain in effect for two years (until June 24th, 1950), but was extended multiple times — usually immediately before its two-year period of effectiveness was due to expire. The last group of young men drafted into the U.S. military reported for duty in June 1973. Dwight Elliot Stone was drafted in 1972, but he was not required to report for service until June 30th, 1973.[54] Mr. Stone became known as the last draftee prior to the 1973 transition to an all-volunteer military.

Reforms during the Vietnam War

History informs that a drafting system that selects some and exempts others can easily be criticized for a lack of fairness, especially by those selected. A potential draftee's attitude toward conscription may be similar to a potential taxpayer's attitude regarding taxes. The word "select" may be substituted for the word "tax" in the old ditty. Don't select you, don't select me, select the person behind the tree.[55]

In 1967, there were 18 registration categories, ranging from Class I-A (available for military service) to Class V-A (registrant over the age of liability for military service). There were six categories for the order of call of those in the I-A category. Some potential draftees avoided military service by serving in civilian occupations categorized as critical that, in 1967, included dozens of occupations, such as astronomer and patternmaker. Others proposed to their local board that they were serving in "essential" civilian positions and should not be drafted. In 1967, many civilian jobs were considered to be essential, including, for example, operations of water and sewerage systems. Local draft boards had the power to grant exemptions. An 80-page handbook, produced by the Engineering Manpower Commission of Engineers Joint Council, included forms that potential draftees and their employers could use to attempt to persuade a local board that a young man's civilian occupation was either critical or essential.[56]

In addition to suggested form letters that could be customized to explain a specific situation to the local board, there were several official forms: AFR 45-31 (format for requesting delay), DA 591 (application for delay for educational purposes), SSS Form 104 (request for undergraduate student deferment), SSS Form 109 (student certificate), SSS Form 103 (graduate or professional college student certificate), and DA Form 1140 and DA Form 1140-1 (army reserve qualifications questionnaire and status verification questionnaire). The decision as to whether to select or not to select was left to the discretion of the local draft board. If the local board was not swayed to exempt, a potential well-informed draftee could appeal to an appeal board, and if necessary, to the National Selective Service Appeal Board.

Local boards made the decision. A request to be deferred could be accepted by one board, whereas a nearly identical situation for another potential draftee could be rejected by another board elsewhere. The lack of consistency provided fuel for those who objected to the system.

President Johnson inherited the military draft policies and procedures that were in place when he became President. The most recent extension of the 1948 legislation enabling the draft was due to expire July 1st, 1967.[57] As with most, if not all, prior U.S. military drafts, the draft, as being conducted in 1966, was not fair. The use of a lottery had been discontinued after the U.S. entered World War II. All men were required to register at age 18 and selection was determined by a local draft board.

Any objective observer could easily ascertain that the selection system that had evolved in the years after World War II was problematic. Draft boards across the country were not consistent in awarding deferments. Deferring college students to study English literature but not deferring young men working as apprentices to learn building trades was not fair. Enabling those with wealth and political connections to enlist in the National Guard, allowing them to avoid service in Vietnam, was not fair. Enabling some to have their paid family doctor submit a report declaring them unfit for service and forcing others with less wealth and influence, and perhaps less healthy, to be examined by a physician at an Armed Forces Entrance Examining Station was not fair. Some considered exempting women to be unfair.

President Johnson was aware of the unfairness of the system. He was diplomatic in his call for action. He attributed the unfairness to the fact that the number of draft age men exceeded the number needed to be drafted. He said, "Fairness has always been one of the goals of the Selective Service System. When the present Act was passed in 1948, one of its underlying assumptions was that the obligation and benefits of military service would be equitably borne..."[58]

On July 2nd, 1966, Johnson "appointed a National Advisory Commission on Selective Service, composed of 20 citizens, distinguished and diverse in their representation of important elements of our national life..." Based on the findings of the Commission, President Johnson reported on March 6th, 1967, "I am instructing the Director of Selective Service, working in collaboration with the Secretary of Defense, to develop a Fair And Impartial Random (FAIR) system of selection to become fully operational before January 1st, 1969. This system will determine the order of call for induction of qualified and available 19-year-olds and older men as their deferments expire..."[59]

Johnson's commission recommended a draft lottery. However, in June of 1967, a sufficient number of Representatives and Senators did not support a lottery. Since the end of World War II, the draft system had evolved so that if they chose to do so, those with wealth and political connections could find legal and politically acceptable ways to avoid service in the combat arms. The Senators and Representatives understood that quick implementation of a fairer system would make it more difficult for their sons, nephews, and the sons of their donors to find an acceptable alternative.[60] Rejecting Johnson's lottery plan in 1967 would keep the existing system in place and provide more time for favored constituents to find an alternative. For example, they might be able to negotiate a slot in the National Guard. At the time, National Guard units were not sent to Vietnam.[61]

In a major setback for President Johnson, the Military Selective Service Act of 1967 prohibited a draft lottery without Congressional approval in the form of new legislation.[62] On June 30th, 1967, President Johnson signed a four-year extension of the draft and an executive order to implement it. The legislation thwarted Johnson's plan to reform the system and implement a lottery.

Reform was delayed until November 19th, 1969, when Congress passed, and President Nixon signed, a one-sentence bill that repealed the provision in the 1967 law that prohibited the President from using a random selection system for drafting men.[63] President Nixon signed the bill on November 26th, 1969. On the same day, President Nixon also signed an executive order implementing the lottery system. The first Vietnam era draft lottery was held on December 1st, 1969.[64]

Chapter 44

Paving the Way to an All-Volunteer Force

"We're committed to eliminating unnecessary formations, skin-head haircuts, signing out, signing in, bed checks, and 'make work' projects."

In March of 1969, two months after his inauguration, President Nixon appointed a 15-member committee to develop a plan to transition from the draft to an all-volunteer force. On February 21st, 1970, the Gates Commission, as it became to be known, presented "The Report of the President's Commission on an All-Volunteer Armed Force."[1] The commission presented a framework for transitioning to an all-volunteer military that President Nixon strove to implement. In January of 1973, Defense Secretary Melvin Laird announced the end of the military draft. Men born after 1952 were not subject to being conscripted.[2] The last group of men drafted into the U.S. military reported for duty in June 1973. President Nixon's legal authority to draft expired on June 30th, 1973. He did not request an extension.[3] With the expiration of legal authority to draft, President Nixon presided over the transition to an all-volunteer military.

The transition to an all-volunteer force was facilitated by a number of changes in addition to the reduction of U.S. involvement in Vietnam. Congress agreed to increasing pay, paying enlistment bonuses, and advertising.[4] Substantial quantities were invested in advertising often associated with sporting events, such as National Football League games. Pay for privates was increased more than 260%, from $124.50 per month for an entering private when I was drafted in 1970, to $326.10 per month in 1974.[5] [6]

Pay increases were supplemented with a number of other changes. An Army advertisement to attract volunteers included: "We're committed to eliminating unnecessary formations, skin-head haircuts, signing out, signing in, bed checks, and 'make work' projects..."[7] Cafeteria services and grounds maintenance were contracted out to civilian companies, freeing recruits from routine KP and grounds policing. Most training on Saturdays and Sundays was discontinued. Ward barracks were replaced with semi-private rooms.[8] An Entry Level Separation (ELS) policy was implemented.[9] [10] Volunteers who had been in the military for fewer than 180 days could, with the assistance of an accommodating commander, opt out of their military contract and return to civilian life with no repercussions.[11] In 1993 and 1994, 15% of Army volunteers separated in the first six months.[12]

Legislation also mandated that when necessitated to meet emergencies, the military would be required to activate the Reserves and the National Guard prior to reinstating a draft.[13] Enlistment in the National Guard could no longer be used as a hedge to protect from foreign service.

When the draft was discontinued in 1973, registration of 18-year-old males was no longer required. However, in response to the 1980 Soviet Union invasion of Afghanistan, President Carter issued Proclamation 4771 that reinstated the requirement that all male U.S. citizens and male immigrants, who were 18 through 25, register with the Selective Service System.[14] Failure to register was a felonious offense punishable by a fine of up to $250,000 and/or a prison term of five years.[15] By policy, the birth date lottery machines were to be maintained and routinely tested.[16] [17]

The registration system was designed to be a passive process requiring little thought and little effort. In many states, some registration was facilitated by requiring male state driver's license applicants to check a box following fine print on the state driver's license application form.[18] [19] [20] The cooperating government agencies then provided the information to the Selective Service System, and the licensed driver was officially registered.[21]

UNITED STATES SELECTIVE SERVICE REGISTRATION

In accordance with Federal Law, any male United States citizen or immigrant who is at least 18 years of age but less than 26 years of age must register with Selective Service. You must be registered to qualify for Federal student aid (to include Pell Grant), job training, Federal employment, and citizenship, if an immigrant. In Texas, you must be registered to qualify for state college student aid or state employment. If convicted, failure to register with Selective Service is a felony punishable by up to five years in prison and/or a $250,000 fine. If not registered by age 26, you can no longer register and could permanently lose those benefits associated with registration.

All <u>male</u> applicants from the age of 18 but less than 26 years of age are required to provide a response to this form as part of the application process.

Would you like to register with the United States Selective Service System?

By providing an affirmative response, you are consenting to registration with the Selective Service System.

By providing a negative response, you <u>WILL NOT</u> be registering with the Selective Service System.

*****Please verify your response as recorded on your receipt*****

DL-15 (1/03)

Part of Texas Driver's License Application Form[22]

Some registered when they applied for federal financial college aid.[23] Others, more aware of the requirement and after the development of the internet, registered online.[24] Young men

Draftee

who did not register were not eligible to receive federal student aid and were restricted from applying for a federal job. The Selective Service System estimated that 91% of young men between the ages of 18 and 26 (16,417,042) who were required to be registered in 2019 were registered. Most were registered via the various states driver's license application programs and the federal government's student aid application program.[25] Based on the estimate, more than 1.5 million young men failed to register. The reasons for failing to register are not known. By law, these 1.5 million would be subject to a fine of up to $250,000 and/or a prison term of five years. However, from 1980 to 2018, only 20 men were charged with refusing to register for the draft, and only 14 (less than 0.4 per year) were convicted.[26][27]

For most men under age 26 who did not desire a driver's license, did not seek student aid and loans, and had no interest in employment with the federal government, the data suggests a high probability of zero consequences for failing to register. The percentage of 18-year-olds who were licensed drivers declined from 80.4% in 1983 to 65.4% in 2008.[28] Men younger than 26 who had not registered were permitted to register when and if they chose to apply for a federal job. Men older than 26 who did not register were prevented from applying for a federal government job.

Given that almost 10% failed to register, even when the likelihood of a draft and the cost for registration approached zero, in the event of a national emergency justifying a draft, a much greater percentage may refuse to register.

Chapter 45

Economists and the Draft

"I don't like to hear our patriotic draftees
referred to as slaves."

The theory of market economics is straightforward. If markets are successful, resources, such as labor, will flow to their best use. Potential workers will be free to choose among alternatives. Those individuals for which military service is the best alternative will choose military service. No coercion is required. At some wage rate, the number of workers required by the military will be equal to the number of potential workers (soldiers) who freely choose to work for the military. Conscription is less economically efficient. A draft fails to enable workers to find their comparative advantage and fails to enable workers, and the economy at large, to benefit from specialization. A draft imposes a cost, an in-kind tax, on those who have the alternative of earning a higher wage. One complicating factor is that Congress must approve the wage rate.

With an all-volunteer force, one would freely choose to work as a soldier rather than choosing an alternative, such as working as a butcher at a chicken processing plant, at a school as a teacher, for a business as an accountant, or manager, roofer, plumber, or truck driver. Those for which working as a soldier is the best choice will freely volunteer. The draft enabled the government to employ most of the draftees at a wage lower than what they could have earned in a civilian job, thereby imposing an in-kind tax. The extra funding required to support the higher salaries, bonuses, and more costly amenities required to support an all-volunteer system, must be procured with a tax that presumably is more equitably acquired.[1]

In a 1956 letter to the editor of the *New York Times*, economist John Kenneth Galbraith argued that "the draft survives principally as a device by which we use compulsion to get young men to serve at less than the market rate of pay. We shift the cost of military service from the well-to-do taxpayer, who benefits by lower taxes to the impecunious young draftee. This is a highly regressive arrangement which we would not tolerate in any other area. Presumably freedom of choice here as elsewhere would be worth paying for..."[2] In other words, young, and often poor, men were being oppressed. The draft was a subtle form of transferring wealth from the poor to the rich.

During the Vietnam War, a number of prominent economists, including University of Chicago Economics Professor Milton Friedman, who cited Galbraith, proposed abolishing the draft, as it was being implemented at the time, and transitioning to an all-volunteer military. In a 1967 opinion article published in the *New York Times*, Friedman presented a case for replacing the draft with an all-volunteer force.[3] He argued that economists across the political spectrum found that the draft, as being conducted in 1967, was inequitable, wasteful, undesirable, and unnecessary. The draft was an affront to market economics, the citizen's freedom of choice, and coercion by the state, resulting in the loss of liberty.

In 1969, North Carolina Congressman Lennon articulated

pro-draft sentiments in a speech on the floor of the U.S. House: "Mr. Chairman, the overriding argument against an all-volunteer force for me, and I think this would be true for virtually all members of the committee, is the consideration of morality. As I said, those who attack the inequities of the draft never seem to be bothered about the inequity of an all-volunteer force. But the questions of morality involved are considerable. For the life of me, I cannot see why it would be more equitable to excuse some men from any obligation to their country as long as we can spend enough dollars to buy this service from somebody else. It sounds very nice to say 'all volunteer army'; it does not sound nearly as nice to say 'mercenary army,' but really it says the same thing. Our government would be in a morally untenable position if its international policies in defense of freedom were in any way equated with the ability to buy sufficient forces. Many of those who are criticizing the draft, are also criticizing the government and its involvement in Vietnam. How much more temptation would there be to get involved in what some people call 'international adventures' if we had an all-professional army? You will recall that the Senate, in rejecting the FDL — fast deployment logistic ships — concept, said that it would encourage us to act like policemen to the world. How much more ready might we be to act like policemen of the world; how much less would be the call for restraint if we had an all-volunteer army?"[4]

An exchange that occurred between Professor Friedman and U.S. Army General William Westmoreland has frequently been quoted. In response to a question about an all-volunteer army, General Westmoreland said he did not want to command an army of mercenaries. Dr. Friedman interrupted, "General, would you rather command an army of slaves?"

Mr. Westmoreland replied, "I don't like to hear our patriotic draftees referred to as slaves."

Draftee

Dr. Friedman then retorted, "I don't like to hear our patriotic volunteers referred to as mercenaries. If they are mercenaries, then I, sir, am a mercenary professor, and you, sir, are a mercenary general; we are served by mercenary physicians, we use a mercenary lawyer, and we get our meat from a mercenary butcher..."[5] Perhaps General Westmoreland should have reminded Professor Friedman that there is a national holiday for military veterans, but none for retired professors.

President Nixon appointed both Friedman and economist Alan Greenspan (who later served as Chairman of the Federal Reserve) to the Gates Commission assigned to evaluate consequences of transitioning to an all-volunteer armed force. Both men were celebrated for their powers of persuasion. The economists were heard. The text of the commission's final report includes a chapter titled "Conscription is a Tax."[6] Friedman was a consistent and persistent critic of the draft. He and, to a lesser extent, Galbraith, along with other economists, are credited with providing the Gates Commission, and thereby the Nixon administration, with a strong justification for elimination of the U.S. military draft in 1973. Congressman Lennon and General Westmoreland lost the argument.

If the market for military labor is successful, then the all-volunteer force will be more economically efficient than a draft. There are several issues that could, to use a President Nixon phrase, "throw a monkey wrench" into the market such that it will fail to achieve the most efficient outcome. Recognizing the potential for the market to fail to achieve an efficient outcome substantially complicates the model.

One potential problem is information asymmetry. If the employer (the demander) has more information about the job than the potential worker (the supplier), the worker may freely accept an incorrect (inefficient) wage and make an incorrect job choice. A change implemented after the introduction of the all-volunteer force has the potential to reduce the asymmetric information problem. The Entry Level Separation (ELS) policy enables volunteers who have been in the military for fewer than 180 days, with the assistance of an accommodating commander, to opt out of their military contract and return to civilian life with no repercussions.[7] In 1993 and 1994, 15% of Army volunteers separated in the first six months.[8] For an all-volunteer force, the ELS policy mitigates information asymmetry. However, an economist would expect many draftees to petition for early separation. An effort to reintroduce a military draft could be expected to include changes to the ELS policy.

A second issue that could throw a monkey wrench into the efficiency argument for the military labor market is the existence of externalities. That is, if the hiring of one military worker rather than another potential worker impacts a third party or business other than the worker and the military. Businesses that sell to the military are third parties. Recall President Eisenhower's farewell address: "We have been compelled to create a permanent armaments industry of vast proportions ... In the councils of government, we must guard against the acquisition of unwarranted influence, whether sought or unsought, by the military-industrial complex..."[9]

One potential issue with an all-volunteer system, especially when combined with an up (be promoted) or out (lose your job) policy, is that there are built-in penalties and few, if any, incentives for reporting activities, including waste and corruption, that reflect poorly on the military. A fully-professional, volunteer-only military is incentivized to extract funds from taxpayers. It is facilitated in this activity by private sector defense contractors.

Lucrative positions as employees of defense contractors are more likely for military retirees who, while serving, did not rock the boat. Coyne et al. explain that "U.S. military contracting has been plagued by systematic corruption, fraud, and waste ... These outcomes result from the inherent features of the US military sector which incentivize unproductive entrepreneurship..."[10]

For a specific, entertaining (but frustrating) example, see *The Pentagon Wars* by James G. Burton, in which Burton describes billions of dollars in cost legally transferred from citizens through taxation to the federal treasury, and eventually to defense contractors.[11]

Another complicating issue is that since most U.S. representatives and senators have not served in the military, most are reluctant to voice any criticism. Most would vote to support any type of military expenditures that would flow to their district, even if the expenditure was an obvious waste. Any vote to not support appropriations to the military is likely to be characterized by an opponent in a future election as a failure to support the troops.[12] [13]

President Obama surmised that "'there is yet another dimension to the AVF (all-volunteer force) that is truly an unmentionable ... There is a bias in this town [Washington, D.C.] toward war...' What the president meant was quite clear: powerful forces, such as the military-industrial complex, a less-than-courageous Congress that has abandoned its constitutional duty with respect to the war power, extreme ideologies, and a nation with no skin in the game, work together to persuade all presidents to consider war as the first instrument of national power rather than the last..."[14] [15]

The Afghanistan Papers published by the *Washington Post* in 2019 reported that a forensic evaluation of $106 billion in 2010–2012 military contracts funded to assist in Afghanistan found that about 40% of the funds ended up in the pockets of insurgents, criminal syndicates, or corrupt Afghan officials.[16] [17]

The all-volunteer military incentive structure is for volunteers to keep quiet.

On April 6th, 2020, acting Navy secretary Thomas Modly spoke to the all-volunteer sailors stationed on the USS Theodore Roosevelt aircraft carrier. He explained why he relieved Captain Brett Crozier from command. The Captain, according to Modly, did not follow the proper chain of command in requesting assistance for sailors on the ship suffering from the potentially deadly COVID-19 virus. Modly explained to the volunteers, "That's your duty. Not to complain..."[18] By firing Crozier, Modly reinforced that complaints of any type, even those made in an attempt to save lives, are not good for enhancing a military career. If it is a soldier's duty to not complain about proliferation of a life-threatening disease, would it not also be a duty to ignore waste, fraud, and corruption?

Thus, one potential externality argument is that a volunteer may be more likely to go along to get along, and thus, be more likely to turn a blind eye to activities that inappropriately benefit a third party, such as a defense contractor. Whereas a draftee who has no interest in a military career, or with potential future employment with an interdependent entity, is less likely to be reticent about reporting waste and cases of widespread sickness. Draftees have less incentive to conceal obvious corruption. The economic value of one courageous whistleblower could be sufficient to cover the deadweight losses of hundreds of draftees.[19] However, historically, neither draftees nor volunteers were incentivized to report corruption. Elected federal officials and senior military leaders did not provide a routine procedure for doing so.

If draftees were drawn randomly from the population, some would be brilliant, some would have an abundance of common sense, and during their term of service, may discern

Draftee

more efficient systems. However, in addition to the potential external benefits, there are potential external costs that could result from the loss of productivity if those drafted had remained in the private sector. Time lost in the private sector may reduce inventions and productivity-enhancing contributions of the draftees. Ideas may be lost forever, or simply delayed. On the other hand, military time and experience may serve to incubate new ideas that could produce benefits after separation. Of course, if the draftee is killed, all potential contributions may be lost. Indeed, considering the potential for the market to fail to achieve an economically efficient outcome complicates the model.

Another potential external benefit of a truly random draft is that it facilitates citizens to meet and work with people outside their tribe. That is, the hiring of one military worker rather than another potential worker may impact a future unrelated business transaction. Many draftees in World War II and Vietnam were introduced to and learned to cooperate with fellow soldiers from different parts of the country, different ethnic backgrounds, different prior educational experiences, different political persuasions, and different family and religious traditions. Perhaps this was of no consequence for the wellbeing of the Country. On the other hand, it may have contributed to the level of civility among members of what became known as the greatest generation.

The Iwo Jima flag raisers that are immortalized in the iconic monument displayed in Arlington County, Virginia, provide an example of the diversity of those who served during World War II. Those associated with the monument included Harlon Block, Rio Grande Valley, Texas; Jack Bradley, Appleton, Wisconsin; Rene Gagnon, Manchester, New Hampshire; Ira Hayes, Gila River Indian Reservation, Arizona; Franklin Sousley, Hilltop, Kentucky; Mike Strank, Franklin Borough,

Pennsylvania; Harold Keller, Brooklyn, Iowa; and Harold Schultz of Los Angeles, California (originally from Detroit, Michigan). They were from different ethnic backgrounds. Mike Strank was an immigrant from Czechoslovakia. Rene Gagnon was the son of French-Canadian mill workers. Ira Hayes was a Pima Indian. The soldiers had different religious traditions. Harlon Block was a Seventh-day Adventist. Mike Strank was a Catholic. Harold Keller was a Methodist. Unfortunately, several, including Sergeant Michael Strank, Corporal Harlon Block, and Private First Class Franklin Sousley, were killed in action during the war.

In 1978, 81 of the 100 U.S. senators were military veterans. On April 18th, 1978, 68 senators — 15 Republicans and 53 Democrats — voted for final approval of the treaties that facilitated transfer of the control and management of the Panama Canal to the host country. Two of the Republican Senators, Henry Bellmon of Oklahoma and Mark Hatfield of Oregon, served in World War II. Both spent time at Iwo Jima and may have crossed paths with one or more of the Iwo Jima flag raisers. Bellmon was a marine tank platoon leader who participated in the amphibious landing on Iwo Jima. 9 of the 32 men in his platoon were killed, 10 suffered severe physical injuries, and two suffered severe mental injuries.[20] Mark Hatfield was a Navy landing craft officer at Iwo Jima and was among the first Americans to see Hiroshima, Japan, after the atom bomb blast.[21]

Prior to the vote, Bellmon addressed his Senate colleagues. He was brief. He explained that he "thought we should treat the Panamanians the way we would want to be treated..." Bellmon obviously knew the Christian Golden Rule as reported in Matthew 7:12: "Do to others whatever you would have them do to you."[22]

In his autobiography, Bellmon wrote, "I am afraid that

American servicemen and their families will have a difficult time maintaining a strong fighting spirit when the purpose for their sacrifice is basically commercial. It is difficult to develop a rallying cry around the concept of 'Whip the Panamanians and keep cheap freight..."[23]

Bellmon also wrote, "It is a perversion of the public trust for an elected official to act against the public interest in order to retain office. Legislators who claim to always do their constituents' will are, in effect, trying to follow rather than lead..."

Henry Bellmon and Mark Hatfield both witnessed the carnage of war. No doubt, their lives were changed as a result, and their votes in the Senate were influenced by what they saw. Compare their rhetoric with that of movie actor Ronald Reagan, who fought in imaginary battles with make-believe weapons and fake blood. In Reagan's wars, all killed rose from the dead after the scripted scene. During his campaign against Gerald Ford for the 1976 Republican presidential nomination, he often repeated his mantra: "We bought [the Canal]. We paid for it. It's ours, and we aren't going to turn it over to some tinhorn dictator..."[24] Unlike Bellmon and Hatfield's real war, in which real people bled and died, in Reagan's imaginary wars, those "killed" and "maimed" were instantly "healed" after the scene. They were free to return to their family and later return to the movie studio to fight and win or lose another fictitious glorious battle.

The transition of canal management to Panama ran smoothly, averted a potential military conflict, potentially saving many lives and billions of taxpayer dollars, averted what would have been an effective anti-U.S. colonialist argument by adversaries, and created a stable environment that facilitated improvements enabling passage of more efficient, larger ships. Over the long term, after most of the 68 who voted for the treaties in 1978 have died, U.S. consumers and businesses benefit from the increased efficiency in transportation.[25] Some would dismiss it as foolish to attribute any of these monetary benefits to the existence of a military draft during World War II. There is no standard quantifiable measure of the level of civility and bipartisanship, but there are numerous examples of bipartisan legislation that was passed by Senators and Representatives during times when a greater proportion had experienced military service and during a time when a draft was in effect.

Economists who are biased toward laissez-faire capitalism may be biased toward downplaying the existence of, and potential negative consequences of, market failures. Economists who are more inclined to acknowledge and recognize market failures are hampered because the modeling is more complicated. Also, they may be accused of invoking market failure as a crutch to apply, as the market success solution is inconsistent with their preconceived bias.

Israel drafts Jewish men and women over the age of 18. In discussing the external consequences of the draft, Michael Eisenberg, co-founder of an Israeli venture capital fund, explains that "we're forcing kids to sacrifice on behalf of something greater than themselves. And that creates an esprit de corps, that creates patriotism, that creates comradery and collaboration that I think is missing in a lot of places. And, I think it creates a force and an empowering force in an economy of mutual responsibility to empower other people to be successful as well..."[26]

In discussions of the evils of a military draft, economics textbooks do not mention the potential external benefit of enhanced national civility. Instead, they champion the liberty of personal choice associated with an all-volunteer military. But it could be hypothesized that by purchasing an all-volunteer

Draftee

army, the U.S. transitioned from a citizenry that honored civility, public service, and the citizen soldier, to one that glorifies freeloading, promotes selfishness, facilitates tribalism, and ignores the overall economic efficiency of military service alternatives.

Chapter 46

Push Back

"Even the hard-pressed young proved increasingly difficult to recruit."

The views of many military and elected public officials may be summarized by the following statement. "By many accounts, the All-Volunteer Force (AVF) has been a great success. It has provided the military with high-quality personnel and has proven effective in both peace and war. Military leaders, politicians and the American people themselves all prefer it to the alternative. It is here to stay..."[1]

Critics of the all-volunteer force exist. Ackerman has argued that the all-volunteer army increases militarization. On the other hand: "A draft places militarism on a leash."[2] "With a draft, the barrier to entering new wars would be significantly higher..." Approximately $6 trillion of the U.S. national debt was borrowed from future generations for post-September 11th, 2001, wars.[3] After the World Trade Center and Pentagon attacks, U.S. taxpayers were not asked to pay to confront enemies. They were not asked to send their children to fight. The all-volunteer military, combined with a borrow and spend philosophy, provided U.S. officials with a blank check to conduct war and transfer the cost to future generations.

Draftee

As long as their children were not required to fight and their taxes were not raised to pay for the war, citizens were relatively content to let the volunteers do the fighting and to let their grandchildren pay for it. President Bush suggested that citizens "get down to Disney World in Florida."[4] Not everybody could afford to visit Disney World, but most could wave flags, sing the national anthem, recite the pledge, and greet veterans with a "thank you for your service." Relative to Vietnam, there were few public antiwar (or was it antidraft?) protests. Americans showed strong support for the military.

"Andrew Bacevich, a former army officer, academic and longstanding critic of what he terms the militarism of American society, derides that support as 'superficial and fraudulent.' Sanctified by politicians and the public, he argues, the army's top brass have been given too much power and too little scrutiny, with the recent disastrous campaigns, and similarly profligate appropriations, the almost inevitable result..."[5] Bacevich argues that elimination of the draft and transferring the monetary cost of military operations to the future served to disconnect the vast majority of citizens from the military. Relative to past generations, citizens had much less skin in the game.

Appy reported that "even the hard-pressed young proved increasingly difficult to recruit. Simply to replenish its ranks the military had to increase its recruitment budget from $3.7 billion in 2004 to $7.7 billion in 2008."[6] The all-volunteer military is expensive; most elected officials have not served and most choose to ignore the cost.[7]

Laich and Wilkerson conclude that "recruiting and retaining the force has become far too costly and is ultimately unsustainable ... after 16 years of war it is plain to all but the most recalcitrant that the U.S. cannot afford the AVF — ethically, morally, or fiscally. Fiscally, the AVF is going to break the bank ... the recruiting and retention process and rich pay and allowances are consuming one half of the Army's entire annual budget slice, precluding any sort of affordable increase in its end strength..."

They continue: "A more serious challenge ... is the ethical one ... 1 percent is bleeding and dying for the other 99 percent ... Said more explicitly, if the sons and daughters of members of Congress, of the corporate leadership, of the billionaire class, of the Ivy Leagues, of the elite in general, were exposed to the possibility of combat, would we have less war? From a socio-economic class perspective, the AVF is inherently unfair..."[8]

In other words, a President, Congressman, or Senator may be expected to be more likely to support engagement in military conflicts if the military does not directly include his or her children and grandchildren. In 2018, President Trump allegedly referred to the more than 1,800 U.S. soldiers buried at the Aisne-Marne American Cemetery near Paris as "losers" and "suckers" for being killed in the World War I battle at Belleau Wood.[9] Perhaps he did not understand that most did not have wealthy parents who could protect them from being drafted.

The likelihood that the children and grandchildren of elected officials would be in the military is expected to be greater under a fairly-conducted draft than with an AVF. In the language of economics, the elected officials are third parties who are incentivized to vote for military appropriations.[10][11] The old political requirement of preventing a communist takeover of a country on one's watch has morphed into support the troops and support the local defense contractor. The support the troops rhetoric is reinforced by defense contractors. Since volunteers are less likely to rock the boat and have zero incentive to report graft, corruption, and malfeasance, it is increasingly difficult to heed President Eisenhower's warning to "guard against the acquisition of unwarranted influence, whether sought or unsought, by the military-industrial complex."[12]

Most criticism of the all-volunteer military has fallen on deaf ears. A single Congressman, Charles Rangel, a Korean War veteran, who represented districts in New York from 1971 to 2017, expressed opposition to the all-volunteer army. He opined that the President and Congress would be less inclined to war if there was a chance that their children might be required to serve. He argued that President Bush and his administration would not have ordered the military invasion of Iraq in 2003 if children from their families would have been required to serve. During his time in Congress, Rangel introduced legislation to reinstate a draft seven times. His proposed legislation came up for a vote in the full House once in 2004. It was defeated 2–402. The U.S. Congress was in no mood to implement a military draft.[13] [14]

While they were not supportive of implementing a draft, they were also not in the mood to discontinue the requirement that young men register with the Selective Service System. Over the years, several bills were introduced in the U.S. House of Representatives to repeal the Selective Service Act. Examples include 103 H.R. 2513 and 105 H.R. 2421 by Fortney Stark of California in 1994 and 1997, 108 H.R. 487 by Ronald Paul of Texas in 2003, 114 H.R. 4523 by Mike Coffman of Colorado in 2016, and 116 H.R.5492 by Peter DeFazio of Oregon in 2019. On April 14th, 2021, Representative Peter DeFazio introduced H.R. 2509, the Selective Service Repeal Act, in the House.[15] On April 15th, 2021, Senator Ron Wyden introduced S 1139, the Selective Service Repeal Act of 2021, in the Senate. [16] On September 28, 2021, Representative Owens, Burgess introduced H.R.5392 to amend the Military

Selective Service Act to allow women to elect to register for the draft.[17] In each case, the proposed legislation was referred to a committee where it was left to "die."

Chapter 47

Flawed Plans to Revise the Selective Service System

"The highest income level found a doctor that would say they had a bone spur."

Ackerman proposed what he called a "reverse-engineered draft: those whose families fall into the top income tax bracket would be the only ones eligible..." In Ackerman's plan, all children of families in the top one percent of wealth or income would be drafted and assigned only to specialties within the combat arms — infantry, artillery and armor.[1] It is not clear what measure of wealth or income Ackerman would use. The ability of the ultra-wealthy to manipulate and intimidate government officials may make it difficult to implement his plan.[2] Economists would expect that the wealthy would simply purchase citizenship from some other country for anyone they wanted to shield.[3]

In 2017, U.S. Senators John McCain and Jack Reed championed the establishment of a bipartisan commission to conduct a comprehensive review of military, national, and public service.[4] The Commission released their final report in 2020. The report included 49 recommendations. The first recommendation was that Congress appropriate $450 million per year for civic education and service. The 49th recommendation, and the one that received the most press, was that Selective

Service registration requirements be expanded to require women, as well as men, to register.

Historically, women were not required to register and were not drafted. In 1981, several men filed a lawsuit labeled "Rostker versus Goldberg," alleging that the Military Selective Service Act violated the Due Process Clause of the Fifth Amendment by requiring that only men, and not women, register.[5] The Supreme Court eventually upheld the Act, stating that the "decision to exempt women was not the accidental byproduct of a traditional way of thinking about women," that "since women are excluded from combat service by statute or military policy, men and women are simply not similarly situated for purposes of a draft or registration for a draft, and Congress' decision to authorize the registration of only men therefore does not violate the Due Process Clause," and that "the argument for registering women was based on considerations of equity, but Congress was entitled, in the exercise of its constitutional powers, to focus on the question of military need, rather than equity..." In stating as much, in 1981, the Supreme Court officially recognized that the requirement that only men register with the Selective Service System was unequal, but that the military had the right to enforce this inequality.[6]

The decision was based in part on the Congressional policy at the time that excluded women from combat service. In 2013, the policy that excluded women from combat was rescinded. Thus, it was not surprising that on February 22nd, 2019, U.S. District Court Judge Gray Miller, in Southern Texas, ruled in National Coalition for Men versus Selective Service System that exempting females from the male-only draft was unconstitutional.[7] [8] [9] He ruled that requiring men, but not women, to register violated the Due Process Clause of the Fifth Amendment to the United States Constitution, since the restrictions on women serving in combat roles in the military (that were present at the time of the decision in Rostker versus Goldberg) no longer applied, and men and women are, therefore, similarly situated for purposes of a draft or registration for a draft. Thus, the legal justification for exempting women from registering was in jeopardy. However, in August of 2020, a federal appeals court in New Orleans explained that only the Supreme Court may revise its precedent, thereby overturning the District Court's decision and upholding the constitutionality of the male-only registration requirement.[10][11] The case was appealed to the Supreme Court. The Biden administration asked the Court to decline to hear the suit based on the expectation that "Congress's attention to the question may soon eliminate any need for the Court to grapple with that constitutional question..."[12] In June 2021, the Supreme Court declined to hear the case. Justice Sotomayor wrote, "The Court's longstanding deference to Congress on matters of national defense and military affairs cautions against granting review while Congress actively weighs the issue."[13] However, Congress has been reluctant to address the issue. Rather than require women, as well as men, to register, on September 28, 2021, Representative Burgess Owens introduced H.R.5392 to amend the Military Selective Service Act to allow women to elect to register for the draft.[14] Consistent with prior legislation proposed to change Selective Service registration issues, it was referred to the House Committee on Armed Services to "die".

The McCain-Reed National Commission's recommendations were very much "carrot" based, rather than "stick" based. For example, they recommended enhanced funding to incentivize elementary and high school teachers to expand the teaching of civics. The Commission did not explain what topics should be removed from the curriculum to enable more time for civics. The Commission recommended maintaining the existing Selective Service System, including the legacy system of local draft boards. The final report did not reference the civil disobedience and riots that resulted from drafts conducted during the Civil War, World War I, and the Vietnam War. They did note that some "deferment categories ... were open primarily to those of privileged socioeconomic status, contributed to a perception that the system was unfair and led public opinion about the draft to turn increasingly negative during the 1960s."[15] Their recommended solution was to "ensure a fair, equitable, and transparent draft." Their reluctance to incorporate penalties for failing to register is evident in the following statement: "Should an individual unknowingly or mistakenly fail to register, a mechanism to allow corrective registration is necessary to mitigate unduly harsh lifelong penalties to which they would otherwise be subject."

The Commission failed to fully acknowledge the blatant unfairness of prior drafts, the lack of consistency in interpreting the rules among the many draft boards, and the level of civil disobedience that it instigated. Given the existence of the internet, potential draftees would quickly learn that for many of wealth and power, there were no negative consequences for using their connections to avoid service. Based on historical activities, any future military draft that had as much as one category enabling exemption would be exploited, compromise fairness, and provide fuel for civil disobedience.

The Commission recommended maintaining the existing draft board and birth date lottery systems. However, history informs that to achieve the Commission's goal of a "fair, equitable, and transparent draft," it would be necessary to eliminate the discretion of local draft boards. Historically, local boards interpreted and implemented differently deferment policies. The vast majority of board members were honorable citizens. They were often placed in an untenable predicament. If one registrant was exempted, another was selected. Each board member, perhaps unwittingly, was another point of potential conflict of interest. The Commission's report did not address this systemic flaw.

Examples of inconsistency among local draft boards abound. For example, professional boxer Muhammad Ali (Cassius Marcellus Clay Jr.), who claimed conscientious objector status, was selected to be drafted. When he refused, he was arrested, found guilty of draft evasion charges, and stripped of his boxing titles. On the other hand, different draft boards in different locales chose not to draft professional National Football League quarterbacks Joe Namath and Jack Kemp, presumably because of physical limitations.

Examples of exemptions available for those with wealth, power, and the desire to use it to avoid service abound. Radio personality Rush Limbaugh lost his student deferment when he dropped out of college. There are no records indicating that Limbaugh was examined by an Armed Forces Entrance Examining Station physician, however, his local draft board changed his classification and elected to defer him, almost certainly based on a report Limbaugh had his own doctor prepare and submit to his draft board. According to a physician paid for by his family, Limbaugh had a pilonidal cyst. His local draft board used the diagnosis to enable the son of a prominent local family to be exempted from service.[16]

Former New York City mayor Rudy Giuliani used student deferments during his years of undergraduate study at Manhattan College and his years in law school at New York University. After he graduated in 1968, at the height of the War in Vietnam, his local board classified him as available for military service. That is, until a local judge interceded on his behalf, arguing that Giuliani was an essential employee.[17] Thus, Giuliani was an essential worker before they became famous in the movie *Schindler's List*.

President Bill Clinton used student deferments during his years of undergraduate study at Georgetown. However, unlike Giuliani, access to a student deferment during graduate school was eliminated as an option in 1968 when, in his senior year, he was one of 32 American men selected to receive Rhodes Scholarships to study at Oxford University in England. His local draft board elected to delay action and permit Clinton to go to Oxford. It was not unusual for local boards to give special consideration to Rhodes Scholars. For most, perhaps all, of the 32 1968 Rhodes class, local draft boards managed to find a way to enable their local celebrity to attend Oxford. Tom Williamson, of Alameda County, California, was granted a graduate school deferment, even though such deferments had been eliminated. Darryl Gless, from Nebraska, was also given a special deferment. John Isaacson, of Lewiston, Maine, convinced his local board to permit him to go to Oxford. Scholar Mike Shea was given a standard student deferment, even though he was no longer an undergraduate.[18]

When Clinton returned to Arkansas, he found that the local Army National Guard and Reserve units were full. Clinton's only available out seemed to be joining the advanced Reserve Officers' Training Corps (ROTC) program at the University of Arkansas, which had no quotas and was open to graduate students. He made arrangements to join the ROTC program, which was complicated, since he had already received an order to report for military service. In the December 1969 lottery, his number, based on his birth date, was 311, and thus he knew that he would not be drafted. He then decided that he did not want to be in the ROTC. There is no doubt that Clinton went to great lengths to avoid being drafted. Perhaps if he had been the son of a more prominent and wealthy family and had lived in a different draft board district, it would have been much easier to do so.[19]

Draftee

Some cases are extremely curious. Actor Sylvester Stallone was born on July 6th, 1946, 44 days before Bill Clinton. So, given most draft boards and the fact that he was not from a wealthy family, unless he, similar to Clinton, had made a substantial effort to avoid being drafted, Stallone would most certainly have been a prime candidate for being drafted prior to the December 1969 lottery. Stallone was once accused of dodging the draft during the Vietnam War by a British magazine writer. Stallone sued and won the case for an undisclosed settlement.[20] How he managed to avoid being drafted is not clear. His first starring role in the U.S. was in the 1970 adult film *The Party at Kitty and Stud's*. But there was no published deferment classification for pornographic film actors. He did not serve, but he did manage to exploit and profit from the war and those who served, via the *Rambo* movies.

Supreme Court Justice Clarence Thomas received a lottery number of 109 in the 1969 lottery. Others with a lottery number of 109 were drafted in 1970. However, Thomas failed his medical exam, due to curvature of the spine.[21]

Senator Mitt Romney receive three student deferments, one for serving as a minister of religion while performing Mormon missionary work in France.[22]

President Joe Biden received several student deferments. After undergoing a Selective Service physical exam in 1968, Biden was exempted due to having had asthma as a teenager.[23] He was able to participate in high school football, work as a lifeguard at a Wilmington, Delaware pool, and confront Corn Pop in spite of the asthma, but it rendered Biden unfit for military service.[24]

President Donald Trump received four student deferments. After he graduated from college, he was susceptible to being drafted, but a physical examination in 1968 found that he was not qualified for unspecified reasons. Years later, it was posited that he had a sore foot — a bone spur.[25] After he was elected President, one of Donald Trump's associates testified that Trump acknowledged to advisors that he made up a fake affliction to avoid military service.[26]

Senator John McCain graduated from the U.S. Naval academy, served as a naval aviator, piloted ground-attack aircraft from aircraft carriers, and while on a bombing mission over Vietnam in October 1967, was shot down, seriously injured, and captured by the North Vietnamese. McCain's plane was one of more than 8,500 U.S. aircraft lost during the war.[27] He was held captive as a prisoner of war for five and a half years, experienced episodes of torture, and sustained wounds that left him with lifelong physical disabilities. He lost the 2008 presidential election to Barack Obama. In July of 2015, candidate Donald Trump, in a reference to Senator John McCain, said, "I don't like losers."[28] [29]

Trump continued, "He's a war hero because he got captured. I like people who don't get captured..."[30] [31]

Senator McCain died in 2018. In an interview broadcast on C-Span 3's American History TV on October 18th, 2017, when discussing the Vietnam War, he said, "One aspect of the conflict ... that I will never, ever countenance ... is that we drafted the lowest income level of America and the highest income level found a doctor that would say they had a bone spur. That is wrong. That is wrong. If we are going to ask every American to serve, every American should serve..."[32] [33]

This list of those who used their wealth, power, and political influence to avoid being drafted and serving in the military could be extended. The point is that local draft boards had discretion that enabled them to apply policies in an inconsistent manner. This lack of consistency and unfairness was apparent to those of draft age. We knew who was being selected and who was being exempted. Some who could not convince their draft board that they deserved an exemption, but had sufficient means to do so, fled to other countries, such as Canada and Sweden.

President Carter graduated from the Naval Academy in 1946. He served on both Navy surface ships and submarines. After his father died in 1953, Carter resigned from the Navy and returned home to manage his family's business. On January 21st, 1977, one day after he was inaugurated, President Carter granted a pardon to almost all Vietnam-era draft evaders. Senator Barry Goldwater said that the pardon was "the most disgraceful thing that a President has ever done ... it will utterly destroy" any effort to reinstate the draft.[34][35]

The 2020 National Commission on Military, National, and Public Service, which had been established in response to efforts by Senator McCain in cooperation with Senator Reed, recommended that the draft board system be maintained.[36] There are more than 2,000 local draft boards, comprised of approximately 11,000 volunteer civilian board members, across the U.S.[37] In the event of a draft, these civilian board members would decide who to select and who to exempt.[38] Historically, the local draft board system shielded federal officials and provided a semblance of local control.[39] Based on prior drafts, these local volunteers could be expected to be under a great deal of pressure to exempt some based on the wealth, power, and political connections of parents.

The Commission did not provide a solution for the lack of consistency among local draft boards. If draft boards are involved, based on the historical record, implementation of any policies for granting of exemptions will not be consistently applied. As with prior drafts implemented by local draft boards, the system is not designed to facilitate fairness. Given the historical widespread abuse of the exemption system and the common knowledge that many prominent people managed to avoid service, some with no legitimate reason, with no apparent penalty, it is very likely that attempts to reinstate the draft would be welcomed with civil disobedience.

Potential draftees would be aware, or made aware, that under prior drafts, many prominent people avoided service and suffered no negative consequences. They could be expected to have a keen interest in the history of prior U.S. military drafts. Many potential draftees would know that President Trump acknowledged to advisors that he made up a fake affliction to avoid military service.[40] Many would know that the same President made disparaging comments regarding Senator McCain, who, as a consequence of service, endured more than five years as a prisoner of war. They may know that in 2018, President Trump allegedly referred to the more than 1,800 U.S. soldiers buried at the Aisne-Marne American Cemetery near Paris as "losers" and "suckers" for serving and sacrificing their lives in the World War I battle at Belleau Wood.[41] Potential draftees are also likely to know that in 1977, President Carter granted a pardon to almost all Vietnam-era draft evaders. The subtle message is that only fools would not be sufficiently clever to avoid being drafted.

History informs that the Selective Service System, as structured with local draft boards, did not result in fair, equitable, transparent drafts. The first recommendation to fulfill the Commission's objective of a fairer, more equitable, and more transparent system than prior U.S. military drafts would be to dismantle and eliminate the Selective Service System and local draft boards.

I propose an alternative that has potential to address both the civic education and the framework for a draft in the event that Congress and the President would authorize one. The alternative framework has two components. The first would provide for a replacement of the current Selective Service registration requirement. It would be designed to address the civic education issue and to provide citizens with the opportunity to freely and publicly acknowledge their citizenship and their willingness to serve their country. The second is designed to replace the existing Selective Service policies, including both the legacy birth date selection procedure and the systematically flawed exemption system.

Chapter 48

Free to Choose on Citizenship Acknowledgement Day

"Claiming the right to get drunk without being interfered."

In 1756, Edmund Burke wrote, "Nine parts in ten of the whole race of mankind drudge through life."[1] Nasar reminded us that "the eighteenth century founders of economics ... assumed that nine out of ten human beings were sentenced by God or nature to lives of grinding poverty and toil."[2] Opportunities for my ancestors who were born into the European peasant class were extremely limited. My great-great-grandfather Sebastian Epplin left France in 1853. My great-grandfather Joseph Bruns emigrated from Germany in 1883 with his family, including my grandfather Henry Bruns. My ancestors freely chose to leave what were almost certain to be lives of poverty, tyranny, and misery, and for some, the potential for being drafted into military service.

An article in an 1854 edition of the *Edinburgh Review* described the emigration of Europeans to America as "the modern 'Exodus' from famine, want, and plethora of labor."[3] In 1855, a U.S. German immigrant explained that "Germans who found the restricted, enslaved life of their Fatherland no longer endurable took up the wanderer's staff ... as they do at this very

Draftee

day."[4] The immigrant continued, "We [German immigrants] are enthusiastic for personal freedom ... claiming the right to get drunk without being interfered with by anybody..."

My ancestors left their extended families, and their almost-certain condemnation to poverty, and emigrated to America. They chose to come. After they arrived, they freely chose to become citizens. My immigrant ancestors benefited immensely from living in a system that permitted successful markets to flourish. Indeed, for many decisions, they were free to choose.[5]

A major difference between my immigrant ancestors and those of us born in the U.S. is that, while my ancestors deliberately, freely, and publicly chose U.S. citizenship, it was granted to us at birth. The 14th amendment to the U.S. Constitution specifies that "All persons born ... in the United States, and subject to the jurisdiction thereof, are citizens of the United States." I was not required to think about citizenship; I was not required to consider the benefits and costs. U.S. citizenship was an incredibly valuable birthright freely granted to me. The birthright is such that for an entire lifetime, if a citizen so chooses, they may remain ignorant of its value. Perhaps the first time I considered its cost was when I turned 18 and registered for the draft. I was not permitted to vote until age 21.

Court decisions regarding the legality of exempting women from the Selective Service registration requirement, and recommendations provided by the National Commission on Military, National, and Public Service, provide an opportunity for bipartisan action to fundamentally change U.S. civic education. Legislation could be produced to provide those endowed with birthright citizenship an opportunity to publicly and formally acknowledge it, and in so doing, also state their willingness to subject themselves to a small probability of providing military service.

Legislation could be designed to provide every U.S. citizen, between their 18th and 19th birthdays, the opportunity to publicly and freely choose to simultaneously acknowledge their citizenship and their willingness to serve. The proposal is in keeping with the philosophy of President George Washington. In a May 2nd, 1783, letter to Alexander Hamilton, Washington wrote that, "It may be laid down as a primary position, and the basis of our system, that every citizen who enjoys the protection of a free government, owes not only a portion of his property, but even of his personal services to the defense of it..."[6][7]

Patriot Thomas Paine, author of *Common Sense*, wrote that: "Those who expect to reap the blessing of freedom must ... undergo the fatigue of supporting it..."[8]

Legislation could be designed and implemented to replace the Selective Service System registration requirement. I propose a once-in-a-lifetime irrevocable decision with lifetime-lasting consequences. Knowledge of an upcoming lifetime, irrevocable decision could be used by educators to motivate elementary and high school students to strive to become proficient, as defined by the National Assessment of Educational Progress (NAEP) civics test, as recommended by the National Commission on Military, National, and Public Service.[9]

Citizenship Acknowledgement Day

To increase the likelihood that all citizens would be aware of their opportunity to choose, a national holiday, Citizenship Acknowledgement Day, could be instituted. Citizenship Acknowledgement Day could be co-celebrated each year with the celebration of independence on July 4th. Parties and public patriotic celebrations, that are traditionally conducted in large cities, small towns, and suburban centers across the country to commemorate independence, could be enhanced to enable thousands of 18-year-olds to freely and voluntarily celebrate their U.S. citizenship. Indeed, as was the case for my European-born ancestors, they would be free to choose.

Draftee

Events could be held in public venues across the country on Citizenship Acknowledgement Day. Federal and state government officials could demonstrate their support for public service by volunteering their time to officially sanction the citizenship acknowledgement choice. Each 18-year-old would be given the opportunity to freely walk, ride, or, if disabled, be carried across a stage in front of family, friends, neighbors, and fellow citizens and sign an official document affirming their desire to acknowledge their citizenship. Every U.S. citizen, between their 18th and 19th birthdays, could be provided the opportunity to freely choose to simultaneously acknowledge their citizenship and their willingness to serve in the event of a national emergency of such enormity that Congress and the President implement a draft. Consistent with the declaration "that all ... are created equal," all would be provided the opportunity to acknowledge citizenship.

Some may freely choose to not acknowledge their willingness to provide military service. To prevent freeloading, a price for not confirming willingness to serve would be required. The traditional penalty for males not registering with the Selective Service System has been the loss of opportunity for federal student aid and loans, and the loss of opportunity to apply for a federal government job. In addition, technically, failure to register was legislated as a felonious offense, punishable by a fine of up to $250,000 and/or a prison term of five years.[10] However, more than 30 years have elapsed since the Justice Department prosecuted anyone for failing to register.[11][12] The historical record informs that a more costly penalty would be required to incentivize citizenship acknowledgement and willingness to serve.

Rather than a fine of up to $250,000 and/or a prison term of five years, both of which are costly to implement, I propose an alternative.

1. Between their 18th and 19th birthdays, all would be free to choose to acknowledge their citizenship and willingness to provide military service at a locally held Citizenship Acknowledgement Day ceremony, officiated by a federal or state government official. This would be a once-in-a-lifetime, irrevocable decision with consequences lasting their lifetime. They would publicly sign an official document that could be witnessed by family, friends, and an official representative of the government. In the event of a national emergency of such enormity that Congress and the President deem to warrant a draft, the public act of freely choosing to confirm citizenship on Citizenship Acknowledgement Day would facilitate a fairer, more equitable, and more transparent selection process.

2. Those who freely choose to acknowledge their willingness to subject themselves to a very small probability of providing military service if randomly selected.

a. Affirm that they would be subject to selection for military service and would willingly serve.

b. Retain eligibility for any paid or unpaid position with the federal government.

c. Retain eligibility for federal student aid and student loans.

d. Retain all legitimate claims to payments from the Social Security Administration, including disability, family, and retirement benefits.

e. Retain legitimate claims to federal transfer payments, including agricultural program payments, federal disaster payments, flood insurance subsidies, health insurance subsidies, housing subsidies, reparations payments, SNAP (food stamps), small business loans, and all other federal transfer payments.

Draftee

    f. Retain the right to fund or to provide funding and any in-kind services for federal elections.

    g. Retain eligibility for participation in federally funded grants and contracts.

3. Those who reject founding father George Washington's vision that one "who enjoys the protection of a free government, owes not only a portion of his property, but even of his personal services to the defense of it," and freely choose to acknowledge their refusal to subject themselves to a very small probability of providing military service if randomly selected, would face consequences that would be in effect for the remainder of their life.

    a. They would relinquish eligibility for any paid or unpaid position with the federal government.

    b. They would not be eligible for federal student aid and student loans.

    c. They would forfeit all claims to payments from the Social Security Administration, including disability, family, and retirement benefits.

    d. As long as they retained U.S. citizenship, they would be required to pay all federal taxes, including all taxes based on income, including FICA (Federal Insurance Contributions Act, social security, Medicare) taxes.

    e. They would forfeit all claims to federal transfer payments, including agricultural program payments, federal disaster payments, flood insurance subsidies, health insurance subsidies, housing subsidies, reparations payments, SNAP (food stamps), small business loans, and all other federal transfer payments.

    f. They would not be permitted to fund or to provide funding and any in-kind services for federal elections.

g. They would not be eligible for participation in federally funded grants and contracts.

4. Those who fail to freely and publicly participate in the Acknowledgement Day ceremony would endure the same consequences as those who freely and publicly refuse their willingness to subject themselves to a very small probability of providing military service.

The consequences for refusing to acknowledge citizenship and confirm willingness to provide military service could be designed for easy implementation. No arrest, no prosecution, and no collection of fines would be required. Computer programs used to facilitate transfers from federal government agencies to individuals, firms, and federally funded grants and contracts, could be programmed to block transfers to those who chose to freely and publicly refuse their willingness to acknowledge their citizenship.

Prior to and during the Citizenship Acknowledgement Day ceremony, the rights, benefits, privileges, and potential service responsibilities of citizenship could be enumerated, discussed, and learned in civics classes. Students would have an incentive to learn. Individuals would be free to weigh the expected benefits against the expected costs. The ceremony would explicitly acknowledge that those who freely choose to retain eligibility for the listed federal benefits would be made aware that, by doing so, they would freely affirm that they could be subject to a very small probability of selection for military service, and they would willingly serve if randomly selected.

If the specified consequences were insufficient to incentivize acknowledgement of citizenship, Congress could consider increasing the consequences by revoking citizenship for those unwilling to freely and publicly confirm their citizenship. There is precedent for legally revoking citizenship. Section 21 of the Enrollment Act of 1865 imposed denationalization (loss of citizenship) as a penalty for draft evasion or desertion. Justice John Marshall Harlan II's dissent in the 1967 Afroyim versus Rusk case cited the Enrollment Act of 1865 as an example of a law in which Congressional action sanctioned revoking citizenship without a person's consent.[13]

The proposal is for a Citizenship Acknowledgement Day to replace the Selective Service registration requirement. It is independent of any proposal for a military draft. However, in the event of a national emergency of such enormity that Congress and the President deem to warrant a draft, the public act of freely choosing to confirm citizenship on Citizenship Acknowledgement Day would facilitate a fairer, more equitable, and more transparent selection process.

Chapter 49

A More Random Selection System

"Fair, equitable, and transparent draft process."

I do not advocate the reinstatement of a peacetime military draft. The probability of the U.S. government establishing a military draft under any set of rules — in the absence of a very serious military conflict and a declared war or natural disaster — is exceedingly slim. Given the unfairness of prior drafts, given the arguments against a draft from economists, and given the propensity of power in the U.S. to be concentrated in the hands of wealthy people, a truly random military draft is not likely to be implemented. However, in the event of a national emergency that, in the view of Congress and the President, necessitates an increase in military personnel in excess of volunteers, the National Commission on Military, National, and Public Service recommended "a fair, equitable, and transparent draft."[1]

Every prior U.S. military draft has had some components that were blatantly unfair. The systems were designed, whether intentionally or not, to enable those with wealth, power, and political connections to avoid service if they desired to do so. This unfairness was widely recognized and resulted in civil disobedience during the Civil War, World War I, and the Vietnam War. Prudence would dictate that any future selection for military service be designed to reduce unfairness.

Rather than using the Selective Service System to obtain personnel, it is likely that Congress and the President would increase bonuses to a level necessary to meet enlistment goals. If that is the case, why does the U.S. continue to spend more than $25 million annually to support the Selective Service System and, historically, more millions for the legal fees defending its constitutionality? My hypothesis is that a switch from the current Selective Service System to a Citizenship Acknowledgement Day could be done without increasing costs. Plus, for every citizen who refuses to acknowledge their willingness to serve, government outlays for transfer payments will be reduced. A time of relative peace would be prudent for replacing the flawed Selective Service System.

For most in our society the words "draft," "Selective Service," and "conscription" carry very negative connotations. It is not surprising that Congressman Rangel's 2004 proposed legislation to reinstate a draft was defeated in the House of Representatives by a vote of 2–402. The U.S. Congress is highly unlikely to support a military draft resembling those that existed in the U.S. prior to 1973.[2,3]

An issue that would complicate fairness is that, according to the National Commission on Military, National, and Public Service, "under current standards, 71 percent of Americans ages 17 through 24 do not meet the qualifications for military service. Medical issues, weight, body art, a history of drug use, educational attainment, or a criminal record may disqualify a person from military service..."[4] A tattoo on the head or face may disqualify one from service. Thus, a potential draftee could obtain a tattoo and avoid service. In the event of a draft for which tattoos guaranteed exemption, economists would expect that a market would develop for temporary tattoos that could be removed after one was disqualified from service.

History informs that the legacy system with more than 2,000 local draft boards — with 11,000 volunteer civilian board members selecting some and exempting others — did not, and likely could not, achieve fairness and equity. A completely random — with zero exemptions and zero deferments — draft would more nearly approximate a fair, equitable, and transparent system.

Assume that each year, 4,000,000 residents (female and male) celebrate their 18th birthday, and they freely and publicly choose to confirm their willingness to provide military service on Citizenship Acknowledgement Day. Suppose that 80,000 mentally and physically fit draftees are required each year. Assume that 20% of 18-year-olds are either mentally or physically challenged to the extent that there is no military occupation they could perform. However, to more approximately attain fairness, there would be no pre-draft examination, no draft boards, and zero exemptions (except for those who freely choose to accept the consequences of refusing to serve and those currently serving after having volunteered). Thus, to achieve the 80,000 requirement, a total of 100,000 could be randomly selected from the total population of 4,000,000. Each 18-year-old who confirmed their willingness to serve would have a 2% chance of being selected.

After Citizenship Acknowledgement Day, all who freely confirmed their willingness to serve (an expected 4,000,000) could be assigned a truly random number.[5] After all are assigned a truly random number, if a draft was authorized, a second step could be conducted in which another 100,000 truly random numbers could be selected. The selected second-step numbers would then be matched with the corresponding first-step numbers assigned to the citizens in the pool. Thus, selection could be based on two separate random draws conducted at different times. The legacy birth date lottery machines that are maintained and routinely tested could be scrapped.[6] [7] No mother should be saddled with the guilt that her son or daughter was drafted only because she and her physician scheduled a Cesarean-section birth on the wrong day.

All 100,000 selected in the second step would be summoned and required to appear for service. Those who refuse to appear would be subject to the same consequences as those who refused to confirm their willingness to serve. Teams of medical and cognition experts could be used to visit and conduct on-site evaluations for those who are legitimately confined, such as in an extended care facility, hospital, or prison. To approximate a fair, equitable, and transparent system, as recommended by the National Commission on Military, National, and Public Service, there would be zero exceptions. Everyone whose number was randomly selected in the second step, no matter mental or physical limitations, would be required to report for service, or otherwise be subject to the same consequences as those who refused to confirm their willingness to serve.

Nothing, including AmeriCorps, anorexia, asthma, attention deficit hyperactivity disorder, autism, blindness, bone spur, children, conscience, criminal record, curved spine, cyst, deafness, dependents, diabetes, Down's syndrome, essential worker, family hardship, fatherhood, flat feet, marriage, missionary work, motherhood, obesity, Olympic sports participant, paralysis, Peace Corps, polio, political influence, porn star, pregnancy, professional sports player, religious beliefs, Rhodes scholarship, sexual preference, sole-surviving child, sore feet, student status, tattoo, wealth, or any other mental or physical attribute could be used to avoid reporting for service.

All 100,000 would be inducted and issued the military oath. Economists would expect that a market would develop to facilitate those with wealth to train a selectee how to fake a malady in an attempt to result in early dismissal. Thus, after induction, a period of time (perhaps four weeks) could be used to determine which of the 100,000 are genuinely afflicted with a mental or physical limitation such that they could provide no useful service. Based on the historical record, it could be expected that some would go to extraordinary means to fake a condition to avoid service, even after confirming their willingness to serve on Citizenship Acknowledgement Day, having been fairly selected in a random process, and taking the military oath.[8][9][10][11]

Rather than an immediate transition from civilian to military life, to identify fakers, an orientation/observation period would be warranted and used to identify those with legitimate physical and/or mental deficiencies. Given the potential sophistication of determined fakers, an observation period of four or more weeks may be required. During the orientation period, the draftees could retain and wear their civilian clothes. Most of the training during the observation period could be conducted in classrooms with a heavy dose of civics. U.S. history, world history, and geography could be taught to further facilitate the goals specified by the National Commission on Military, National, and Public Service. During the observation period, those with legitimate mental and or physical limitations that would restrict the draftee from doing any useful service could be identified. Those identified as being unfit could be discharged after the four-week observation period. They would not be subject to any additional penalties and would not have been issued military uniforms.

A draft of 100,000 might be expected to yield 40,000 males and 40,000 females that would be physically and mentally fit for at least one military occupation. Some of those included in the group (2%) of 80,000 — an expected 1,600 — would qualify for membership in Mensa. Those draftees retained after the observation period could be issued military uniforms and continue with military training. The proposal to implement "a fair, equitable, and transparent draft"[12] may be summarized as follows:

Implementation of a Fair, Equitable, and Transparent Draft

1. Eliminate all draft boards.
2. Eliminate all deferments.
3. Eliminate all pre-selection physical and mental examinations.
4. Selection would be from those who freely chose to confirm their willingness to serve on Citizenship Acknowledgement Day and for which a truly random number had been assigned.
5. Each year, a determination would be made as to whether or not the Army, Air Force, Marines, Navy, Coast Guard, and Space Force legitimately required additional personnel to provide for the security and defense of the United States. Congressional hearings could be conducted to enable the Chiefs of each branch to explain and report their findings regarding personnel needs in excess of volunteers.
6. If a Branch Chief reports needs in excess of volunteers, an executive order by the President of the United States could be issued stating the number to be randomly selected for service.
7. For years in which the President certifies needs in excess of volunteers, a random draw lottery could

be conducted to determine who, from among the 19-year-old confirmed citizens and recent immigrants in excess of age 18 that have confirmed that they want to remain eligible for possible citizenship in the future, would be selected to serve.

8. There would be zero exceptions. Everyone whose number was randomly selected, no matter mental or physical abilities, would be required to report for service. Nothing, including AmeriCorps, anorexia, asthma, attention deficit hyperactivity disorder, autism, blindness, bone spur, children, conscience, criminal record, curved spine, cyst, deafness, dependents, diabetes, Down's syndrome, essential worker, family hardship, fatherhood, flat feet, marriage, missionary work, motherhood, obesity, Olympic sports participant, paralysis, Peace Corps, polio, political influence, porn star, pregnancy, professional sports player, religious beliefs, Rhodes scholarship, sexual preference, sole surviving child, sore feet, student status, tattoo, wealth, or any other mental or physical attribute could be used to avoid reporting for service. Those who were legitimately confined, such as in an extended care facility, hospital, or prison, could request to be visited by a team of medical and cognition experts to conduct on-site evaluations.

9. After reporting to serve, an observation period (perhaps four weeks) could be used to determine which, if any from among those randomly selected, are genuinely afflicted with a mental or physical disability that would compromise the mission of the branch. These then could be discharged. Care

Draftee

     should be taken to ensure that no self-inflicted afflictions, such as face tattoos and gunshot wounds to the foot, could be used to avoid service.

10. Those discharged after the preliminary (four-week) period would not be referred to as veterans or eligible for veterans' benefits. They would be treated in a fashion similar to those who had indicated their willingness to serve but who had not been randomly selected for service.

11. A post-selection, self-inflicted anomaly intended to facilitate early discharge should be considered a felony, and it should be prosecuted with a minimum two-year sentence in a federal penitentiary and imposition of those consequences described for those who freely choose to refuse willingness to serve.

12. Immigrants who arrived prior to their 19th birthday would be required to indicate their willingness to serve as a prerequisite for potential future citizenship and for future access to any federal benefits for which they might qualify.

13. Immigrants who arrived after their 19th birthday, and who desired to eventually apply for citizenship, would be assigned a number and entered into the first draft lottery after their arrival regardless of age. (There are military jobs that could be performed by 70-year-old immigrants. Several Commanders-in-Chief have been over 70.)

Over time, every resident would be free to choose to confirm their willingness to serve on Citizenship Acknowledgement Day. They would freely affirm their willingness to be subject to selection for military service and, if selected, would be expected under penalty of law to willingly serve. In the event of action by the President and Congress that mandated a military draft, a truly random selection process from those who freely chose to enter the pool with zero exceptions would eliminate the blatant unfairness that has been associated with every prior U.S. military draft.

The citizenship acknowledgement proposal is for a small probability of a judicious amount of public service in exchange for retaining eligibility for some federal benefits. The proposal is in keeping with the stated philosophy of each of the four American Presidents enshrined on Mount Rushmore. U.S. founder and President George Washington, wrote that, "It may be laid down as a primary position, and the basis of our system, that every citizen who enjoys the protection of a free government, owes not only a portion of his property, but even of his personal services to the defense of it..."[13]

In a letter to James Monroe dated June 19th, 1813, former President Thomas Jefferson wrote: "It is more a subject of joy that we have so few of the desperate characters which compose modern regular armies. But it proves more forcibly the necessity of obliging every citizen to be a soldier. This was the case with the Greeks and Romans and must be that of every free state ... We must train and classify the whole of our male citizens, and make military instruction a regular part of collegiate education. We can never be safe till this is done..."[14]

In 1863, President Lincoln, in reference to the draft implemented during the Civil War, explained, "I do think every patriot should willingly take his chance under a law made with great care in order to secure entire fairness..."[15]

In a speech on November 11th, 1902, President Theodore Roosevelt opined, "The first requisite of a good citizen in this republic of ours is that he shall be able and willing to pull his own weight..."[16] In a letter written after his presidency, he indicated enthusiastic support for "universal obligatory military training and liability to serve in the time of war..."[17]

It is hoped that no military draft is needed. However, in the event that the President and Congress choose to draft, the proposed system would be fairer, more equitable, and more transparent than prior U.S. military drafts. It has the potential to reduce the likelihood of civil disobedience that resulted from prior drafts during the Civil War, World War I, and the Vietnam War. In the event that a draft is needed and conducted, the system as described, relative to prior drafts, has the potential for external benefits, including a reduction in waste, graft, and corruption, and enhanced civility.

Epilogue

Over time, when the topic of Vietnam arose, I found myself classifying people into one of three groups. Group one, perhaps the largest group, preferred that the War be forgotten. The other two groups were — and have remained — deeply divided. Group two was convinced that the War was wrong and immoral. Then there is the third group. Members of group three have been the most vocal; their narrative is that the U.S. lost only because the military was constrained by civilian politicians to fight with one hand tied behind its back. They are sincerely convinced that the U.S. was denied permission to win. Prior to conducting the research used to develop this manuscript, I did not have a response. I now believe that components of the conclusions of all three groups are wrong.

Relative to group one, if the War is forgotten, the mistakes that the U.S. made in attempting to facilitate a thriving democracy in an independent South Vietnam may be buried. There is much that can and should be learned and taught to future decision makers.

Relative to group two, the appropriate response is less clear.

Draftee

Do we, as citizens of planet Earth, have a responsibility to those who live elsewhere on the planet? Ho Chi Minh and Le Duan dictated over a brutal, inhumane, totalitarian regime. The residents of North Vietnam were clearly not free to choose. Dissent was not tolerated. Many who did not succumb to the will of the state were tortured and killed. There was no free press to document atrocities. Some U.S. policy makers recognized the evil and sought to right it. Unfortunately, their arsenal of tools, given the lack of competent, honest, and dedicated South Vietnamese leaders, was not adequate for rectifying the evil.

Relative to group three, it is still common to hear military personnel, some Vietnam veterans, and politicians proclaim with great certainty that South Vietnam would have survived as a thriving democracy if the U.S. military had not been required to fight with one hand tied behind their back. Based on what I had observed in Vietnam, the one-hand-tied-behind-our-back, denied-permission-to-win narrative completely misses the point. From my perspective, even though it is a false narrative, it has been exploited very successfully by the military, defense contractors, and some politicians. The one-hand-tied-behind-our-back narrative may have cost U.S. taxpayers billions of dollars.

The U.S. military that arrived in Vietnam was designed to use overwhelming force to kill and destroy an obvious and visible enemy. The U.S. could claim victory when the winner was determined by the side that killed and destroyed the most. By this measure, by these rules, the U.S. could claim victory in every fire fight. We were trained to kill and destroy. We were good. When funded with the almost-blank checks provided by taxpayers to the U.S. military industrial complex for delivering lethal tools, it was, and is, easy to destroy. It is much more difficult to build.

It is true that, unlike in World War II, the U.S. did not intentionally firebomb large cities and did not use nuclear weapons. But it is very unlikely that additional killing and destruction would have resulted in a thriving democracy in South Vietnam. In the war to which I was drafted, the enemy was not obvious. The ambiguity made it almost impossible to restrict the killing to enemy combatants. People other than soldiers were killed. Any structure could be rationalized as providing enemy support. The U.S. military was not designed and not trained to fight the type of war in which we were engaged.

The war might have been won if the government of South Vietnam had demonstrated to the people who lived in the country that they could provide good government and better public services than had been provided under decades of exploitation by the French. Unfortunately, none of the South Vietnamese governments that were recognized as official by the U.S. were successful in providing good government. Many government officials were more interested in maintaining power and accumulating personal wealth than in building a thriving democracy. They were not successful in convincing the majority of the people that their lives would be worse if the Communists prevailed.

The U.S. government and U.S. military officials were not successful in training South Vietnamese government officials how to win the hearts and minds battle. Ultimately, the failure of the South Vietnamese governments to provide good government service, to treat all citizens fairly, to conduct a fair military draft, and to acknowledge and prosecute corrupt public officials determined the outcome. It was clear to us that the ARVN troops that we observed during our time near the DMZ in 1971 were not motivated to fight. At the time, we did not know that the majority of those soldiers were draftees. They were not well

Draftee

educated, but they were not dumb. No doubt, they understood that the military draft, as implemented in South Vietnam, was not fair. Why would they be motivated to fight to preserve a system that they knew was corrupt? My hypothesis is that South Vietnamese government officials paid insufficient attention to, and lost, the hearts and minds battle. In the end, it was the battle that mattered. It was difficult for the South Vietnamese draftees to develop a strong fighting spirit when the purpose for their sacrifice was to support a corrupt system that appeared content to treat them as second-class citizens.

Maps

Maps

French Indochina consisted of most of present-day Vietnam, Cambodia, and Laos. The 1954 Geneva Accords divided Vietnam near the 17th Parallel, north of Dong Ha.

Maps

South Vietnam: Fire Support Base Wilson (the hill) was located north of Nha Trang, near Ninh Hoa. After the War, Saigon was renamed Ho Chi Minh City.[1]

Notes

1. Introduction

1. Kelley, Michael. *Where We Were in Vietnam: A Comprehensive Guide to the Firebases and Military Installations of the Vietnam War*. Central Point, OR:Hellgate Press. 2002, p. 5-89.
2. Associated Press. U.S. Plane Attacked in North; B-52's Pound Area Below DMZ. *New York Times* July 11, 1971, p. 3.
3. Last U.S. Combat Unit Below DMZ Pulls Out. *New York Times*. July 22, 1971, p. 13.
4. 1/83rd Artillery Association. M-110 8-inch Self-Propelled Howitzer and M-107 175-mm Self-Propelled Gun. http://1stbn83rdartyvietnam.com/Artillery_Info/Artillery_8-inch_175mm.htm
5. *Pacific Stars & Stripes*. September 1, 1971. p. 1.
6. http://www.vvmf.org/Wall-of-Faces/1304/RUEBEN-T-ARAGON
7. McNamara, Robert S. *In Retrospect: The Tragedy and Lessons of Vietnam*. New York, Random House. 1995. p. 321.
8. Ward, Geoffrey C., Ken Burns, and Lynn Novick. *The Vietnam War: An Intimate History*. New York, NY:Alfred A. Knopf. 2017. p. xvii.
9. Semple Jr., Robert B. Nixon Vows to End War with a 'New Leadership'. *New York Times*. March 6, 1968. p. 1.
10. Semple Jr., Robert B. Nixon Withholds His Peace Ideas: Says to Tell Details of Plan Would Sap His Bargaining Position if He's Elected. *New York Times*. March 11, 1968, p. 1, 33.
11. Remarque, Erich Maria. *All Quiet on the Western Front*. New York, NY:The Heritage Press. 1929. p. 206.
12. Appy, Christian G. *American Reckoning*. New York, NY:Viking. 2015. p. 214.
13. Ward, Geoffrey C., Ken Burns, and Lynn Novick. *The Vietnam War: An Intimate History*. New York, NY:Alfred A. Knopf. 2017. p. 326.
14. Ward et al., p. 327.
15. Kelley, Michael. *Where We Were in Vietnam: A Comprehensive Guide to the Firebases and Military Installations of the Vietnam War*. Central Point, OR:Hellgate Press. 2002, p. 5-288.
16. Emerson, Gloria. For Saigon's Diplomatic Set, the War Is Near, and Yet So Far. *New York Times*. September 20, 1971, p. 20.
17. Angrist, J. D. Lifetime Earnings and the Vietnam Era Draft Lottery: Evidence from Social Security Administration Records. *American Economic Review* 1990. 80, p. 313-335.

Notes

2. A Child During the Cold War

1. Leviero, Anthony. McCarthy Breaks with Eisenhower; Rues 1952 Support: Issue Is the Reds. *New York Times*. December 8, 1954, p. 1, 18.
2. Stalin vs. Church. *New York Times*. February 13, 1949. p. E1.

3. December 1969 Draft Lottery

1. The Draft Lottery. CBS News Special Report. December 1, 1969. https://www.youtube.com/watch?v=XhLbysRh8XY
2. Lakeshore Public Radio. International Guard: How The Vietnam War Changed Guard Service. Weekend Edition Saturday April 25, 2015. https://www.npr.org/2015/04/25/402045128/ international-guard-how-the-vietnam-war-changed-guard-service
3. Champagne unit. https://en.wikipedia.org/wiki/Champagne_unit
4. Trillin, Calvin. A Short History of Someone Who Failed to Get into The Champagne Unit of the Texas Air National Guard in 1968. *The Nation*. Vol. 279, Iss. 10. October 4, 2004, p. 6.
5. Schmidt, Dana Adams. Guard Is Widening Its Defense Role. *New York Times*. March 14, 1971, p. 1, 17.
6. Rutenberg, A.J. *Rough Draft: Cold War Military Manpower Policy and the Origins of Vietnam-Era Draft Resistance*. Cornell Univ. Press, 2019, p. 175.

4. May 1970 Kent State University Tragedy

1. Keatley, Robert. Nixon Sends U.S. Force into Cambodia to Eliminate Key Red Base; Terms Action Test of American 'Will'. *Wall Street Journal*. May 1, 1970, p. 3.
2. Southern Illinois University student newspaper. *Daily Egyptian*. May 5-15, 1970. https://opensiuc.lib.siu.edu/de/
3. Dill, Emma. Campus Protests Cost the Class of 1970 Its Commencement. Now Covid-19 Has Taken Away Its 50th Reunion. *The Chronicle of Higher Education*. May 08, 2020.
4. Champagne unit. https://en.wikipedia.org/wiki/Champagne_unit
5. Schmitt, William E. Some Now in Congress Joined Reserve or Guard. *New York Times*. August 20, 1988, p. 1, 9.
6. Walsh, Steve. International Guard: How The Vietnam War Changed Guard Service. *National Public Radio Weekend Edition Saturday*. April 25, 2015.

Notes

5. Report for Induction

1. United States Census Bureau. Table 199. Years of School Completed by Persons 14 Years Old and Over by Race, Sex, and Age: 1970. Last Revised: November 22, 2016. https://www2.census.gov/programs-surveys/demo/tables/educational-attainment/1970/pc-s1-36/tab-199.pdf

6. KP (Kitchen Police) – Spilled Milk and Guilty Bystander

1. U.S. Army Training Center *Company A, First Battalion, Second Basic Combat Training Brigade Pictorial Review Book*. Atlanta, GA:Albert Love Enterprises, Inc. Publishers. 11 September 1970.

7. Fitness, Blisters, and Poison Ivy

1. Luke 22:50-51. http://www.usccb.org/bible/luke/22
2. Police call was the term used to describe an order to form a line, walk slowly forward, and pick up all trash including items such as cigarette butts, gum wrappers, and paper scraps. It was not uncommon for a missed piece of scrap paper, that was planted by those in charge after the line passed, to be found by the NCO in charge who could then mete out punishment.
3. Warren, James A. U.S. combat advisers in Vietnam knew the score and got ignored. *The Daily Beast*. February 3, 2018. https://www.thedailybeast.com/us-combat-advisers-in-vietnam-knew-the-score-and-got-ignored

8. Advanced Individual Training 13E20, Field Artillery Fire Direction Control

1. Dickinson, Elizabeth R. *The Production of Firing Tables for Cannon Artillery*. U. S. Army Materiel Command Ballistic Research Laboratories, Aberdeen Proving Ground, Maryland. November 1967.
2. U.S. Army Artillery and Missile School. Artillery Trends. Instructional Aid Number 10. June 1959. http://sill-www.army.mil/firesbulletin/archives/1959/JUN_1959/ JUN_1959_FULL_EDITION.pdf
3. U.S. Army Artillery and Missile School. Artillery Trends. Instructional Aid Number 10. June 1959. https://tradocfcoeccafcoepfwprod.blob.core.usgovcloudapi.net/fires-bulletin-archive/1959/JUN_1959/JUN_1959_FULL_EDITION.pdf

Notes

4. U.S. Army Artillery and Missile School. Artillery Trends. Instructional Aid Number 10. June 1959. https://tradocfcoeccafcoepfwprod.blob.core.usgovcloudapi.net/fires-bulletin-archive/1959/JUN_1959/JUN_1959_FULL_EDITION.pdf
5. Roberts, William. Theory and Practice of Gunnery. *The British Review, and London Critical Journal*. December, 1822, p. 283-300.
6. Gleckler, Jim. *Redleg: An American Artilleryman's Personal Account of the Vietnam War*. Miami, OK:Northeastern Oklahoma A&M College. 1985.
7. Price, Thomas J. Technical Note TN-1119 Computer, Gun Direction Ml8 (FADAC) Applications Manual. United States Army Frankford Arsenal Philadelphia, PA. May, 1967. https://apps.dtic.mil/dtic/tr/fulltext/u2/664137.pdf
8. Artillery Trends. United States Army Artillery and Missile School Instructional Aid Number 40. May 1968. https://sill-www.army.mil/fires-bulletin/archives/1968/MAY_1968/MAY_1968_ FULL_EDITION.pdf
9. https://en.wikipedia.org/wiki/Gun_data_computer
10. U.S. Army Technical Manual TM 9-1220-221-34/7
11. Weik, Martin H. U.S. Department of the Army Ballistic Research Laboratories Report No. 1115, Aberdeen Proving Ground, Maryland FADAC, March 1961 p. 254.
12. US Army, Technical Manual, TM 5-6115-271-24P, Generator Set, Gasoline Engine Driven, Skid Mounted, Tubular Frame, 3 Kw, 3 Phase, AC.

9. Next Stop, Vietnam

1. Kelly, John. No needle, but the damage was done: Here's why jet injectors fell from favor. *Washington Post*. February 2, 2021. https://www.washingtonpost.com/local/jet-injectors/2021/02/02/23f3b8b0-6578-11eb-886d-5264d4ceb46d_story.html
2. Seattlepi. Ask the Mayo Clinic: Whatever happened to 'jet injectors?' https://www.seattlepi.com/lifestyle/health/article/Ask-the-Mayo-Clinic-Whatever-happened-to-jet-1293851.php. December 7, 2008.

10. Replacement Battalion to Artillery Battery

1. U.S. Army Technical Manual No. 43-0001-28. Army Ammunition Data Sheets for Artillery Ammunition. Washington, DC. April 28, 1994. https://www.militarynewbie.com/wp-content/uploads/2013/11/TM-43-0001-28-Army-Data-Sheets-Guns-Howizers-Mortars-Rifles-Gren-Launchers-Arty-Fuzes.pdf

2. Artillery Ammunition Department of the Army Technical Manual TM 9-1300-203. Headquarters, Department of the Army. April 1967. https://bulletpicker.com/pdf/TM%209-1300-203,%20Artillery%20Ammunition.pdf#page=158

11. Fire Support Base Wilson

1. QL is an abbreviation for quốc lộ that translates in English to highway.
2. Kelley, Michael. *Where We Were in Vietnam: A Comprehensive Guide to the Firebases and Military Installations of the Vietnam War*. Central Point, OR:Hellgate Press. 2002, p. B-10.

13. Life at Wilson

1. Kitchen, Lynn W., David W. Vaughn, and Donald R. Skillman. Role of US Military Research Programs in the Development of US Food and Drug Administration–Approved Antimalarial Drugs. *Clinical Infectious Diseases*, Volume 43, Issue 1, July 1, 2006, p. 67–71.

15. Life at Wilson: Neighboring Rice Paddies

1. Brigham, Robert K. *ARVN: Life and Death in the South Vietnamese Army*. Lawrence, KS:University Press of Kansas. 2006, p. 14.
2. Ellen T. Chang, Ellen T, Paolo Boffetta, Hans-Olov Adami, Philip Cole, and Jack S. Mandel. A critical review of the epidemiology of Agent Orange/TCDD and prostate cancer. *European Journal of Epidemiology*. July 27, 2014, p. 667–723.
3. Banout, Jan, Ondrej Urban, Vojtech Musil, Jirina Szakova, and Jiri Balik. Agent Orange Footprint Still Visible in Rural Areas of Central Vietnam. *Journal of Environmental and Public Health*. February 3, 2014.

16. Calm at Wilson, Disasters Near the DMZ

1. World History Project. Operation Lam Son 719 Begins, February 8, 1971. https://worldhistoryproject.org/1971/2/8/operation-lam-son-719-begins
2. Sorley, Lewis. *Vietnam Chronicles: The Abrams Tapes 1968-1972*. Lubbock, TX:Texas Tech University Press. 2004, p. 560.

Notes

3. Beecher, William. U.S. Warns Hanoi On DMZ Build-Up: Threatens Air Raids if Foe Fires from Neutral Zone. *New York Times.* March 26, 1971, p. 9.
4. Sorley, Lewis. *Vietnam Chronicles: The Abrams Tapes 1968-1972.* Lubbock, TX: Texas Tech University Press. 2004, p. 560.
5. Beecher, William. U.S. Warns Hanoi On DMZ Build-Up: Threatens Air Raids if Foe Fires from Neutral Zone. *New York Times.* March 26, 1971, p. 9.
6. Associated Press. 30 U.S. Soldier Killed in Attack On Vietnam Base. *New York Times.* May 22, 1971. p. 1, 12.
7. Kolb, Richard K. Deadly blast on Firebase Charlie 2. *VFW, Veterans of Foreign Wars Magazine;* May 1996, p. 32.
8. Sorley, Lewis. *Vietnam Chronicles: The Abrams Tapes 1968-1972.* Texas Tech University Press. Lubbock. 2004. p. 629.
9. Associated Press. Saigon Troops Push Drive Near DMZ. May 26, 1971.
10. Shuster, Alvin. Crossing of DMZ by 2 Regiments of Foe Reported: First Major Move Across Zone in 3 Years Leads to Increased Attacks. *New York Times.* June 28, 1971, p. 1.
11. Associated Press. Charge by Enemy Reported Halted: 300 Said to Be Repulsed at Fire Base Near DMZ. *New York Times.* July 3, 1971, p. 5.
12. Sorley, Lewis. *Vietnam Chronicles: The Abrams Tapes 1968-1972.* Lubbock, TX: Texas Tech University Press. 2004, p. 629-630.

17. Vacating Fire Support Base Wilson

1. Dictionary of American Naval Fighting Ships. https://military.wiki-a.org/wiki/USS_LST-546

18. Ship to Shore to the Cam Lo Cemetery

1. Associated Press. 30 U.S. Soldiers Killed in Attack On Vietnam Base. *New York Times.* May 22, 1971. p. 1, 12.
2. Associated Press. B-52's Pound Enemy. *New York Times.* June 22, 1971, p. 6.
3. Peterson, Iver. Saigon Retakes Key Base at DMZ: U.S. Copters Land Troops in Counterattack on Post After Heavy Bombing. *New York Times.* June 25, 1971, p. 1.
4. Associated Press. U.S. Plane Attacked in North; B-52's Pound Area Below DMZ. *New York Times.* July 11, 1971, p. 3.
5. Last U.S. Combat Unit Below DMZ Pulls Out. *New York Times.* July 22, 1971, p. 13.

Notes

19. Camp Carroll – Keystone of the McNamara Line

1. U.S. Abandons Artillery Base Near DMZ in a Shift of Tactics *New York Times*. December 29, 1968, p. 6.
2. Sorley, Lewis. *Vietnam Chronicles: The Abrams Tapes 1968-1972*. Lubbock, TX:Texas Tech University Press. 2004, p. 110.
3. Dee, Micky. A "Tale" Of Camp Carroll-The DMZ-Vietnam. https://hubpages.com/politics/A-Tale-Of-Camp-Carroll-The-DMZ-Vietnam. Accessed 2-5-2019.
4. Peterson, Iver. Saigon Retakes Key Base at DMZ: U.S. Copters Land Troops in Counterattack on Post After Heavy Bombing. *New York Times*. June 25, 1971, p. 2.
5. Shore II, Captain Moyars S. *The Battle for Khe Sanh*. Washington DC: U.S. Marine Corps Historical Branch, 1969. p. 7.
6. Baldwin, Hanson W. Guerrillas in South Vietnam Get More Modern Soviet Arms. *New York Times*. December 3, 1967, p. 6.
7. Associated Press. U.S. Plane Attacked in North; B-52's Pound Area Below DMZ. *New York Times* July 11, 1971, pg. 3.
8. Last U.S. Combat Unit Below DMZ Pulls Out. *New York Times*. July 22, 1971, p. 13.
9. Whitney, Craig R. A Bitter Little War Raging Just Below the DMZ *New York Times*. August 20, 1971, p. 2.
10. Ott, David Ewing. Vietnam Studies, Field Artillery, 1954-1973. Department of the Army
    Washington, D.C., 1995, p. 61.

20. Rookie Aerial Observer

1. Beecher, William. U.S. Warns Hanoi On DMZ Build-Up: Threatens Air Raids if Foe Fires from Neutral Zone. *New York Times*. March 26, 1971, p. 9.
2. Peterson, Iver. U.S. Jets Attack in North Vietnam: 200 Planeloads of Bombs Dropped in 8-Hour Raid. *New York Times*. September 22, 1971, p. 1, 9.
3. Hastings, Max. 2018. *Vietnam: An Epic Tragedy, 1945-1975*. New York, NY:Harper Collins. 2018, p. 358.

21. Duck and Cover

1. S&S Vietnam Bureau. Action Reaches Low Point During Vietnam Elections. *Pacific Stars & Stripes*. September 1, 1971, p. 6.

22. ARVN (Army of the Republic of Vietnam) – the South Vietnamese Army

1. Streba, James. Saigon Troops Will Leave Secure Villages. *New York Times.* February 23, 1970, p. 14.
2. Fulghum, David and Terrence Maitland. *The Vietnam Experience: South Vietnam on Trial, Mid-1970 to 1972.* Boston, MA:Boston Publishing Company. 1984, p. 54.
3. Langguth, Jack. 30% of Vietnam Draftees Desert Within 6 Weeks. *New York Times.* January 19, 1965, p. 8.
4. Brigham, Robert K. *ARVN: Life and Death in the South Vietnamese Army.* Lawrence, KS:University Press of Kansas. 2006, p. 7.
5. Brigham, p. 21.
6. Brigham, p. 22.
7. Brigham, p. 23.
8. Helton, Clinton. *Religious Politics in South Vietnam: A Study of the Religious Nature of Vietnamese Politics.* Washington, D.C.:The American University, M.A. Thesis, 1968.
9. Hastings, Max. 2018. *Vietnam: An Epic Tragedy, 1945-1975.* New York, NY:Harper Collins. 2018, p. 680.
10. Hastings, p. 751.
11. Hastings, p. 741.
12. Hastings, p. 23.
13. Hastings, p. 23.
14. Hastings, p. 742.
15. Ward, Geoffrey C., Ken Burns, and Lynn Novick. *The Vietnam War: An Intimate History.* New York, NY:Alfred A. Knopf. 2017, p. 527.
16. Johnson, Lyndon. Remarks at a Dinner Meeting of the Texas Electric Cooperatives, Inc. May 04, 1965. https://www.presidency.ucsb.edu/documents/remarks-dinner-meeting-the-texas-electric-cooperatives-inc

23. Leaving Carroll

1. Department of The Army Headquarters. 8th Battalion 4th Artillery Operational Reports. San Francisco, CA. November 12, 1971. https://www.8th-4th-arty.com/or15.html
2. Kelley, Michael. *Where We Were in Vietnam: A Comprehensive Guide to the Firebases and Military Installations of the Vietnam War.* Central Point, OR:Hellgate Press. 2002, p. xx.

24. Albright's Forecast

1. Willbanks, James H. *Abandoning Vietnam: How America left and South Vietnam Lost its War*. Lawrence, KS:University Press of Kansas. 2004, p. 133.
2. Hastings, p. 611.
3. Willbanks, p. 133.
4. Hastings, p. 611.
5. Ott, David Ewing. *Vietnam Studies, Field Artillery, 1954-1973*. Washington, D.C.:Department of the Army, 1995, p. 222.
6. Willbanks, p. 134
7. United Press International. Nixon On Bombing Recorded in Tape. *New York Times*. June 30, 1974, p. 27.
8. Ward, Geoffrey C., Ken Burns, and Lynn Novick. *The Vietnam War: An Intimate History*. New York, NY:Alfred A. Knopf. 2017, p. 520.
9. Hastings p. 622
10. Butterfield, Fox. Saigon Restricts Its Press On War: Tells Papers to Carry Only Official Reports On Fighting. *New York Times*. April 4, 1972, p. 9.
11. United Press International. Nixon On Bombing Recorded in Tape. *New York Times*. June 30, 1974, p. 27.

25. Leaving Vietnam

1. For other U.S. soldier accounts of Vietnam experiences see:
    Garrison, Mark. *Guts 'N Gunships: What it was Really Like to Fly Combat Helicopters in Vietnam*. 2015.
    Gillam, James T. *Life and Death in The Central Highlands: An American Sergeant in the Vietnam War, 1968–1970*. Denton, TX:University of North Texas Press. 2010.
    Gleckler, Jim. *Redleg: An American Artilleryman's Personal Account of the Vietnam War*. Miami, OK:Northeastern Oklahoma A&M College. 1985.

26. Headed for Home

1. Appy, Christian G. *American Reckoning*. New York, NY:Viking. 2015. p. 214.
2. Ward, Geoffrey C., Ken Burns, and Lynn Novick. *The Vietnam War: An Intimate History*. New York, NY:Alfred A. Knopf. 2017. p. 326.
3. Remarque, Erich Maria. *All Quiet on the Western Front*. New York, NY:The Heritage Press. 1929. p. 132.
4. Remarque, p. 132.

5. Peterson, Iver. Foe Seizes Post Near DMZ, Inflicting Heavy Losses. *New York Times.* August 17, 1971, p. 3.
6. Whitney, Craig R. A Bitter Little War Raging Just Below the DMZ *New York Times.* August 20, 1971, p. 2.

27. Fort Hood

1. 'Another Korea'? Indo-China the Problem. *New York Times.* April 18, 1954, p. E1.
2. Semple Jr., Robert B. Nixon Vows to End War with a 'New Leadership'. *New York Times.* March 6, 1968. p. 1.
3. Semple Jr., Robert B. Nixon Withholds His Peace Ideas: Says to Tell Details of Plan Would Sap His Bargaining Position if He's Elected. *New York Times.* March 11, 1968, p. 1
4. Kenworth, E.W. Nixon Would Outlaw Lewd Mail to Young. *New York Times.* October 10, 1968, p. 1, 50.
5. Kimball, Jeffrey. *Nixon's Vietnam War.* Lawrence, KS:University Press of Kansas. 1998, p. 101.
6. Berman, Larry. *No Peace, No Honor: Nixon, Kissinger, and Betrayal in Vietnam.* New York, NY:The Free Press. 2001.

28. Jesuits Following their Call

1. Mark 16:15-16. *The New American Bible, Revised Edition.* March 9, 2011.
2. Llewellyn, Jennifer, Jim Southey, and Steve Thompson. Europeans in Vietnam. Alpha History. January 5, 2018. https://alphahistory.com/vietnamwar/europeans-in-vietnam
3. Owen, Norman G. *The Emergence of Modern Southeast Asia: A New History–Vietnam 1700–1885.* Honolulu:University of Hawaii Press. 2005.
4. Llewellyn, Jennifer, Jim Southey, and Steve Thompson. Europeans in Vietnam. Alpha History. January 5, 2018. https://alphahistory.com/vietnamwar/europeans-in-vietnam
5. Carver, George A, Jr. The real revolution in South Viet Nam. *Foreign Affairs.*; Vol.43, No.3. April 1965, p. 391.
6. Norman, Henry. The Future of Siam. *The Contemporary Review*, London Vol. 64, July 1893, p. 2.
7. A French Lesson. *Blackwood's Edinburgh Magazine.* October 1893, p. 577.
8. Yokeley, Richard. French colonization in Indochina: A study of the decline of Vietnamese social and economic life, 1930–1954. M.A. Thesis. California State University, Dominguez Hills. 2006.
9. Source: https://www.u-s-history.com/pages/h1863.html

Notes

10. Source: http://what-when-how.com/western-colonialism/french-indochina-western-colonialism/
11. Carver Jr., George A. The Real Revolution in South Viet Nam. *Foreign Affairs* 43(3). April 1965.
12. Hastings, p. 110.

29. World War II Intervened

1. Stavisky, Sam. Indochina Eight Years of War. *Nation's Business* 42(6). June 1954. p. 34-37.
2. Hastings, Max. *Vietnam: An Epic Tragedy, 1945-1975*. New York, NY:Harper Collins. 2018, p. 3-4.
3. Paterson, Thomas G. and Dennis Merrill. Franklin Roosevelt Memorandum to Cordell Hull, January 24, 1944. *Major Problems in American Foreign Policy, Volume II: Since 1914*, 4th edition. Lexington, MA:D.C. Heath and Company. 1995, p. 189.
4. Herring, George C. *America's Longest War: The United States and Vietnam, 1950-1975*. New York, NY:McGraw Hill, 1986.
5. United Press International. Puppet State to Fight. *New York Times*. Aug 18, 1945, p. 5.
6. Neu, Charles E. *American's Lost War Vietnam: 1945-1975*. Wheeling, IL:Harlan Davidson, Inc. 2005, p. 5.
7. Congressional Record. Causes, Origins, And Lessons of the Vietnam War. May 9-11, 1972. P. 201.
8. Pertinax. French Progress on Indo-China Seen: Allies Said to Favor Speedy Re-establishment of Their Prerogatives in Colony. *New York Times*. August 17, 1945. P. 7.
9. Paterson, Thomas G. and Dennis Merrill. Franklin Roosevelt Memorandum to Cordell Hull, January 24, 1944. *Major Problems in American Foreign Policy, Volume II: Since 1914*, 4th edition. Lexington, MA:D.C. Heath and Company. 1995, p. 189.
10. http://www.worldwar2facts.org/world-war-2-casualties.html.
11. Callender, Harold. Votes Belie Split of Reds in France. *New York Times*. March 30, 1947. p. 39.
12. Ward, Geoffrey C., Ken Burns, and Lynn Novick. *The Vietnam War: An Intimate History*. New York, NY:Alfred A. Knopf. 2017, p. 25.
13. Congressional Record –Senate, April 6, 1954, p. 4676.
14. Adams, Frank S. Truman Rejects Any Backing of Wallace and Communists. *New York Times*. March 18, 1948, p. 1, 30.
15. Mr. Truman to The Country. *New York Times*. July 20, 1950, p. 20.
16. Ward, Geoffrey C., Ken Burns, and Lynn Novick. *The Vietnam War: An Intimate History*. New York, NY:Alfred A. Knopf. 2017, p. 25.
17. Soustelle, Jacques. Indo-China and Korea: One Front. *Foreign Affairs*. October 29, 1950, p. 56.
18. Soustelle, p. 63.

Notes

19. Soustelle, p. 65.
20. President Truman's Radio Address on Korea, U.S. Far Eastern Policy. *New York Times.* April 12, 1951, p. 4.

30. U.S. Leaders Discuss

1. Ward, Geoffrey C., Ken Burns, and Lynn Novick. *The Vietnam War: An Intimate History.* New York, NY:Alfred A. Knopf. 2017, p. 27.
2. United Press International. Firm Indochina Step Held Radford View. *New York Times.*
   June 2, 1954, p. 2.
3. Congressional Record –Senate, April 6, 1954, p. 4644-4681.
4. Congressional Record –Senate, April 6, 1954, p. 4644-4681.
5. Congressional Record –Senate, April 6, 1954, p. 4644-4681.
6. White, William S. Senate Weighs Indo-China; Bipartisan Stand Shapes Up: Knowland Demands Allies Take Full Role if Asian War Comes -- Kennedy Bids France Grant Liberty to People. *New York Times.* April 7, 1954, p. 1-2.
7. What's News: Business and Finance World Wide. *Wall Street Journal.* April 7, 1954, p. 1.
8. Transcript of President Eisenhower's Press Conference, With Comment on Indo-China. *New York Times.* April 8, 1954, p. 18.
9. Leviero, Anthony. President Warns of Chain Disaster If Indo-China Goes. *New York Times.* April 8, 1954, p. 1, 3.
10. Falling Dominoes. *New York Times.* April 8, 1954, p. 26.
11. Falling Dominoes. *New York Times.* April 8, 1954; p. 26.
12. Cart and Horse: Freedom for Indo-China Depends Upon Security. *Barron's National Business and Financial Weekly.* April 12, 1954, p. 1.
13. Digest of Nixon's Talk on Indo-China. *New York Times.* April 18, 1954; p. 3.
14. 'Another Korea'? *New York Times.* April 18, 1954, p. E1.
15. White, William S. Bipartisan Policy On Asia Is Sought: Nixon Puzzles Senators. *New York Times.* April 20, 1954, p. 10.

31. 1954 Geneva Accords

1. What and How? *New York Times,* July 25, 1954, p. E1.
2. What and How? *New York Times,* July 25, 1954, p. E1.
3. Abouzahr, Sami. The Tangled Web: America, France and Indochina 1947-50. *History Today* Vol. 54, No. 10. October 2004.
4. Fall, Bernard B. *Political Development of Viet-Nam. VJ-Day to The Geneva Cease-Fire.* Syracuse University, Ph.D. dissertation. October 1954
5. Appy, Christian G. *American Reckoning.* New York, NY:Viking. 2015. p. 3.

Notes

6. Halberstam, David. Vietnam's Faiths Underlie Rising: Buddhist-Catholics Disputes Sharpen under Diem. *New York Times.* September 14, 1964, p. 15.
7. Dooley, Thomas A. *Deliver Us from Evil: The story of Viet Nam's Flight to Freedom.* New York: Farrar, Straus and Cudahy. 1956.
8. Appy, p. 8.
9. Hastings, p. 97.
10. Appy, p. 11.
11. Hastings, p. 39.
12. Paterson, Thomas G. and Dennis Merrill. Franklin Roosevelt Memorandum to Cordell Hull, January 24, 1944. *Major Problems in American Foreign Policy, Volume II: Since 1914,* 4th edition. Lexington, MA:D.C. Heath and Company. 1995, p. 189.
13. Douglas, Paul H. The Bad and the Good in Us. *Foreign Affairs* Vol. 33, Iss. 4, July 1955, p. 535.

32. Bao Dai and Ngo Dinh Diem

1. Hastings, Max. 2018. *Vietnam: An Epic Tragedy, 1945-1975.* New York, NY:Harper Collins. 2018, p. 11.
2. Hastings, p. 25-26.
3. Leviero, Anthony. McCarthy Breaks with Eisenhower; Rues 1952 Support: Issue Is the Reds. *New York Times.* December 8, 1954, p. 1, 18.
4. https://religion.wikia.org/wiki/Pierre_Martin_Ngô_Đình_Thục
5. Adams, Frank S. Truman Rejects Any Backing of Wallace and Communists. *New York Times.* March 18, 1948, p. 1, 30.
6. Sulzberger, C.L. Indochina Clouds American Relationships with France. *New York Times,* January 22, 1955, p. 10.
7. South Viet Nam: The Beleaguered Man Ngo Dinh Diem. *Time Magazine.* April 4, 1955.
8. Hastings, p. 107.
9. Lieberman, Henry R. Diem Wins Poll in South Vietnam, Ousting Bao Dai. *New York Times.* October 24, 1955, p. 1, 7.
10. Fall, Bernard B. *Political Development of Viet-Nam. VJ-Day to The Geneva Cease-Fire.* Syracuse University, Ph.D. dissertation. October 1954, p. 141
11. Kauffman, Christopher J. Politics, Programs, And Protests: Catholic Relief Services In Vietnam, 1954-1975. *Catholic Historical Review.* Vol. 91, Issue 2. April 2005, p. 223-231.
12. Heneghan, George Martin. *Nationalism, Communism and The National Liberation Front of Vietnam: Dilemma for American Foreign Policy.* Stanford University, Ph.D. Dissertation, 1970.
13. Kauffman, Christopher J. Politics, Programs, And Protests: Catholic Relief Services in Vietnam, 1954-1975. *Catholic Historical Review.* Vol. 91, Issue 2. April 2005, p. 223-231.
14. Hastings, p. 115.

15. Helton, Clinton. *Religious Politics in South Vietnam: A Study of the Religious Nature of Vietnamese Politics.* Washington, D.C.:The American University, M.A. Thesis, 1968.
16. Wulff, Erich. The Buddhist Revolt: Diem's New Opponents Deserve US Support. *New Republic.* Vol. 149 Issue 9/10, August 31, 1963, p. 11-14.
17. Hastings, p. 105.
18. The Pentagon Papers. Gravel Edition Volume 1, Chapter 5, Origins of the Insurgency in South Vietnam, 1954-1960. Boston: Beacon Press, 1971.
19. The Pentagon Papers. Gravel Edition Volume 1, Chapter 5, Origins of the Insurgency in South Vietnam, 1954-1960. Boston: Beacon Press, 1971.
20. Bigart, Homer. Vietnam Victory Remote Despite U.S. Aid to Diem. *New York Times.* July 25, 1962, p. 1, 4.
21. Bigart, p. 4.
22. Bigart, p. 4.
23. Telegram from the Embassy in Vietnam to the Department of State, Saigon, May 18, 1963. https://history.state.gov/historicaldocuments/frus1961-63v03/d129
24. Kenworthy, E.W. Kennedy Warns Buddhist Dispute Imperils Vietnam: Doubts Regime Can Defeat Reds Unless Diem Gains Support of the People. *New York Times.* September 3, 1963, p. 1, 3.
25. Halberstam, David. Coup in Saigon: A Detailed Account. *New York Times.* November 6, 1963, p. 1, 16.

33. Pawn in a Cold War

1. Ward, Geoffrey C., Ken Burns, and Lynn Novick. *The Vietnam War: An Intimate History.* New York, NY:Alfred A. Knopf. 2017, p. 27.
2. Price, Mark J. Local history: President Lyndon B. Johnson's 1964 Akron speech came back to haunt nation. *Akron Beacon Journal.* October 19, 2014.
3. White, William S. Bipartisan Policy On Asia Is Sought: Nixon Puzzles Senators. *New York Times.* April 20, 1954, p. 10.
4. Tannenwald, Nina. Nuclear Weapons and the Vietnam War. *The Journal of Strategic Studies* 2006. 29-4, p. 675–722.
5. Ward, Geoffrey C., Ken Burns, and Lynn Novick. *The Vietnam War: An Intimate History.* New York, NY:Alfred A. Knopf. 2017, p. 520.
6. Truman Doctrine speech to Congress. March 1947. https://alphahistory.com/coldwar/truman-doctrine-congress-speech-1947
7. Associated Press. Communist Leader Pledges Drive to Ruin Marshall Plan. *New York Times.* October 23, 1947, p. 1.
8. What's News:World-Wide. *Wall Street Journal.* November 19, 1956, p. 1.
9. Welles, Benjamin. Khrushchev Bangs His Shoe on Desk. *New York Times.* October 13, 1960, p. 1, 14.
10. McNamara, Robert S. *In Retrospect: The Tragedy and Lessons of Vietnam.* New York, Random House. 1995. p. 32-33.

Notes

11. Hastings, p. 39.
12. Bueno de Mesquita, Bruce and Alastair Smith. *The Spoils of War: Greed, Power, and the Conflicts That Made Our Greatest Presidents.* New York, NY:Public Affairs. 2016.
13. Gen. Smith, Back From Geneva, Denies That Indochina Accord Was a Munich. New York Times. July 24, 1954, p. 4.
14. Republican Party Platform of 1952. July 7, 1952.
15. Republican Party Platform of 1952. July 7, 1952.
16. 'Another Korea'? *New York Times.* April 18, 1954, p. E1.
17. Abouzahr, Sami. The Tangled Web: America, France and Indochina 1947-50. *History Today* Vol. 54, No. 10. October 2004.
18. Republican Party Platform of 1956. August 20, 1956.
19. Congressional Record-Senate. July 21, 1959, p. 13769.
20. Appy, p. 23.
21. Fall, Bernard B. *Political Development of Viet-Nam. VJ-Day to The Geneva Cease-Fire.* Syracuse University, Ph.D. dissertation. October 1954.
22. Republican Party Platform of 1960. July 25, 1960.
23. 1960 Democratic Party Platform. July 11, 1960.
24. Republican Party Platform of 1956. August 20, 1956.
25. Record, Jeffrey. *The Wrong War, Why We Lost in Vietnam.* Annapolis, Maryland:Naval Institute Press. 1998.
26. National Security Action Memorandum No 263. South Vietnam. https://irp.fas.org/offdocs/nsam-jfk/nsam-263.htm
27. Sarnoff Backed in 'Cold War' Plea. *New York Times.* May 16, 1955; p. 2.
28. McNamara, Robert S. *In Retrospect: The Tragedy and Lessons of Vietnam.* New York, Random House. 1995. p. 29.
29. Jones, H. *Death of a Generation: How the Assassinations of Diem and JFK Prolonged the Vietnam War.* New York:Oxford. 2003.

34. President Johnson

1. McNamara, p. 101.
2. McNamara, p. 102.
3. McNamara, p. 32-33.
4. Maddow, Rachel. *Drift: The Unmooring of American Military Power.* New York, NY:Crown Publishers. 2012.
5. McMaster, H.R. *Dereliction of Duty.* New York, NY:Harper Collins Publishers. 1997.
6. Goldwater - The Positions He Has Taken. *New York Times.* July 5, 1964, p. E10.
7. Hamill, Pete. When the Client Is a Candidate: Five TV Commercials. *New York Times.* October 25, 1964, p. SM30.
8. Price, Mark J. Local history: President Lyndon B. Johnson's 1964 Akron speech came back to haunt nation. *Akron Beacon Journal.* October 19, 2014.

Notes

9. Goldwater Bids Johnson Concede U.S. Is at War. *New York Times.* November 2, 1964, p. 19.
10. Associated Press. Many Are Injured: Deputy Envoy Johnson Cut - Blast Set Off in Front of Building. *New York Times.* March 30, 1965. p. 1, 14.
11. United Press International. Marine Units Join the Build-Up at Bases in Vietnam. *New York Times.* April 11, 1965, p. 1, 4.
12. Text of the President's Address on U.S. Policies in Vietnam. *New York Times.* April 8, 1965, p. 16.
13. Text of the President's Address on U.S. Policies in Vietnam. *New York Times.* April 8, 1965, p. 16
14. Hastings, p. 371.
15. Li, Xiaobing. China's intervention and the end of the communist alliance in Vietnam. In *Beyond the Quagmire: New Interpretations of the Vietnam War.* Geoffrey W. Jensen and Matthew M. Stith, editors. Denton, TX:University of North Texas Press, 2019, p. 215.
16. Text of the President's Address on U.S. Policies in Vietnam. *New York Times.* April 8, 1965, p. 16
17. Johnson, Lyndon. Remarks at a Dinner Meeting of the Texas Electric Cooperatives, Inc. May 04, 1965. https://www.presidency.ucsb.edu/documents/remarks-dinner-meeting-the-texas-electric-cooperatives-inc
18. McNamara, p. 321.
19. van Dinh, Tran. Ky v Buddhists--Round 2. *New Republic.* Vol. 156 Issue 19, August 13, 1967, p. 15-19.
20. Apple Jr., R.W. Ky Gives up Race for Presidency, Bowing to Junta Runs with Thieu Premier Takes Second Place on Ticket for 'Good of Nation'. *New York Times.* July 1, 1967, p. 1.
21. Associated Press. Ky Is Said to Term Aims of U.S. Selfish. *New York Times.* April 1, 1968, p. 11.
22. Fear, Sean. The Feud That Sank Saigon. *New York Times.* Mar 3, 2017.
23. Neu, Charles E. *American's Lost War Vietnam: 1945-1975.* Wheeling, IL:Harlan Davidson, Inc. 2005, p. 129.
24. After the Tet Offensive. *New York Times.* February 8, 1968, p. 42.
25. After the Tet Offensive. *New York Times.* February 8, 1968, p. 42.
26. Congressional Record –Senate, April 6, 1954, p. 4644-4681.
27. Armstrong, Hamilton Fish. Power in a Sieve. *Foreign Affairs,* Vol. 46, No. 3. April 1968, p. 467-475.
28. Preston, H.L. CAP,Yes; Civil Affairs, No. *Marine Corps Gazette,* Vol. 52, No. 8. August 1968, p. 9-10.
29. Neu, p. 148.
30. Text of the President's Address on U.S. Policies in Vietnam. *New York Times.* April 8, 1965, p. 16.
31. https://learnodo-newtonic.com/lbj-accomplishments
32. Price, Mark J. Local history: President Lyndon B. Johnson's 1964 Akron speech came back to haunt nation. *Akron Beacon Journal.* October 19, 2014.

35. Nixon Elected

1. Berman, Larry. *No Peace, No Honor: Nixon, Kissinger, and Betrayal in Vietnam.* New York, NY: The Free Press. 2001, p. 45.
2. Nixon, Richard M. Statement Submitted to Republican National Convention Committee on Resolutions: "Vietnam". August 1, 1968.
3. Semple Jr., Robert B. Nixon Withholds His Peace Ideas: Says to Tell Details of Plan Would Sap His Bargaining Position if He's Elected. *New York Times.* March 11, 1968, p. 1, 33.
4. Kenworthy, E.W. Nixon Would Outlaw Lewd Mail to Young. *New York Times.* October 10, 1968, p. 1, 50.
5. Baker, Peter. Nixon Looked for 'Monkey Wrench' in Vietnam Talks to Help Win Race. *New York Times.* January 3, 2017, p. A.11.
6. Berman, Larry. *No Peace, No Honor: Nixon, Kissinger, and Betrayal in Vietnam.* New York, NY: The Free Press. 2001.
7. Berman, p. 33.
8. Schudel, Matt. Obiturary:Anna Chennault Formidable Washington Hostess and Secret Emissary Dies at 94. *Washington Post.* April 3, 2018.
9. Neu, p. 152.
10. Berman, p. 35-36.
11. Hughes, Ken. LBJ Thought Nixon Committed Treason to Win the 1968 Election. George Washington University History News Network. https://historynewsnetwork.org/article/146770 June 15, 2012.
12. White, William S. Bipartisan Policy On Asia Is Sought: Nixon Puzzles Senators. *New York Times.* April 20, 1954, p. 10.

36. President Nixon

1. Kenworth, E.W. Nixon Would Outlaw Lewd Mail to Young. *New York Times.* October 10, 1968, p. 1, 50.
2. Berman, p. 45.
3. Kimball, p. 101.
4. Kimball, p. 101.
5. Berman, p. 46.
6. Berman, p. 46.
7. Hastings, p. 551.
8. Demmer, Amanda, Richard A. Moss, Scott Laderman, Luke A. Nichter, David F. Schmitz, Robert K. Brigham. A Roundtable on Robert K. Brigham, *Reckless: Henry Kissinger and the Tragedy of Vietnam. Passport.* April 2019, p. 19-32.
9. Ellsberg, Daniel. Lying About Vietnam. *New York Times,* June 29, 2001, p. A, 23.
10. Kimball, p. 73.
11. Ward et al., p. 365.

Notes

12. Prentice, David L. Choosing "the Long Road": Henry Kissinger, Melvin Laird, Vietnamization, and the War over Nixon's Vietnam Strategy. *Diplomatic History*, Vol.40 (3), June 2016, p.445-474.
13. Brigham, p. 12.
14. Johnson, Lyndon B. Special Message to the Congress on Selective Service. March 6, 1967.

37. Fair and Impartial Random (FAIR) Draft Lottery

1. Bueno de Mesquita, Bruce and Alastair Smith. *The Spoils of War: Greed, Power, and the Conflicts That Made Our Greatest Presidents*. New York, NY:Public Affairs. 2016 , p. 212.
2. Johnson, Lyndon B. Executive Order 11289—National Advisory Commission on Selective Service. July 2, 1966.
3. Flynn, George Q. *The Draft, 1940-1973*. Lawrence, KS:University Press of Kansas. 1993.
4. Johnson, Lyndon B. Special Message to the Congress on Selective Service. March 6, 1967.
5. Rutenberg, A.J. *Rough Draft: Cold War Military Manpower Policy and the Origins of Vietnam-Era Draft Resistance*. Cornell Univ. Press, 2019, p. 171.
6. Sheehan, Neil. Draft Extended Under Old Rules Four More Years. *New York Times*. July 1, 1967, p. 1, 6.
7. Flynn, George Q. *The Draft, 1940-1973*. Lawrence, KS:University Press of Kansas. 1993, p. 244.
8. Bueno de Mesquita, Bruce and Alastair Smith. *The Spoils of War: Greed, Power, and the Conflicts That Made Our Greatest Presidents*. New York, NY:Public Affairs. 2016.
9. Congressional Record –Senate, June 14, 1967. p. 15758.
10. Congress Clears Bill Permitting a Draft Lottery. *New York Times*. November 20, 1969, p. 1, 15.
11. The Draft Lottery. CBS News Special Report. December 1, 1969. https://www.youtube.com/watch?v=XhLbysRh8XY
12. Rosenbaum, David E. Lottery Is Held to Set the Order of Draft in 1970. *New York Times*. December 2, 1969, p. 1, 20.
13. 'Another Korea'? *New York Times*. April 18, 1954, p. E1.
14. White, William S. Bipartisan Policy On Asia Is Sought: Nixon Puzzles Senators. *New York Times*. April 20, 1954, p. 10.
15. Nixon, Richard M. Text of President Nixon's Address to Nation on U.S. Policy in the War in Vietnam. *New York Times*. November 4, 1969, p. 16.
16. Kimball, p. 73.
17. President Nixon's explanation of decisions is included in: Nixon, Richard. *No More Vietnams*. New York, NY:Arbor House. 1985.

18. Secretary Kissinger's interpretation of events is included in: Kissinger, Henry. *Ending the Vietnam War*. New York, NY:Simon and Schuster. 2003.
19. Willbanks, p. 65.
20. Kimball, p. 101.
21. Congress Clears Bill Permitting a Draft Lottery. *New York Times*. November 20, 1969, p. 1, 15.
22. Naughton, James M. Nixon Signs Draft Change; First Lottery Due Monday. *New York Times*. November 27, 1969, p. 1, 21.

38. No Secret Plan Only Secret Bombing

1. Hastings, p. 593.
2. Hastings, p. 594.
3. Neu, p. 174.
4. Willbanks, p. 86.
5. Associated Press. U.S. Aides Assert Vietcong Rule Population of 184,700. *New York Times*, September 22, 1970, p. 8.
6. Kimball, p. 101.
7. Kimball, p. 10.
8. Tannenwald, Nina. Nuclear Weapons and the Vietnam War. *The Journal of Strategic Studies* 2006. 29-4, p. 675–722.
9. Hastings, p. 597.
10. United Press International. Nixon On Bombing Recorded in Tape. *New York Times*. June 30, 1974, p. 27.
11. Willbanks, p. 134
12. Hastings, p. 645.

39. Official Paris Talks and Unofficial Kissinger-Le Duc Tho Meetings

1. Berman, p. 59.
2. Berman, p. 44.
3. Sheehan, Neil. U.S. Waging Wider Air War Than in '68. *New York Times*. June 10, 1972, p. 1, 10.
4. Sheehan, Neil. U.S. Waging Wider Air War Than in '68. *New York Times*. June 10, 1972, p. 1, 10.
5. Whitney, Craig R. Giap Teaches Us a Lesson but It's Over Our Heads. *New York Times*. September 24, 1972, p. SM16-17, 76-78, 82-86.
6. Berman, p. 172.
7. Neu, p. 148.

40. Kissinger's October Surprise

1. Berman, p. 172.
2. Gwertzman, Bernard. Kissinger Asserts That 'Peace is at Hand'. *New York Times*, October 27, 1972. p. 1, 16-19.
3. Berman, p. 185.
4. Gwertzman, Bernard. Kissinger Asserts That 'Peace is at Hand'. *New York Times*, October 27, 1972. p. 1, 16-19.
5. Semple Jr., Robert B. Nixon Withholds His Peace Ideas: Says to Tell Details of Plan Would Sap His Bargaining Position if He's Elected. *New York Times*. March 11, 1968, p. 33.
6. Gwertzman, Bernard. Kissinger Asserts That 'Peace is at Hand'. *New York Times*, October 27, 1972. p. 1, 16-19.
7. 1972 Democratic Party Platform. July 10, 1972.
8. Republican Party Platform of 1972. August 21, 1972.
9. Berman, p. 189.
10. Berman, p. 170.
11. Whitney, Craig. U. S. Reports Loss of 16th B-52. *New York Times*. January 5, 1973, p. 71.
12. https://www.worldatlas.com/articles/operations-linebacker-1-and-2-vietnam-war.html.
13. Berman, p. 216.
14. Lewis, Flora. Vietnam Peace Pacts Signed; America's Longest War Halts. *New York Times*. January 28, 1973, p. 1, 24.
15. Kahin, George McT. The Other Paris Accords, Vietnam. *New York Times*. January 18, 1987, p. A.11.
16. Snepp, Frank. *Decent Interval: An Insider's Account of Saigon's Indecent End Told by the CIA's Chief Strategy Analyst in Vietnam.* Lawrence, KS:University Press of Kansas. 2002.
17. Austin, Anthony, Sylvan Fox, Bernard Gwertzman, and R.W. Apple Jr. Cease Fire End and Beginning, To Give Peace a Chance. *New York Times*. January 28, 1973, p. 201.
18. Hastings, p. 645.
19. Hastings, p. 645.
20. Neu, p. 215.
21. Hastings, p. 682.
22. Kahin, George McT. The Other Paris Accords, Vietnam. *New York Times*. January 18, 1987, p. A.11.
23. Neu, p. 217.
24. Hastings, p. 714.
25. The Gilded Exiles? *TIME Magazine*. Vol. 105, Issue 16, April 21, 1975.
26. Thieu Said to Try to Send Out Gold. *New York Times*. April 14, 1975, p. 18.
27. Bass, Thomas A. Nguyen Van Thieu, B. 1924: Exile On Newbery Street, The Leader of South Vietnam said he felt Betrayed by the U.S. Though he

Notes

didn't Mind Living Here. *New York Times*. December 30, 2001, p. SM25.
28. 'Another Korea'? *New York Times*. April 18, 1954, p. E1.
29. Butterfield, Fox. How South Vietnam Died - By the Stab in the Front. *New York Times*. May 25, 1975, p. 30-32, 210.
30. Butterfield, Fox. How South Vietnam Died - By the Stab in the Front. *New York Times*. May 25, 1975, p. 30-32, 210
31. Appy, p. 182.
32. Johnson, Lyndon. Remarks at a Dinner Meeting of the Texas Electric Cooperatives, Inc. May 04, 1965.
33. Text of the President's Address on U.S. Policies in Vietnam. *New York Times*. April 8, 1965, p. 16
34. Dickinson, Elizabeth. A Bright Shining Slogan:How "hearts and minds" came to be. *Foreign Policy Insider Access*. August 22, 2009. https://foreignpolicy.com/2009/08/22/a-bright-shining-slogan/

41. Rationalizing a Loss

1. Reagan, Ronald. *A Time for Choosing*. Speech. Los Angeles, CA. October 27, 1964. https://www.azquotes.com/quote/561632
2. Weaver Jr., Warren. Reagan Charges Johnson Is Silent On Vietnam Gains: Contends News Is Withheld for Campaign. *New York Times*. October 16, 1967, p. 1, 21.
3. United Press International. U.S. Is Criticized in Vietnam's Fall. *New York Times*. August 19, 1975, p. 13.
4. Weisman, Steven. Reagan Vows to Help Salvadorans but Says U.S. Won't Be Locked In. *New York Times*. February 25, 1981, p. A1-A4.
5. Remarque, Erich Maria. *All Quiet on the Western Front*. New York, NY:The Heritage Press. 1929. p. 132.
6. Ward et al., p. 327.
7. Emerson, Gloria. For Saigon's Diplomatic Set, the War Is Near, and Yet So Far. *New York Times*. September 20, 1971, p. 20.
8. Remarque, p. 132.
9. Remarque, Erich Maria. *All Quiet on the Western Front*. New York, NY:The Heritage Press. 1929. p. 132.
10. https://www.history.com/this-day-in-history/firebombing-of-tokyo
11. https://www.history.com/topics/world-war-ii/bombing-of-hiroshima-and-nagasaki
12. Bellmon, Henry. *The Life and Times of Henry Bellmon*. Tulsa OK:Council Oak Books. 1992, p. 67.
13. Ward et al., p. 27.
14. Congressional Record –Senate, April 6, 1954, p. 4644-4681.
15. Johnson, Lyndon. Remarks at a Dinner Meeting of the Texas Electric Cooperatives, Inc. May 04, 1965.
16. Paterson, Thomas G. and Dennis Merrill. Franklin Roosevelt Memorandum to Cordell Hull, January 24, 1944. *Major Problems in American*

Notes

Foreign Policy, Volume II: Since 1914, 4th edition. Lexington, MA:D.C. Heath and Company. 1995, p. 189.
17. Paterson, Thomas G. and Dennis Merrill. Franklin Roosevelt Memorandum to Cordell Hull, January 24, 1944. *Major Problems in American Foreign Policy, Volume II: Since 1914*, 4th edition. Lexington, MA:D.C. Heath and Company. 1995, p. 189.
18. Fall, Bernard B. *Political Development of Viet-Nam. VJ-Day to The Geneva Cease-Fire*. Syracuse University, Ph.D. dissertation. October 1954
19. Hess, David Lazear. The Educated Vietnamese Middle Class of Metropolitan Saigon and Their Legacy of Confucian Authority, 1954-1975. New York University, Ph.D. dissertation. 1977. p. 374-375.
20. https://obamawhitehouse.archives.gov/omb/budget/Historicals
21. Appy, p. 246-247.
22. Appy, p. 246-247.
23. Clodfelter, Mark. *The Limits of Air Power: The American Bombing of North Vietnam*. New York, NY:The Free Press. 1989.
24. Clodfelter, Mark. The Limits of Airpower or the Limits of Strategy: The Air Wars in Vietnam and Their Legacies. *Joint Force Quarterly* 78, 3rd q. 2015, p. 111-124.
25. Clodfelter, Mark. American Bombing of North Vietnam. Presented at the Vietnam Air War Symposium on C-SPAN. October 15, 2015. https://www.c-span.org/video/?328755-1/american-bombing-north-vietnam
26. Clodfelter, Mark. The Limits of Airpower or the Limits of Strategy: The Air Wars in Vietnam and Their Legacies. *Joint Force Quarterly* 78, 3rd q. 2015, p. 113.
27. Schandler, Herbert Y. *U.S. Military Victory in Vietnam: A Dangerous Illusion?* Chapter 7 in *Argument without end: In search of answers to the Vietnam tragedy*. Edited by McNamara, Robert S., James G. Blight, and Robert K. Brigham. New York, NY:Public Affairs. 1999, p. 318.
28. Schandler, p. 318.
29. Schandler, p. 319.
30. Schandler, p. 319.
31. Schandler, p. 367.
32. Schandler, p. 368.
33. Schandler, p. 368.
34. Appy, p. 242.
35. Hastings, p. 739.
36. Hartung, William D. Defense Contractors Are Tightening Their Grip on Our Government. *The Nation*. July 16, 2019. https://www.thenation.com/article/archive/military-industrial-complex-defense-contractors-raytheon-united-technologies-merger/
37. Coyne, C.J., C. Michaluk, and R. Reese. Unproductive entrepreneurship in US military contracting. *Journal of Entrepreneurship and Public Policy*. Vol. 5 No. 2. 2016, p. 221-239.
    Burton, James G. *The Pentagon Wars: Reformers Challenge the Old*

Notes

Guard. Annapolis, MD:Naval Institute Press. 1993.
38. Novak, Viveca. The Center for Responsive Politics. Washington, DC. August 2013. https://www.opensecrets.org/industries/background.php?cycle=2020&ind=D
39. Defense: Lobbying, 2019. The Center for Responsive Politics. Washington, DC
    https://www.opensecrets.org/industries/lobbying.php?cycle=2020&ind=D
40. Horton, Michael. Welcome to the Military-Industrial Pandemic. *The American Conservative.* May 9, 2020. https://www.theamericanconservative.com/articles/welcome-to-the-military-industrial-pandemic/

42. Family Tradition

1. Moody, Walton Smith. *The Introduction of Military Conscription in Napoleonic Europe, 1798-1812.* Durham, NC:Duke University, Ph.D. Dissertation.

43. Military Drafts in the United States

1. Gold, Philip. *Evasions: The American Way of Military Service.* New York, NY: Paragon House Publishers. 1985, p. 55.
2. https://www.mountvernon.org/library/digitalhistory/quotes/article/it-may-be-laid-down-as-a-primary-position-and-the-basis-of-our-system-that-every-citizen-who-enjoys-the-protection-of-a-free-government-owes-not-only-a-proportion-of-his-property-but-even-his-personal-services-to-the-defence-of-it-and-consequently-that-th/
3. Congressional Record. September 30, 1969, p. 4726.
4. Congressional Record. September 30, 1969, p. 4687.
5. Basler, Roy P. editor. *Collected works of Abraham Lincoln 1809-1865.* Volume 6. New Brunswick, N.J:Rutgers University Press, 1953.
6. Cooper, Douglas G. *Stumbling Toward Total Civil War: The Successful Failure of Union Conscription 1862-1865.* Carlisle Barracks, PA:U.S. Army War College. 1997.
7. The Enforcement of the Draft. *New York Times.* July 20, 1863, p. 4.
8. Terrible Riots In New York City. Resistance to the Draft. *New York Observer and Chronicle.* July 16, 1863; p. 230.
9. Clifford, J. Garry and Samuel R. Spencer, Jr. *The First Peacetime Draft.* Lawrence, KS:University Press of Kansas. 1986, p. 32.
10. Facts and Incidents of the Riot. The Murder of Colored People in Thompson and Sullivan Streets. *New York Times.* July 16, 1863, p. 1.
11. The Great Riot. *The Continental Monthly,* September 1863, p. 302.
12. The Great Riot. *The Continental Monthly,* September 1863, p. 302.

Notes

13. Frank, Robert. *Falling Behind: How Rising Inequality Harms the Middle Class.* Berkeley, CA:University of California Press, 2007.
14. Affairs at The West.: Progress of Recruiting in Illinois -The Hegira to Canada. *New York Times.* August 14, 1862, p. 3.
15. From Chicago: The Labors of Logan and McClernand-General News. *New York Times.* August 9, 1863, p. 2.
16. Affairs in the West: The Copperheads the Excess Furnished by Illinois. *New York Times.* September 6, 1863, p. 8.
17. The Great Riot. *The Continental Monthly,* September 1863, p. 302.
18. The Great Riot. *The Continental Monthly,* September 1863, p. 302.
19. Brooklyn News the Draft. *New York Times.* July 27, 1863, p. 3.
20. From Chicago: The Labors of Logan and McLennan - General News. *New York Times.* August 9, 1863, p. 2.
21. The Military Draft. *The Friend, A Religious and Literary Journal.* July 18, 1863, p. 367.
22. The Military Draft. *The Friend, A Religious and Literary Journal.* July 18, 1863, p. 367.
23. Desertion No Bar to Pension. No Distinction Between Good Soldiers and Bad. One-third of Union Army Deserted. *New York Times.* May 28, 1894, p. 8.
24. Desertion No Bar to Pension. No Distinction Between Good Soldiers and Bad. One third of Union Army Deserted. *New York Times.* May 28, 1894, p. 8.
25. Senate Passes Draft Bill 65 To 8, Wilson May Proclaim It Tomorrow, New Army to Mobilize in September. *New York Times.* May 18, 1917, p. 1.
26. Clifford, J. Garry and Samuel R. Spencer, Jr. *The First Peacetime Draft.* Lawrence, KS:University Press of Kansas. 1986, p. 35.
27. President Signs 18 To 45 Draft Bill and Gives Out Ringing Proclamation. *New York Times.* September 1, 1918, p. 1, 8.
28. Sellars, Nigel Anthony. Green Corn Rebellion. *The Encyclopedia of Oklahoma History and Culture.* https://www.okhistory.org/publications/enc/entry.php?entry=GR022.
29. Clifford, J. Garry and Samuel R. Spencer, Jr. *The First Peacetime Draft.* Lawrence, KS:University Press of Kansas. 1986, p. 35.
30. Cunningham, William. *The Green Corn Rebellion.* New York:Vanguard Press, 1935.
31. *Gale Encyclopedia of U.S. Economic History,* 2nd Edition Farmington Hills, Michigan Gale-Cengage. 2015.
32. https://www.law.cornell.edu/supremecourt/text/245/366
33. Clifford, J. Garry and Samuel R. Spencer, Jr. *The First Peacetime Draft.* Lawrence, KS:University Press of Kansas. 1986.
34. Highlights of Willkie Speech. *New York Times.* August 18, 1940, p. 33.
35. Hinton, Harold B. Industrial Draft Chief House Issue. *New York Times.* September 4, 1940, p. 1.
36. Hinton, Harold B. Industrial Draft Chief House Issue. *New York Times.* September 4, 1940, p. 1.

Notes

37. Clifford and Spencer, p. 208.
38. Clifford and Spencer, p. 214.
39. Clifford and Spencer, P. 218.
40. Catledge, Turner. Roosevelt Remains Paramount Campaign Issue. *New York Times.* October 20, 1940, p. 73.
41. President's Appeal to Those Called in Draft. *New York Times.* October 30, 1940, p. 15.
42. President's Appeal to Those Called in Draft. *New York Times.* October 30, 1940, p. 15.
43. Associated Press. Minister Arrested as Draft Violator. *New York Times.* November 19, 1940, p. 10.
44. President's Appeal to Those Called in Draft. *New York Times.* October 30, 1940, p. 15.
45. President's Appeal to Those Called in Draft. *New York Times.* October 30, 1940, p. 15.
46. The Selective Service Act. *New York Times.* September 27, 1940, p. 10.
47. Woods, Lewis. Conscientious Objectors Total Only 6,277 of Millions Called Up. *New York Times.* January 7, 1943, p. 1, 5.
48. Flynn, George Q. The Draft, 1940-1973. Lawrence, KS:University Press of Kansas. 1993.
49. Clifford, J. Garry and Samuel R. Spencer, Jr. The First Peacetime Draft. Lawrence, KS:University Press of Kansas. 1986.
50. Curtin SC, Sutton PD. Marriage rates in the United States, 1900–2018. NCHS Health E-Stat. 2020. https://www.cdc.gov/nchs/data/hestat/marriage_rate_2018/marriage_rate_2018.pdf
51. Associated Press. Text of the President's New Draft Proclamation. *New York Times.* January 6, 1942, p. 10.
52. 13,000,000 Registered in 4th Draft, Including 911,630 in New York. *New York Times.* April 28, 1942, p. 1, 10.
53. Selective Service Act of 1948. June 19, 1948. https://www.loc.gov/rr/frd/Military_Law/pdf/act-1948.pdf
54. Last Draftee Glad He's Out. *New York Times.* May 31, 1982, p. B2
55. Eisner, Robert. Tax Incentives for Investment. *National Tax Journal* Vol. 26, Iss. 3, September 1973, p. 397.
56. U.S. Department of Health, Education & Welfare Office of Education. *Selective Service and Military Policies on Classification, Deferment and Delay, Third Revision.* Engineering Manpower Commission, October. 1967.)
57. Congress Extends Selective Service Law for Four Years, but Rejects Proposals for Comprehensive Draft Reform. In *CQ Almanac 1967,* 23rd ed., 09-261-09-280. Washington, DC: Congressional Quarterly, 1968. http://library.cqpress.com/cqalmanac/cqal67-1314194.
58. Johnson, Lyndon B. Special Message to the Congress on Selective Service. March 6, 1967. http://www.presidency.ucsb.edu/ws/index.php?pid=28685

59. Johnson, Lyndon B. Special Message to the Congress on Selective Service. March 6, 1967. http://www.presidency.ucsb.edu/ws/index.php?pid=28685
60. Bueno de Mesquita, Bruce and Alastair Smith. *The Spoils of War: Greed, Power, and the Conflicts That Made Our Greatest Presidents*. New York, NY:Public Affairs. 2016.
61. Congressional Record, June 14, 1967, p. 15758
62. Sheehan, Neil. Draft Extended Under Old Rules Four More Years. *New York Times*. July 1, 1967, p. 1, 6.
63. Congress Clears Bill Permitting a Draft Lottery. *New York Times*. November 20, 1969, p. 1, 15.
64. President's Draft Lottery Approved by Congress. In *CQ Almanac 1969*, 25th ed., 350-55. Washington, DC: Congressional Quarterly, 1970. http://library.cqpress.com/cqalmanac/cqal69-1248194.

44. Paving the Way to an All-Volunteer Force

1. The President's Commission on an All-Volunteer Armed Force. Washington, D.C.:U.S. Government Printing Office. February 1970.
2. Rosenbaum, David E. Nation Ends Draft, Turns to Volunteers. *New York Times*. January 28, 1973, p. 1, 28.
3. Associated Press. Draft No. 95 Set as Highest in '72: 15,900 Men to Be Called Up Beginning in October. *New York Times*. Sep 2, 1972, p. 13.
4. President Urges Military Pay Rise to Help End Draft. *New York Times*. January 29, 1971, p. 1, 7.
5. 1970 US Military Basic Pay Charts for the active duty personnel of the United States Army, Navy, Air Force, Marines and Coast Guard. https://www.navycs.com/charts/1970-military-pay-chart.html
6. 1974 US Military Basic Pay Charts for the active duty personnel of the United States Army, Navy, Air Force, Marines and Coast Guard. https://www.navycs.com/charts/1974-military-pay-chart.html
7. Bailey, Beth. The Army in the Marketplace: Recruiting an All-Volunteer Force. *The Journal of American History*; Vol. 94, No.1. June 2007, p. 47-74.
8. Bailey, Beth. The Army in the Marketplace: Recruiting an All-Volunteer Force. *The Journal of American History*; Vol. 94, No.1. June 2007, p. 47-74.
9. Tully, Matthew B. Entry-level separation offers a way out for troubled recruits. *Army Times*. November 3, 2008, p. 30.
10. The National Defense Authorization Act for Fiscal Years 1998 And 1999 (105 H.R. 1119) became public law on November 18, 1997 (P.L. 105-85). Section 531 number 6 of P.L. 105-85 "... Require(s) the Secretary of each military department to implement policies and procedures to ensure the

Notes

prompt separation of recruits who are unable to successfully complete basic training and to remove those recruits from the training..."
11. Powers, Rod. What Is an Entry Level Separation (ELS) in the Military? *The Balance Careers*. December 05, 2019 https://www.thebalancecareers.com/entry-level-separations-what-is-an-els-3356960
12. Government Accounting Office. Military Attrition: DOD Could Save Millions by Better Screening Enlisted Personnel. GAO/NSIAD-97-39. January 6, 1997. https://www.govinfo.gov/content/pkg/GAOREPORTS-NSIAD-97-39/html/GAOREPORTS-NSIAD-97-39.htm
13. Rosenbaum, David E. Nation Ends Draft, Turns to Volunteers. *New York Times*. January 28, 1973, p. 1, 28.
14. National Archives. Proclamation 4771--Registration Under the Military Selective Service Act
    45 FR 45247, 3 CFR, 1980 Comp. July 2, 1980, p. 82.
15. Selective Service System, Who Needs to Register. https://www.sss.gov/register/who-needs-to-register/
16. Schmidt, Michael S. Draft Registration for Women Would Stir a Sleepy Government Agency. *New York Times*. February 8, 2016, p. A.10.
17. https://www.sss.gov/about/return-to-draft/lottery/
18. https://www.sss.gov/registration/state-commonwealth-legislation/
19. National Public Radio Morning Edition. Selective Service Registration Comes Under Fire Again. May 27, 2019.
20. Hawkinson, B. and J.C. Hall. Cross-State Variation in Selective Service Compliance: A Research Note. *Romanian Economic and Business Review*. 9-3 Fall 2014, p. 7-9.
21. Seago, Laura. Automatic Registration in The United States: The Selective Service Example. New York:Brennan Center for Justice at New York University School of Law. 2009.
22. https://www.dps.texas.gov/DriverLicense/documents/reqdFormsOOS-NonMilDuplPkg.pdf
23. https://studentaid.gov/apply-for-aid/fafsa/filling-out#options
24. https://www.sss.gov/register/
25. Benton, Donald (Director). *Selective Service System Annual Report to the Congress of the United States*. Arlington, VA:Office of Public and Intergovernmental Affairs. 2019. https://www.sss.gov/wp-content/uploads/2020/03/Annual-Report-FY2019.pdf
26. Korte, Gregory. For a Million U.S. Men, Failing to Register For The Draft Has Serious, Long-Term Consequences. *USA Today*. April 3, 2019.
27. https://www.npr.org/2019/05/27/727260693/selective-service-registration-comes-under-fire-again
28. Sivak, Michael and Brandon Schoettle. Recent Changes in the Age Composition of U.S. Drivers: Implications for the Extent, Safety, and Environmental Consequences of Personal Transportation, *Traffic Injury Prevention*. Vol. 12, No. 6. 2011, p. 588-592.

Notes

45. Economists and the Draft

1. Lee, Dwight R and Richard B. McKenzie. Reexamination of the Relative Efficiency of the Draft and the All-Volunteer Army. *Southern Economic Journal.* Vol. 58, No. 3; January 1992, p. 644-654.
2. Galbraith, John Kenneth. Debate on Draft Favored. *New York Times.* October 14, 1956, p. E10.
3. Friedman, Milton. The Case for Abolishing the Draft--And Substituting for it an All-Volunteer Army. *New York Times.* May 14, 1967, p. SM11.
4. Congressional Record - House. September 30, 1969, p. 4687.
5. Congressional Record – House. December 6, 2006, p. 8793-8798.
6. The President's Commission on an All-Volunteer Armed Force. Washington, D.C.:U.S. Government Printing Office. February 1970.
7. Powers, Rod. What Is an Entry Level Separation (ELS) in the Military? December 05, 2019 https://www.thebalancecareers.com/entry-level-separations-what-is-an-els-3356960
8. Government Accounting Office. Military Attrition: DOD Could Save Millions by Better Screening Enlisted Personnel. GAO/NSIAD-97-39. January 6, 1997. https://www.govinfo.gov/content/pkg/GAOREPORTS-NSIAD-97-39/html/GAOREPORTS-NSIAD-97-39.htm
9. Eisenhower, President Dwight D. Farewell Address. Washington, D.C.:U.S. National Archives & Records Administration. January 17, 1961.
10. Coyne, C.J., C. Michaluk, and R. Reese. Unproductive entrepreneurship in US military contracting. *Journal of Entrepreneurship and Public Policy.* Vol. 5 No. 2. 2016, p. 221-239.
11. Burton, James G. *The Pentagon Wars: Reformers Challenge the Old Guard.* Annapolis, MD:Naval Institute Press. 1993.
12. Brenes, Michael. *For Might and Right: Cold War Defense Spending and the Remaking of American Democracy.* Amherst, MA:University of Massachusetts Press, 2020.
13. Heefner, Gretchen. *The Missile Next Door: The Minuteman in the American Heartland.* Cambridge, MA:Harvard University Press, 2012.
14. Laich, Dennis and Lawrence Wilkerson. The Deep Unfairness of America's All-Volunteer Force. *The American Conservative.* October 16, 2017.
15. Obama, Barack. *A Promised Land.* New York, NY: Crown Publishing, 2020.
16. Whitlock, Craig. The Afghanistan Papers a Secret History of the War. *Washington Post.* December. 9, 2019.
17. Commission on Wartime Contracting. Transforming Wartime Contracting Controlling costs, Reducing Risks Final Report to Congress. August 2011. www.wartimecontracting.gov
18. https://www.cnn.com/2020/04/06/politics/thomas-modly-transcript/index.html

Notes

19. Marshall, Alfred. *Principles of Economics.* New York, N.Y.:Macmillan and Co., 1890.
20. Bellmon, Henry. *The Life and Times of Henry Bellmon.* Tulsa OK:Council Oak Books. 1992. P. 67.
21. Sweeney, Louise. Senator Mark Hatfield, He Waves a Mean Olive Branch. *The Christian Science Monitor.* June 17, 1982.
22. Matthew 7:12. *The New American Bible, Revised Edition.* March 9, 2011.
23. Bellmon, Henry. *The Life and Times of Henry Bellmon.* Tulsa OK:Council Oak Books. 1992.
24. Hakes, Jay. History's Perspective on the Panama Canal Treaties. *Real Clear World.* April 19, 2018. https://www.realclearworld.com/articles/2018/04/19/historys_perspective_on_the _panama_-canal_treaties__112781.html
25. Hakes, Jay. History's Perspective on the Panama Canal Treaties. *Real Clear World.* April 19, 2018. https://www.realclearworld.com/articles/2018/04/19/historys_perspective_on_the _panama_-canal_treaties__112781.html
26. Russ Roberts, Russ. Econtalk Podcast. Michael Eisenberg on the Start-Up Nation, Storytelling, and the Power of Technology. January 25, 2022. https://www.econtalk.org/michael-eisenberg-on-the-start-up-nation-storytelling-and-the-power-of-technology/#audio-highlights

46. Push Back

1. Punaro, Arnold. Building a F.A.S.T. Force: A Flexible Personnel System for a Modern Military. Bipartisan Policy Center Task Force On Defense Personnel. Senate Armed Services Subcommittee on Personnel Hearing. Congressional Documents and Publications; Washington, May 3, 2017.
2. Ackerman, Elliot. Why Bringing Back the Draft Could Stop America's Forever Wars. *Time.* October 10, 2019. https://time.com/5696950/bring-back-the-draft/
3. Ackerman, Elliot. Why Bringing Back the Draft Could Stop America's Forever Wars. *Time.* October 10, 2019. https://time.com/5696950/bring-back-the-draft/
4. Orwall, Burce. Travelers Bypass the Bright Lights-Disney Launches TV Push to Lure Visitors to Its Parks. *Wall Street Journal*, October 26, 2001, p. B.1.
5. Anonymous. *The Economist.* Who will fight the next war? October 24, 2015, p. 25-28.
6. Appy, p. 313.
7. Anonymous. *The Economist.* Who will fight the next war? October 24, 2015, p. 25-28.
8. Laich, Dennis and Lawrence Wilkerson. The Deep Unfairness of America's All-Volunteer Force. The American Conservative. October 16, 2017.

Notes

9. Goldberg, Jeffrey. Trump: Americans Who Died in War Are 'Losers' and 'Suckers'. *The Atlantic*. September 3, 2020.
10. Fallows, James. The Draft, Why the Country Needs It. *The Atlantic*. April 1980.
11. Webb, James. The Draft, Why the Country Needs It. *The Atlantic*. April 1980.
12. Eisenhower, President Dwight D. Farewell Address. Washington, D.C.:U.S. National Archives & Records Administration. January 17, 1961.
13. Shane III, Leo. Why One Lawmaker Keeps Pushing for A New Military Draft. *Military Times*. March 30, 2015.
14. Rangel, Charles B and Ron Paul. Should The U.S. Bring Back the Draft? *New York Times Upfront*. January 14, 2008, p. 28.
15. https://www.congress.gov/bill/117th-congress/house-bill/2509
16. https://www.congress.gov/bill/117th-congress/senate-bill/1139
17. https://www.congress.gov/bill/117th-congress/house-bill/5392

47. Flawed Plans to Revise the Selective Service System

1. Ackerman, Elliot. Why Bringing Back the Draft Could Stop America's Forever Wars. *Time*. October 10, 2019. https://time.com/5696950/bring-back-the-draft/
2. Buettner, Russ, Susanne Craig, and Mike Mcintire. President's Taxes Chart Chronic Losses, Audit Battle and Income Tax Avoidance. *New York Times*. October 10, 2020, p. A.1, A11-A16.
3. Borden, Taylor. Nine Countries Where You Can Easily Buy Citizenship and How to Do It. *Business Insider*, US edition. October 1, 2020.
4. National Commission on Military, National, and Public Service. *Inspired to Serve Final Report*. Arlington, VA. March 2020. https://inspire2serve.gov/reports
5. https://supreme.justia.com/cases/federal/us/453/57/
6. https://www.law.cornell.edu/supremecourt/text/453/57
7. https://law.justia.com/cases/federal/district-courts/texas/txsdce/4:2016cv03362/1396506/87/
8. Lardieri, Alexa. Judge: Male-Only Military Draft Unconstitutional. *U.S. News and World Report*. February 25, 2019.
9. United States Court of Appeals for the Fifth Circuit. Case No. 19-20272. National Coalition for Men versus Selective Service System. Appeal from the United States District Court for the Southern District of Texas. USDC No. 4:16-CV-3362. August 13, 2020. https://law.justia.com/cases/federal/appellate-courts/ca5/19-20272/19-20272-2020-08-13.html
10. https://law.justia.com/cases/federal/appellate-courts/ca5/19-20272/19-20272-2020-08-13.html

Notes

11. McGill, Kevin. Federal appeals court: Male-only draft is constitutional. *Associated Press.* August 13, 2020.
12. https://www.supremecourt.gov/DocketPDF/20/20-928/175759/20210414181101718_20-928%20National%20Coalition%20for%20Men%20Opp.pdf
13. https://www.supremecourt.gov/opinions/20pdf/20-928_e1p3.pdf
14. https://www.congress.gov/bill/117th-congress/house-bill/5392
15. National Commission on Military, National, and Public Service. *Inspired to Serve Final Report.* Arlington, VA. March 2020, p. 90. https://inspire2serve.gov/reports
16. https://www.snopes.com/fact-check/draft-notice/
17. Gray, Geoffrey. Rudy and 'Nam. *New York.* Vol. 40, Iss. 14, April 23, 2007, p. 18.
18. Schaeper, Thomas J. and Kathleen Schaeper. *Rhodes Scholars, Oxford, and the Creation of an American Elite.* New York, NY:Berghahn Books. 2010, p. 169-218.
19. https://www.snopes.com/fact-check/felon-groovy/
20. Hollywood Tough Guys and Their Military Service, Studs and Duds. http://robertheston.expertscolumn.com/article/hollywood-tough-guys-and-their-military-service-studs-and-duds
21. Simon, Martin. Supreme Mystery. *Newsweek.* September 15, 1991.
22. https://www.snopes.com/fact-check/war-stories/
23. Graham, Michael. Joe Biden's Draft Record Looks a Lot Like Donald Trump's. Do Democrats Care? *TCA Regional News Chicago.* June 7, 2019.
24. Graham, Michael. Does Joe Biden Have an Age Problem? Ask 'Corn Pop.' *TCA Regional News Chicago.* September 17, 2019.
25. https://www.snopes.com/news/2016/08/02/donald-trumps-draft-deferments/
26. Shane III, Leo. Trump made up injury to dodge Vietnam service, his former lawyer testifies. *Military Times.* February 27, 2019.
27. Associated Press. 8,500 Aircraft Lost by U. S. In Indochina. *New York Times.* December 31, 1972, p. 6.
28. Schmidt, Grayson. Trump calls McCain 'loser' at Family Leadership Summit. *TCA Regional News Chicago.* July 18, 2015.
29. Haberman, Maggie. Donald Trump Denies Saying What He Said About John McCain. *New York Times.* February 8, 2016.
30. What Donald Trump Said -- About McCain, Obama, Immigrants, His Hair. *Dow Jones Institutional News.* July 19, 2015.
31. Dumain, Emma. Texas Congresswoman to Trump: Have You No Decency? *Roll Call Washington.* July 21, 2015.
32. McCain, John. C-SPAN Interview. October 18, 2017. https://www.c-span.org/video/?435879-1/senator-john-mccain-reflects-vietnam-war-career-2017
33. Pengelly, Martin. Trump's Salute to Vietnam Veterans Meets with Thanks – And Scorn. *The Guardian.* March 29, 2020.

Notes

34. Mohr, Charles. 10,000 Affected Now: Action Postponed On Nearly 100,000 Who Fled Armed Forces During the War. *New York Times*. January 22, 1977, p. 1, 10.
35. https://history.com/news/carter-draft-dodger-pardon-half-returned
36. National Commission on Military, National, and Public Service. *Inspired to Serve Final Report*. Arlington, VA. March 2020, p. 90. https://inspire2serve.gov/reports
37. https://www.sss.gov/about/agency-structure/
38. https://www.sss.gov/about/agency-structure/
39. Clifford, J. Garry and Samuel R. Spencer, Jr. The First Peacetime Draft. Lawrence, KS:University Press of Kansas. 1986. p. 35.
40. Shane III, Leo. Trump made up injury to dodge Vietnam service, his former lawyer testifies. *Military Times*. February 27, 2019.
41. Goldberg, Jeffrey. Trump: Americans Who Died in War Are 'Losers' and 'Suckers'. *The Atlantic*. September 3, 2020.

48. Free to Choose on Citizenship Acknowledgement Day

1. Burke, Edmund. *A Vindication of Natural Society: Or, A View of the Miseries and Evils Arising to Mankind from Every Species of Artificial Society: Letter to Lord **** By a Late Noble Writer*. London:M. Cooper, 1756, p.93.
2. Nasar, S. *Grand Pursuit: The Story of Economic Genius*. New York:Simon & Schuster, 2011, p. 461.
3. European Emigration to The United States. *The Edinburgh Review*. September 1854, p. 58-73.
4. The Future of the German Element in America – Germans Speaking for Themselves. *New York Daily Times*. January 20, 1855, p. 2.
5. Friedman, Milton and Rose D. Friedman. *Free to Choose: A Personal Statement*. New York, NY:Harcourt, Brace, Jovanovich, 1980.
6. https://www.mountvernon.org/library/digitalhistory/quotes/article/it-may-be-laid-down-as-a-primary-position-and-the-basis-of-our-system-that-every-citizen-who-enjoys-the-protection-of-a-free-government-owes-not-only-a-proportion-of-his-property-but-even-his-personal-services-to-the-defence-of-it-and-consequently-that-th/
7. Congressional Record. September 30, 1969, p. 4726.
8. Congressional Record. September 30, 1969, p. 4687.
9. National Commission on Military, National, and Public Service. *Inspired to Serve Final Report*. Arlington, VA. March 2020, p. 90. https://inspire2serve.gov/reports
10. Selective Service System, Who Needs to Register. https://www.sss.gov/register/who-needs-to-register/

Notes

11. https://www.npr.org/2019/05/27/727260693/selective-service-registration-comes-under-fire-again
12. Korte, Gregory. For a Million U.S. Men, Failing to Register For The Draft Has Serious, Long-Term Consequences. *USA Today*. April 3, 2019.
13. https://www.law.cornell.edu/supremecourt/text/387/253

49. A More Random Selection System

1. National Commission on Military, National, and Public Service. *Inspired to Serve Final Report*. Arlington, VA. March 2020, p. 90. https://inspire2serve.gov/reports
2. Shane III, Leo. Why One Lawmaker Keeps Pushing for A New Military Draft. *Military Times*. March 30, 2015.
3. Rangel, Charles B and Ron Paul. Should The U.S. Bring Back the Draft? *New York Times Upfront*. January 14, 2008, p. 28.
4. National Commission on Military, National, and Public Service. *Inspired to Serve Final Report*. Arlington, VA. March 2020, p. 90. https://inspire2serve.gov/reports
5. Kumar, G. Sathesh and V. Saminadan. Fuzzy Logic Based Truly Random Number Generator for High-Speed BIST Applications. *Microprocessors and Microsystems – Kidlington*. September 2019, p. 188.
6. Schmidt, Michael S. Draft Registration for Women Would Stir a Sleepy Government Agency. *New York Times*. February 8, 2016, p. A.10.
7. https://www.sss.gov/about/return-to-draft/lottery/
8. Paralympics: Officials Investigate Fake Disabilities. *New York Times*. November 28, 2000, p. D7.
9. Paralympic Group Orders Suspensions. *New York Times*. January 30, 2001, p. 7.
10. Bray, Thomas J. Young Men Dream Up Some Ingenious Ways to Avoid the Draft. *Wall Street Journal*. April 11, 1966, p. 1, 22.
11. Levitas, Mitchel. 2-S--Too Smart to Fight? *New York Times*. April 24, 1966, p. 27, 125-134.
12. National Commission on Military, National, and Public Service. *Inspired to Serve Final Report*. Arlington, VA. March 2020, p. 90. https://inspire2serve.gov/reports
13. Congressional Record. September 30, 1969, p. 4726.
14. Letter from Thomas Jefferson to James Monroe. National Archives. June 19, 1813. https://founders.archives.gov/documents/Jefferson/03-06-02-0188
15. Basler, Roy P. editor. *Collected works of Abraham Lincoln 1809-1865*. Volume 6. New Brunswick, N.J:Rutgers University Press, 1953.
16. Theodore Roosevelt Speech, New York, N.Y., November 11, 1902. https://wist.info/roosevelt-theodore/34244/
17. Letter from Theodore Roosevelt to William Hutchinson Cowles. Theodore Roosevelt Papers. Library of Congress Manuscript Division.

Notes

June 7, 1918. https://www.theodorerooseveltcenter.org/Research/Digital-Library/Record?libID=0290562.

Maps

1. U.S. CIA. The World Factbook https://www.cia.gov/static/313b9d934a5ff68f4a34d8e10919cbb7/vietnam-admin.jpg)

www.ingramcontent.com/pod-product-compliance
Lightning Source LLC
Chambersburg PA
CBHW052043220426
43663CB00012B/2417